ADVENTURES IN PENN'S WOODS

Planning Your Own Journey While Enjoying Our Quest to Visit All Pennsylvania State Parks

JOSEPH F. BROSKY

Copyright © 2025 Joseph F. Brosky

All rights reserved. No part of this book may be reproduced in any form or by any electronic or mechanical means, including information storage and retrieval systems, without permission in writing from the publisher, except by a reviewer who may quote brief passages in a review.

Trailheads and Byways Publishing

ISBN 979-8-9926891-0-5

Printed in the United States of America

This book is dedicated to Donna Brosky, my Wife, my Companion in Life, and my Quest Partner—
Thank You for being there always and for urging me to write this book.

Love Always, Joe

CONTENTS

Prologue
1

Life Experiences Leading to Our Big Decision to Take Up Our Quest
3

Staying On Track: Motivators to Maintain Momentum and Finish the Quest
21

Planning for Success
39

Preparing to Hit the Road
53

Gearing Up for the Quest
69

124 Pennsylvania State Parks, Here We Go!
93

Pennsylvania's 20 Mighty State Forests
281

Emptying My Shirt Pocket Notes
and Final Thoughts on Achieving Our Quest
309

About the Author
315

Prologue

Since I retired in 2017, I have been attempting to spread the word about the joys of the outdoors that await our aging population in Pennsylvania. I have been motivated both by my own outdoor experiences and by Donna, my companion and wife who always reminds me to keep moving. This book is part of my focus on bringing the outdoors to my peers and bringing my peers to the outdoors through both the use of technologies like Zoom and by physically meeting and enjoying the outdoors as a group. With this in mind, I believe the guide you are holding in your hands is perfect for both young families that are discovering the great Pennsylvania outdoors together and for people my age and beyond that yearn to see more of the natural wonders that are just beyond our doorsteps. Others are welcome to explore these pages but folks that are always exploring the outdoors might find my advice and instructions on how to prepare and undertake this quest to be rudimentary. However, I am sure they will enjoy our trek through all the parks and forests as well as my picks for parks in ten categories. I enjoyed picking my favorites because everyone can join in with their picks as well and so the fun begins!

At this point, I urge everyone to see their physicians to determine their health status and to gain knowledge on how to physically prepare for this quest. Remember, developing a more active lifestyle does not happen overnight and the fun, joy, and inspiration that awaits your participation in this quest will be waiting and welcoming no matter when you begin.

Plus, your visits to each park are easily tailored to both your physical abilities and interests. This means as long as you are able to drive or someone accompanying you can drive, your quest awaits. Just keep in mind that your park visits can range from simply stopping in at the park office for your passport stamp and having a picnic lunch with a scenic view at a nearby picnic table to an intense hiking or kayaking adventure. A bonus might include sleeping the night in your tent after cooking a great outdoor meal at the campfire. Any of these options, or something in-between, guarantees fun, laughter, and contentment. Enjoy and have fun as you work on your quest and be prepared for a healing touch or two along the way.

Life Experiences Leading to Our Big Decision to Take Up Our Quest

I KNOW IN MY HEART THAT EVERYONE GOING ON THIS QUEST HAS A BIG "WHY" BEHIND THEIR DECISION AS WELL—ALWAYS PERSONAL, SPECIAL, AND UNIQUE.

The big "Why" behind our quest and achieving it within five years, is our mutual, lifelong love of the outdoors. I know in my heart that everyone taking on this quest has a big "Why" behind their decision as well—always personal, special, and unique. Donna and I were lucky to be living in the "country" during our respective childhoods, which enabled us to discover and explore nature early in life. My parents moved to Ross Township in 1947 since Babcock Boulevard was zoned commercial and this enabled my dad to purchase an existing home, and build an addition containing both a warehouse and office. His new office space acted as a bridge between the warehouse and home.

The side of our home was near a small stream with the woods beyond while the front sat above Girty's Run. This was prior to the housing boom in the North Hills so the environment formed a great playground for us adventuresome kids. I joined the Boy Scouts but my interest waned when our weekly meetings just happened to be the same day and evening every week as the time slot on television when the *Beverly Hillbillies* appeared. I guess my stern scoutmaster was no competition for Elly May Clampett (Donna Douglas) lounging by the cement pond in her bathing suit. After my Scouting days unceremoniously came to an end, I went to Camp Fatima in the summers because this religious-based camp had an affiliation with Saint Teresa Grade School in Perrysville where I attended school from 1958 to 1966–all five of us siblings graduated from St. Teresa. I loved this camp because of several "first time experiences" including shooting a 22-rifle, shooting a bow and arrow, using a compass, boxing, rowing a boat, and sleeping under the stars.

Thanks to our little neighborhood of six homes that included a small farm, there were enough kids around to explore our surroundings just as if we were a bunch of Boy Scouts and Girl Scouts going on field trips together. We neighborhood kids spent hours roaming the woods, building treehouses for overnight stays, and camping out in our backyards, but there was much more. To go to our mailbox or to catch the school bus, or visit the donut shop across Babcock Boulevard, I just crossed over Girty's Run on our footbridge—Girty's Run was a major key to our adventures. This stream and its banks held a cornucopia of wildlife including water snakes, crayfish, salamanders, minnows, muskrats, and raccoons which popped out at night. At the same time, our hikes through the woods always fascinated me because of all the different types of trees and plants—I always wanted to know more but this was a long time before I learned about field guides. However, my constant yearning for knowledge about the natural world was fostered on those hikes.

With the passing of our dad in 1959, Mom was very busy running the family business and she lost interest in her flower garden. I took over weeding her garden by our gravel road that led to our paved driveway and warehouse where the semi-trailers came to make deliveries and pick up shipments. At the same time, I started my own flower garden—I always loved plants and was especially fascinated by watching young peony and spiderwort plants sprout in early spring and produce blooms in June. Also, I enjoyed watching my brother, Paul, plant and harvest a vegetable garden in our side yard. When he married and bought the house next door to our warehouse, he started his own vegetable garden and I took over his garden.

In the winter, I loved looking at seed catalogs with him and finding unique new vegetables to grow. Hiking and gardening seemed to help heal the pain I felt over losing my dad.

In high school, I was into my 10-speed bike, hiking, tobogganing, Nordic skiing and gardening. At that time, our go-to family parks included North Park (County Park), McConnells Mill State Park, and Presque Isle State Park. Although all of this outdoor activity engendered a love for the outdoors, the most important influence during my childhood, and to this very day, is a beautiful painting that hung on the wall of the bedroom that Paul and I shared. This same painting now resides on our living room wall where I see it several times a day walking to and from my desk.

This wonderful nature-portal arrived in our house through my dad's mom and it was brought to America from Poland. All four of my grandparents immigrated from Poland and my Grandmother Brzozowski is the only grandparent that survived into my childhood; the others all passed before the 1930s receded into history. The wondrous, nature-inspiring theme shows rays of the Moon reflecting on a tranquil lake with mountains as a backdrop and in the foreground a rocky shoreline with a path leading from the placid lakeshore to a canvas tent with its flaps open and a huge campfire burning. In both good times and bad, this painting beckons me to enter the refuge of the tent after a long day of exploration by foot or by water or exit through the flaps, tell stories by the campfire, and later, in the prolonged moonlight, launch my canoe once again. On countless occasions I have found solace in that scene as I let my imagination run wild and let nature heal my troubled spirit.

As I write these words, I turn around in my desk chair and once again become lost in the awe-inspiring vista that greets me as I awaken early in the morning, step through the tent flaps, have a hearty, campfire breakfast, and follow the trails into the woods to summit the surrounding mountain peaks. I know since I was a kid, I have been seeking this place during all my excursions into the natural world which always beckons me to explore around the next bend in the trail. Maybe, someday, in one of Pennsylvania's State Forests or a lake in northern Maine or in the mountains of Poland it is waiting for me to discover it. If not, I have this amazing painting and all the memories of immersing in nature with Donna and so many of our family and friends.

Donna and I met while attending La Roche College (now University) in 1974. We were both biology majors when we completed a Biology Practicum together. Through this Practicum, we worked for McKeever Environmental Learning Center which was relatively new in 1976, opening in 1974. Under the direction of McKeever staff, we hunted wildflowers in Allegheny County, captured their images on hundreds of slides, made pressings of the very common varieties (through a permit issued by the County), and developed lesson plans utilizing these images and pressings. All of this was provided to McKeever to complete our Practicum and we paid to have a set of these slides duplicated for our own use which we still have in our possession.

Having our own set of slides was fortuitous because in August 1977, I read an article in the *Pittsburgh Press* about Deputy Principal W. R. Crawshaw asking for help in securing information on the United States. This struck a chord with the two of us and we duplicated another set of slides and sent them along with our lesson plans to Buller High School in Westport, New Zealand. This started an enjoyable correspondence between Deputy Crawshaw and us that lasted for several years. We just love wildflowering so much that sharing with a school in another country brought us much joy.

Our first date at a Pennsylvania state park was at McConnells Mill in the fall of 1975. It was a magical fall day with plenty of sunshine, sparkling waters, enjoyable hiking trails, and a historical mill and covered bridge to explore. Donna and I brought bagged lunches that day, enjoying them as we sat in the sunshine on a wall leading up to the interior of the covered bridge.

I never grow tired of the exciting experience of descending through the woods and boulders into the Slippery Rock Gorge area to find parking and begin exploring this beautiful park. When I was a kid, my brother, Paul, would bring us here to enjoy a day of picnicking and exploring. This continued for many years after he married and had kids of his own.

Donna and I would have never guessed that day that within ten years of visiting McConnells Mill, we would be sharing our love for the outdoors with our own children, Joseph and Laura. Our favorite family vacation destination was Acadia National Park in Maine where we exhausted ourselves biking on the carriage trails, hiking granite-lined trails to wide-open peaks, and kayaking in ocean waters surrounding Mount Desert Island. We returned to this park with Laura and our grandkids, Mason and Sophia, in 2019. Needless to say, we all had a blast and Mason and Sophia enjoyed the famous Jordan Pond popovers as much as us and they just flew up the mountain trails like a couple of mountain goats. Along with exploring Acadia, the five of us have visited many Pennsylvania state parks as well as Shenandoah, Yellowstone, Badlands, Indiana Sand Dunes, New River Gorge, Bryce Canyon, Zion, Great Sand Dunes, Mesa Verde, Arches, Capital Reef, and Canyonlands National Parks. We have enjoyed, biking, geocaching, hiking, horseback riding, kayaking, tent-camping, tobogganing, and wildflowering with our grandkids—we think this is our most important legacy since they will have lasting memories of exploring the great outdoors with their grandparents.

As a couple, Donna and I have enjoyed many hiking adventures including Rim to Rim in the Grand Canyon, trails in Mount Rainier National Park, trails in Isle Royale National Park, hut to hut in New Hampshire's White Mountains, the Trans Mount Blanc trail in Europe, the West Highland Way in Scotland, portions of the Wild Atlantic Way in Ireland, and segments of the Cornwall Coast Path in England. Our longest bike adventure brought us from Pittsburgh to Washington, DC by way of the Great Allegheny Passage and C & O Canal. We were weekend warriors on this trail since we were both working as were our companions on this adventure, our good friends John and Sue Hofrichter. Our most exciting kayaking adventure was our paddle out to Allegheny Islands State Park for obvious reasons but my favorite paddle occurred at the Quemahoning Family Recreation Area. This is a wonderful campground set on a flat plot of land projecting into the waters of Quemahoning Reservoir which consists of 899 acres. Our campsite was on the shoreline with our tent looking out onto the water and we kayaked to and from our campsite. Lots of fun.

These outdoor adventures have taken place before, during, and after our quest but the overriding fact is we have been immersed in the outdoors together since we met in college. I can say with confidence that the great outdoors will remain a central part of our lives as we grow old together. I retired on May 31, 2017, and Donna retired on May 31, 2018. What happened on June 1, 2018, is a reflection of the joy our engagement with the outdoors continues to bring us. Our first day of freedom as a couple found us at one of our favorite state parks, Laurel Hill. With so many astonishing memories of this park bouncing around in our minds, I believe we came face to face with kismet when walking into the park's gift shop, we spied the book that is responsible for shaping our first five years as a retired couple. This passport to bliss is entitled "Pennsylvania State Parks and State Forests Passport" and is produced by the Pennsylvania Parks and Forests Foundation (PPFF). The concept is not new to us since we enjoy using our national parks passport but we were instantly excited that the Pennsylvania state parks system has a passport book as well.

June 1, 2018 was an amazing moment in time for the two of us. Purchasing our passport, starting our quest, and targeting a completion date, were our way of drawing a line through our work experiences and metaphorically holding hands and jumping feet first into a new existence punctuated by all the magic that the natural environment has to offer. As I type this sentence, my mind is flooded by the enchantment of the peaceful, fog-shrouded views that greeted us at the Grand Canyon of Pennsylvania on a stormy spring morning. Yes, these and so many other spellbinding views never left our mind's eye as we pursued our quest through the years.

When we successfully finished our quest at the Point on May 21, 2023, we quickly told our family and friends in an effort to spread the joy that filled our hearts and souls. I know, in a reality check, this accomplishment is not on the level of winning an Olympic gold medal or flying on a commercial rocket or winning the lottery but for us, it was like all three experiences combined! In a flurry of activity, I also contacted La Roche University, the University of Pittsburgh, and North Catholic High School since each maintained an alumni newsletter and I believe that spreading the word will motivate and encourage others in our age bracket to spend more time outdoors and not be limited by their ages. Donna and I also submitted the required application forms to the PPFF to become members of the "Passport Hall of Fame" by notifying the organization that we completed their "Seen 'Em All Challenge" on May 21st. They sent us neat bandannas (Seen 'Em All Challenge theme) and certificates recognizing our accomplishment. They further recognized us by including an article in the Foundation's "Take Five Fridays with Pam" newsletter. This was very exciting because reading Pam's newsletter is always a great motivator for us. Thank you, Pam!

Our final bit of recognition came by making a request through the office of the Honorable Frank Burns, representing our 72nd Legislative District. I knew that one can obtain Pennsylvania House of Representatives citations for such personal events as special birthdays and anniversaries but this accomplishment was different so I was not sure if it was even possible. Donna and I have met Frank at different functions over the years and have come to know him as a great supporter of the outdoors—hunting, trail development, and parks—so we thought he would understand the importance of our request. He and his staff came through and our citation arrived in the mail on January 4, 2024 and it was beautifully worded. It was a wonderful ending to our big year and a boost as we look forward to new outdoor adventures in 2024.

During the last three years of our journey, I kept a special group informed of our progress. I host "Cupa Joe with Joe" on the Virtual Senior Academy (VSA) which is part of AgeWell Pittsburgh at the Jewish Community Center (JCC) of Greater Pittsburgh. The JCC through AgeWell Pittsburgh does a wonderful job of serving the elderly community of all faiths. Cupa Joe is an hour-long gathering during which I normally take Zoom participants on a virtual hike and afterwards, we have a conversation that goes in many different directions but is always filled with smiles and laughter. We have a wonderful core group with others dropping in on a month-to-month basis. My goal with this program is to spread the message that no matter what physical limitations one is facing in their sixties and beyond, there are ways that the treasures found in the outdoors can be experienced—through physical adaptations or the use of Zoom and similar technologies. I think this message dovetails nicely with AARP's Disrupt Aging campaign and the goals of AgeWell Pittsburgh.

As Donna and I ended 2022 with only five parks remaining, I promised my VSA students that we would have an in-person gathering when we crossed the finish line in 2023. On Thursday, August 10th, I conducted a hybrid Cupa of Joe class with Donna. The JCC provides a room with the necessary technology where a hybrid class can be held—both a Zoom component and an in-person one. This was lots of fun and led to another speaking engagement—amazing how that works when it is free of charge; but seriously, it provided another venue where I presented my message that the natural environment can become a playground for older adults when they are properly motivated and prepared for the experience. My hope is that the publishing of this book will lead to many more such opportunities.

When Donna and I loaded our kayak on our truck during the sunshine-filled morning of May 21st, we had only one objective: namely, to paddle to Allegheny Islands State Park. Much earlier in the year, we told Laura that our plan was to have the whole family join us at Point State Park to celebrate the end of our quest. They live in Pittsburgh's South Side so they are just a few minutes from this state park. However, emotions intervened when we landed on the island and we became so enthusiastic on our paddle back to the launch site that we entered a state of euphoria and found ourselves driving to Point State Park instead of our home in the Laurel Highlands. You would think two older adults would have enough sense to keep to the plan and not disappoint our family, but no, not us! Sorry Laura,

Eric, Mason, and Sophia—Pappy Joe and Grams acted like kids instead of mature adults. We are grateful you forgave us and appreciate the support you provided us along the way.

During the five years we were immersed in our adventure, reaching this river park always loomed large. Ideally, Allegheny Islands and Point State Parks would be the last two stamps in our passport since Pittsburgh is our hometown and filled with childhood, dating, and new parent memories. Our allegiance to this plan wavered at times because of our need to find river transportation. However, Point State Park as our final destination was set in concrete from day one because it was such a fitting venue both steeped in world history as well as our personal family history.

We followed many false trails over the years to obtain our river passage to the islands but as fate would have it, our original plan remained intact. What were some of those false trails? A friend's son had a boat on the Allegheny River and he was willing to transport us but schedules never lined up; a relative had a kayak but plans to use it never jelled; one adventure company had planned trips to the park but the means of transport were stand-up paddle boards which are beyond our skill sets; and a local non-profit with a stated goal of helping older folks and others to enjoy the outdoors turned down our request for help. Anyway, Donna and I were tired of all the false starts so I decided that for my 70th birthday, I would buy myself a kayak and lock down our plans to visit Allegheny Islands State Park as a worthy prelude to crossing the finish line at the Point.

We rented kayaks many times over the years on various vacations so Donna and I knew the basics of operating them safely. I researched the subject and came up with the perfect tandem kayak. A 70-year-old buying a kayak for the first time might seem odd to some people; however, in my own defense, it was not just a necessity but fulfilled a lifelong dream. As I mentioned earlier, we lived along Girty's Run when I was a kid and this stream became a special playground for all the kids in our little neighborhood of six homes. We raised the level of our portion of Girty's Run by building a dam of old railroad ties and large stones found along the stream. The water easily topped our makeshift dam but the key is that it raised the water level to the point that it would support our rafts.

Rafts? Yes, we built wooden rafts and attached huge, tractor-trailer inner tubes underneath their decks. Crawford Tire on Babcock Boulevard was a B. F. Goodrich tire dealer and was our source for old inner tubes that needed patches. Now we had our rafts and simultaneously, our little dam enabled us to both float along and formed a destination for our fun. The increased water level flowed around a high spot in Girty's Run where a couple willow trees grew, creating a cool little island. We played pirates by using our rafts to go to our island where we proudly flew our Jolly Roger from one of the willows. I had a Yancy Derringer cap gun which was perfect for our pirate theme. For those not familiar with Yancy Derringer, he was a character on a television show of the same name, circa 1958/59, set in New Orleans after the Civil War. The toy itself was a belt with a belt buckle hiding the derringer which could be swung away from the buckle, detached, and immediately fired. Anyway, since this childhood experience, my dream is to have my very own boat. So, about 60 years later, my opportunity finally arrives to fulfill my lifelong dream and there are no leaking, patched inner tubes anywhere! Plus, my finances got off easy—much cheaper compared to a Chevy Corvette or a Harley hog that headlines some others' lifelong dream list.

Arriving downtown, we could not park in an indoor parking garage with our kayak on top of our truck so we parked in an open-air parking lot across from the Heinz History Center and began our fairly long trek to

Point State Park and the completion of our quest. The Point was authorized as a state park in 1945, seven years before I was born, and was completed in 1974, when I was 22. The first parcel of the 36 acres that form the park was purchased in 1946. I do not know the details but I am sure the extended time necessary to complete the park resulted from the fact that it was not only a historical site but it was an industrial site with numerous property owners. To compound the problem, the Point and Manchester Bridges and the established traffic flows had to be eliminated and replaced by the Portal, Fort Pitt, and Fort Duquesne Bridges. Massive time and money were needed to accomplish this amazing transformation.

When Donna and I started dating in 1975, Point State Park was brand new and provided a backdrop to so many of our visits to downtown and the North Side for sporting events. Over the years, we were drawn to many events held in the park and visits to the Point have produced numerous cherished family memories. These memories span the gamut from picnicking with Paul and his family on one of his annual visits after he moved to Florida in 1979 to viewing the giant rubber duck with little Mason in 2013.

The picnic we had at Point State Park with Paul and his crew was based on take-out food from the Original Oyster House in Market Square. On every visit, Paul and I made it a goal to have some oysters there and wash them down with Iron City beer; however, with our families in tow, we decided on a spontaneous picnic in our local state park. We love the oysters and giant fish sandwiches but there is another reason for our loyalty to the Oyster House and it is not just the fact that it has been around since 1870. If you are from Pittsburgh, you might be thinking, well it is just because it is a Pittsburgh thing, but you would be wrong. To explain it, we are going to walk down memory lane again.

I have a small, sports-themed bar in our family room designed not really for drinking but as a setting for my sports memorabilia hanging on the wall behind it. Well, the largest hanging, not including my shadow-box homage to Super Bowl 43, is a poster of Rocky Marciano. Rocky was before my time but the reason it made my sports wall goes back to 1958. Our dad took Paul and I to the Oyster House for lunch sometime in the fall of 1958– Paul and I remember Dad having buttermilk with his oysters and us having Cokes. The big deal is that our presence at this bar-cafe is the only time we remember being together at a bar with our dad (I was six and Paul 16). Behind the bar at the Original Oyster House you still see the same Rocky Marciano poster that I have on my wall but in a larger size. That moment in time always remained precious to both of us and visits to the Oyster House or sitting at my home bar always sparked wonderful memories.

Lucky for me, years ago, the Oyster House maintained a special deal for members of their birthday club. Within 30 days of my birthday, I received a discount coupon to use towards a meal and an opportunity to receive a birthday gift—the Marciano poster, an Oyster House coffee mug or an Oyster House T-shirt. In 2017, I picked the poster as my birthday gift and Donna framed it for me. So now you know why the Oyster House was always so special to us brothers; unfortunately, Paul passed in 2014, so now I never look at the poster behind my bar or eat at the Oyster House without thinking of Paul and that special day when we were together with our dad. Over the years, my son, Joseph, and I have visited the Oyster House on many occasions before or after sporting events and traditionally, I hoist an Iron City to that memory and Joseph hoists a Coke.

By the way, below my Rocky poster is a photo showing Mohammed Ali standing over Sonny Liston. I bought it because Ali is the best boxer in my lifetime and it shows the end of his return match with Liston. I know it was controversial but I think Ali was just that good of a boxer and it was not a dive on the part of Liston. Ali stood strong for his beliefs and was never the same boxer when he returned to the ring after being incarcerated. I think the head blows he received after resuming his boxing career were the cause of his brain injuries which he dealt with for years prior to his passing. His lighting of the Olympic flame is locked into my memory but it remains a sad reminder of how much this great man gave up to stay true to himself and how much he and his family endured prior to his death.

I hope my jaunts down memory lane are not a bother, but for now, back to May 21, 2023. I can only imagine what Donna was thinking when we went through the doors of the Fort Pitt Museum together to collect our final stamp. For my part, it was a mixture of shared joy and a bit of sadness because we had reached the end of such an amazing quest and I was realizing nothing else would ever compare to this adventure. We were like young college kids again, just laughing, holding hands, having an accommodating Fort Pitt Museum staff member take our photo with Donna's iPhone, and afterwards running through the park taking selfies. What a great day to be alive and the weather was amazing with blue skies and sunshine providing the perfect backdrop to us finally filling our passport with all 144 stamps! I believe that if this well-loved passport could speak, it would keep repeating the words "amazing," "beautiful," "fun," "joy," and "tranquility." In my mind, the whole idea of setting out to visit all the parks and forests is encompassed in these five words. No matter what appeals to individuals about the outdoors, it awaits everyone in our parks, forests, and game lands. I added game lands just to say we in Pennsylvania are truly blessed with our public lands of all stripes.

Although I have done a bit of hunting and fishing in Pennsylvania, this definitely is not a hunting and fishing guide. However, as most know, there is a huge overabundance of deer causing maximum damage to our forest ecology, destroying ornamental landscaping in suburban and urban areas alike, spreading Lyme disease through deer ticks, and causing death and destruction on the highways through deer strikes. Strange situation because gun ownership in Pennsylvania is steeply increasing while hunting is continuing a long-term decline. Please advocate for hunters because they have a positive impact on the out-of-control deer population and annually supply over 100,000 pounds of deer meat to food banks around the state. Go hunters!

Along with hunting and fishing, we are blessed with many ways to enjoy all our public lands in Pennsylvania. For example, Donna and I love tent-camping and for us it is not just a thing from the past but is chock full of fun in the present. We love sitting by the campfire, making s'mores, playing cards and reading by lantern light, smelling percolating coffee and bacon frying in the early morning hours, tasting fresh blueberry and buttermilk pancakes just off the griddle, cooking up all sorts of hearty camp stove dinners, the twin flavors of burgers smothered in onions and slightly singed corn on the cob smothered in butter, falling asleep listening to a full orchestra of insects, hearing rain patter on the tent ceiling and experiencing the flashes and booms of a passing summer thunderstorm, waking up to a chill in the air in the spring or fall and quickly dressing to run through the tent flap and start the coffee, lounging in our camp chairs and alternately holding hands and sipping freshly brewed coffee during the day and tea at night, and laying in our sleeping bags while our minds drift along to the sounds of nature amplified by the darkness enveloping our tent. Oh, the many joys of tent camping!

On the topic of fun, the joy-filled memories of our nearly five years of exploring are filled with amazing road trips. Depending on the season and what gear we hung on our truck racks or slid into the truck bed, we had many options to increase our outdoor fun. Most of the time, we just depended on good hiking boots and trekking poles, other times we made use of Nordic skis, snowshoes, a tandem kayak, and hybrid bicycles. No matter how we experienced the joy and serenity of being outdoors, we continuously found ourselves enveloped in the beauty found in the various landscapes including bogs, boulder fields, lakescapes, meadows, mountain tops, river banks, stream banks, wetlands, and woods.

Staying On Track: Motivators to Maintain Momentum and Finish the Quest

Motivators are critical; without them, our quest could easily have spun into an endless march with hardships working overtime to upset our rhythm to the point where the quest becomes never-ending.

COMPANIONSHIP

The number one motivator for achieving our quest was each other. Metaphorically speaking, we held hands and ran through the years of this quest together. On some occasions, when the fun and joyful moments waned, we pushed each other to keep grinding away by embracing discipline and hard work in equal measures. In other words, motivators are critical; without them, our quest could have easily spun into an endless march with COVID and other hardships working overtime to upset our rhythm to the point where May 21, 2023, turns into a non-event with the quest never-ending.

So task one, find a companion for this big adventure—spouse, significant other, or friend. I know some people prefer to be on their own but I have my fingers crossed that everyone reading this book will have the fun, joy, and inspiration of human companionship. Donna and I learned the importance of sharing in the splendor of all the natural wonders we encountered as well as the setbacks—the awe, smiles, and laughter went hand-in-hand with mutual frustration and discouragement. In those times, mutual words of encouragement and support kept us moving forward on our quest. Also, please keep in mind that it is much safer to be in the woods with another person—just in case something goes wrong.

Special Opportunity: For those couples in their sixties and above, consider going on this quest with your grown children or grandchildren. I know it requires more coordination but what a special opportunity to pass along a love of nature to the next generations. I know with our own grandchildren we keep this in the forefront of each and every visit.

To convey how much importance I place on finding a companion for this big adventure, I will describe my saddest experience while being surrounded by nature in all its glory. I can remember it very clearly, just like it was yesterday! I was on a Temporary Duty (TDY) assignment at the New England High Intensity Drug Trafficking Area (NE HIDTA) in the winter. The location, near Boston, is very convenient for weekend drives to the lower Maine coastal region and I looked forward to taking full advantage of a wonderfully, snowy New England winter through both snowshoeing and Nordic skiing. Before I continue relating this story, I am going to pause and discuss Nordic skiing since many readers are likely unfamiliar with this term.

Nordic skiing is any type of skiing that requires the heel of the ski boot to remain free and unattached to the ski—unlike Alpine skiing where both ends of the boot are locked onto the ski. Under the broad category of Nordic skiing, I do both cross-country skiing and back-country skiing. In cross-country skiing, I use touring-style skis designed for groomed trails where tracks are set for skiers to follow. The bindings have automatic boot locks, accommodate less wide rod clips, and rely on a less robust boot. On the other hand, my back-country skis are heavy-duty, wider and shorter, steel-edged with a less pronounced upward curve in the front. The bindings lock manually (less chance of failure) and accommodate wider and thicker rod clips that hold heavily insulated boots to the skis. These boots are essential for back-country skiing because when breaking a new trail, the skis tend to submarine under a layer of snow unlike skiing on groomed trails, where the skis tend to float on top of the snow. Although I do some cross-country skiing, I much prefer the freedom of back-country skiing where I make my own trails.

Back in 1968, I read an article about Nordic skiing and from that very day, I was hooked on the sport. Let me add a bit of cocktail trivia. The ski binding system that accomplishes the task of attaching boots to skis continues to evolve. When I first started skiing, a Nordic binding system included a u-shaped spring that went around the heel of the ski boot and was fixed to that portion of the binding which attached the front of the boot to the ski. Later, I replaced my spring binding system with a three-pin binding structure in which the boot is attached to the ski by aligning three round holes in the toe-section of the boot to three pins residing on a metal bracket attached to the ski. Today, it seems the majority of bindings revolve around the New Nordic Norm (NNN) which uses a thin metal rod residing in an open section just beyond the toe area of the boot, automatically locking the boot to a binding mechanism anchoring the front of the boot to the ski. My answer to an unasked question: the oldest skis I currently own were manufactured in Norway and I bought them in 1972.

While reading the article in 1968, I learned the key to this sport is a two-way wax. This "magical" wax applied to ski bottoms produces the grip necessary to propel a skier up hills without sliding backwards, while simultaneously providing that extra glide needed for a skier to move effortlessly downhill. In my mind's eye, I saw a whole new world of winter wonders opening before me as I used Nordic skiing equipment and techniques to explore my favorite woodlands in the winter. Based on this article, I convinced my sister, Sandy, a downhill skier, to take Nordic skiing classes at the American Youth Hostel in the Shadyside section of Pittsburgh. Sandy agreed and the rest is history—Sandy did not become addicted like me but returned to Alpine skiing.

My excitement over the discovery of this amazing wax and new winter sport produced an uncontrollable desire to spread the word. The very morning after reading the article on cross-country skiing, I rapidly walked 0.7 miles uphill to my bus stop in Perrysville, Pennsylvania in eager anticipation of talking to my friends.

Unfortunately, my conversation on the school bus was overheard by a member of a ski club. An argument developed when he called me a liar since he knew that the "magical" wax did not exist. In short order, tempers flared and I ended up with a bloody nose. It all happened so fast—I recklessly threw my nose at his ham-like fist, producing a bloody nose which was followed by my use of cat-like reflexes to use my chest to intercept his piston-like punches, resulting in my quick fall to the school bus floor. Just like Vegas, what happened at the back of the bus, stayed at the back of the bus. Some readers may find it difficult to believe that Nordic skiing was so unknown in the United States in 1968 that it produced such ignorance in the downhill skiing crowd. However, a nugget of information clearly illustrates the truthfulness of this long ago memory. The famous American Birkebeiner cross-country ski marathon in Wisconsin did not start until 1973, long after the bloody nose affair, and at that point not even 60 skiers participated.

For the first 20 years of my Nordic journey, I went to groomed trails where I enjoyed the scenery when snow sporadically arrived in the Pittsburgh area. The fun really began in 1988 when we moved to Laurel Hill Mountain, located between Ligonier and Johnstown, and I experienced our first winter in the Laurel Highlands. Of course, I did not endear myself to my long-suffering, winter-adverse neighbors, who had been on the mountain for years and were continually bemused by my wintertime antics, including running around in my front yard screaming thanks to God for all of the beautiful, powdery snow. The location of our home turned out to be a stroke of luck since I was only two miles from the Laurel Highlands Trail, a perfect venue for Nordic skiing. I quickly adapted by buying skis that were designed for both groomed trails and open country. I just loved this sport but an opportunity to fulfill a high school dream never surfaced until my TDY to the NE HIDTA.

Since I was attending North Catholic, my dream had been to ski on a beach along the New England coast. I even purchased a guide to cross-country skiing in New England. During my TDY, I focused on the perfect place to fulfill my dream; namely, the Wells Reserve near Wells, Maine. This location is not far from the New Hampshire/Maine border and it is a gorgeous saltwater farm—perfect for skiing along the coast. I knew about the reserve since Donna and I visited there with our kids, Joseph and Laura, on one of our trips to Acadia National Park, which is further north along the Maine coast. There are some great trails and since it once was a salt water farm, a trail leads out to a beach.

One beautiful, snowy, Saturday in January 2001, I packed my lunch, grabbed my backpack, skis, poles, and boots and off I went. I arrived at the parking lot and skied right onto the beach. I could hardly believe it, I was skiing parallel to the beach, watching the waves rush in and out with the snow in the foreground. My longtime dream was coming true. I stopped skiing, just drinking it all in with my eyes and this incredible view filled my soul with overwhelming joy. I turn to Donna to describe my feelings but she was home in Johnstown with our kids. Oh my goodness, what an overwhelming feeling of sadness! My dream was coming true but I was unable to share this experience with my companion in life—still a joy but I was missing that special human feeling when two souls share a profound experience together. Skiing over to a group of coastal pine trees for shelter, I ate lunch watching the waves crash on the sand and sometimes roll far enough up to engage the snow line, but Donna was not there to make it perfect. Yes, those moments in time have had a profound impact since these feelings remain intact all these years later. The benefit is that Donna's presence throughout this quest was that much sweeter.

To further emphasize this belief of mine in companionship during this quest, I will relate another skiing experience. Long after I had settled into my skiing routine, a chance meeting occurred while watching Laura play volleyball for her high school team, Westmont-Hilltop. I met Tom who was there watching his daughter, Marie—Laura's good friend—play for Westmont as well. Much to the collective relief of our wives, we discovered that we both loved Nordic skiing and usually went out alone on the mountain. We quickly realized we were both crazy about the sport and wanted to go beyond the norm. This meant equipping ourselves with headlamps, backpacks, and back-country skis. We were now geared up to go bushwhacking (skiing through the woods without the use of paths) at night on the top of Laurel Hill Mountain. The parking lot we used to access this section of the Laurel Highlands Trail sits at the peak (2,743 feet) which back in those days (before climate change hit us hard) translated into great amounts of snow throughout the long winter months.

Our friendship was cemented over numerous ski runs during several great winters. We never let the frigid temperatures curb our enthusiasm and usually spent four to five hours exploring various terrain and making our way through numerous laurel thickets with late dinners at the turnaround point. Skiing together was an amazing experience where we found ourselves becoming lost in our own thoughts yet enjoyed pausing at times just for each of us to verbally share our thoughts on the unbelievable beauty we were seeing. Somehow the verbal sharing enhanced our perception of the unbelievable world that unfolded before us.

All of this led to our most amazing time skiing together. We started out on an overcast evening and glided along within a mile or two of the truck, the winds picked up, snow began to fall, and suddenly we were experiencing a white-out on skis. We simultaneously voiced concern but like kids with a new toy, we continued gliding along through the heart of the storm. Each of us were lost in our own thoughts as the winds increased, snow blinded us, and we found ourselves deeply ensconced in our private world of white. Time flowed unhampered by the normal touchstones of reality, muscles remained on automatic pilot continuing to propel us deeper into the landscape that was quickly being overwhelmed by the output of nature's giant flocking machine; suddenly, the storm's fury was spent, no longer blinded, we saw the falling flakes of white replaced by the rays of a full moon. Wordlessly, we stopped, turned off our headlamps and saw a glimpse of heaven in the wondrously transformed landscape—after a very long pause where we each experienced our personal glimpse of heaven, we thanked God for this experience and our friendship and resumed our skiing. Eventually, we reached a turnaround point, had a quick meal, and smoothly regained our skiing rhythm in the direction of the truck. Our senses remained overwhelmed as moonlight revealed a wonderfully altered landscape that spoke to our hearts and souls about God's presence in a palpable and all-encompassing way.

PENNSYLVANIA STATE PARKS AND STATE FORESTS PASSPORT

In second place, just behind human companionship as a motivator, is the treasure trove found within the pages of this state parks passport book. Before I go further, I want to extend my enduring thanks and gratitude to all the people that make the PPFF a superior organization and for this passport as well as so much more. Here are just a few quotes from the organization that say it all. "PPFF's mission is to inspire stewardship of Pennsylvania's state parks and forests." "Working to ensure a place—and an experience—for everyone in Pennsylvania's state parks and forests." "Conserve, enhance, enjoy! Forever." I urge everyone to explore www.PaParksAndForests.org and I know that through this quest your appreciation of their efforts will grow and grow. Please consider donating to this amazing organization!

Now let us dive into the passport. The brief biographies of four historical figures who worked so hard and did so much to establish and grow our amazing state parks and forests system really got us jazzed about our undertaking. Reading about some of the accomplishments of Joseph Rothrock, Mira Lloyd Dock, Gifford Pinchot, and Maurice Goddard really stoked the fire of our desire to achieve our quest and by doing so, in some small way honor all they did for us. The life of Maurice Goddard really intrigued me since he was born the same year as my dad and he retired the year after Donna and I married. Furthermore, he was born in Lowell, Massachusetts where my brother-in-law Gerry was born, and which is one of the towns I got to know during my NE HIDTA assignment. The fact that in 24 years as a Pennsylvania cabinet officer, he was responsible for adding 45 new parks is just astounding and that this all occurred during the early part of my lifetime really makes me feel grateful for his efforts. Being a contemporary of my dad enabled me to place him in some context of age and place.

Another amazing segment of this book provides a means to earn Pennsylvania Parks and Forests Champion tags. These metal tags are about the size of military "dog tags" and have a hole punched into each one for hanging purposes—great for backpacks. To me, earning these tags is another great motivator found in the pages of this passport. There are 14 categories: the Civilian Conservation Corps, Scenic Views and Vistas, Water Rushing By, Big Trees and Special Stands, Flora and Fauna, the Goddard Connection, Wet and Wild, Marvels of Nature, Scenes from History, Learning at One of Pennsylvania's Six Environmental Centers, Let 'Em Roll, Boots and Skis on the Ground, Kid-Sized Amusements, Eating and Contemplating, and Equestrian and Snowmobile Trails. Under each category is a list of things to do within specific parks and forests. All that is necessary to earn a tag is to check off a total of 10 boxes under a category and mark the date each is completed. Lots of fun and a neat way to track visits to various parks and forests. A bonus is that the possibilities under each of these headings are virtually endless so freelancing is possible with personal discoveries easily added during the quest to reach 10. Bravo, PPFF, for providing great locations as well as opening the door to freelancing—freedom to explore dovetails nicely with the personal feelings of freedom generated by being in the great outdoors.

Of course, the best part of the passport is the section where the passport stamps are placed. One-half of each page is devoted to a park or forest. On the upper left section is a photo, below the photo is the name, and below that is a blank space for the stamp itself. The right section begins with a highlight found in that specific park or forest and below that is a small description which is followed by a phone number to obtain more information. As I write this and page through our passport, I am impressed by all the unique stamps as well as the corresponding memories that swim around in my mind. Yes, using this passport and obtaining the stamps is definitely a huge motivator for reaching the finish line.

CANVAS MAP SHOWING PARK AND FOREST OFFICE LOCATIONS

Another nice motivator is a gift from Laura and it is designed for pins to be inserted when a park or forest office is visited. Thanks again, Laura! We are like little kids when we return home from a quest road trip, running to the hanging on the wall, taking it down, and placing our new pins and proudly rehanging our map. Of course, sometimes we are a patient Pappy Joe and Grams and wait for a visit from Mason and Sophia so they can do the honors. Oh what joy as our personal wall hanging map fills with pins of many colors.

PENNSYLVANIA STATE PARKS & FORESTS RECREATIONAL GUIDE & HIGHWAY MAP

This map and guide is produced by the Pennsylvania Department of Conservation and Natural Resources (PA DCNR). This is the big kahuna (the perfect descriptor since it is a Hawaiian word meaning expert) of DCNR guides since it served many purposes on our quest. One of these purposes was motivation. After returning from each road trip, we unfolded our map and underlined in red the name of the parks and forests we just visited. As you will read later, this simple act serves both as a motivator and as a crucial planning tool. Typing these words, I am chuckling over the condition of our precious map. A critical companion and constantly in use during our five-year quest—its current condition reminds me of *The Velveteen Rabbit* by Margery Williams since Donna and I are loving our map to life. I think it must have a roll of tape holding it together (LOL). By the way, *The Velveteen Rabbit* celebrated 100 years in 2021. We just loved sharing this story with our kids and grandkids and I highly recommend it.

HIKING MEDALLIONS

We not only visit park offices for our passports and to talk to staff but to see if the little gift shops within have hiking medallions. I don't know how many are familiar with these little gems but they are a wonderful motivator for me since I love collecting each one and attaching them to my wooden hiking poles. Not many shops have them but it's very exciting to find some along the way. The history of hiking medallions is very interesting. Collecting and attaching them to hiking poles became popularized in Europe. Roy Klebe, the owner of Hike America, brought the concept to America and has developed a nice little business offering wooden hiking poles and medallions to the public. My first wooden hiking pole is inscribed with "Acadia" and I purchased it at the Acadia National Park Visitor's Center in the early 1990s. My second one has "Joe" inscribed on it and Donna sent it to me when I was on my TDY to the NE HIDTA in 2001. My third is inscribed with "The Great Smokys" and I bought it during one of the Wildflower Pilgrimages we attended at the Great Smoky Mountains National Park. The other two are blank because Roy no longer offers inscriptions, which I discovered when ordering Mason's first hiking pole.

The story of Mason and hiking medallions is a joyful snippet. Several years ago, Laura volunteered me to be a mystery reader at Phillips School (a Pittsburgh Public School on the South Side) where Mason attended first grade. I was very happy with the invitation to select and read a book to his class. Donna and I brainstormed over the book selection and settled on *When Grandma Gatewood Took a Hike*, written by Michelle Houts and illustrated by Erica Magnus. Grandma Gatewood was the first woman to hike the Appalachian Trail. Along with the book, I brought three of my medallion-covered hiking poles that look similar to Grandma Gatewood's and two of my carbon-fiber hiking poles to show the children how hiking equipment has evolved. With my book, hiking poles, backpack, and wearing my hiking boots and hiking clothes, I arrived at Mason's classroom and his teacher introduced me as the mystery reader.

Just to see the smile on Mason's face when I walked into his classroom was all I needed to make the day perfect but the morning held many wonderful surprises. The children were very respectful and hung onto every word I read—they loved Grandma Gatewood's adventure. When I showed them my wooden hiking poles their enthusiasm knew no bounds and I never had a chance to talk to them about my modern hiking gear and compare it to Grandma Gatewood's. I was surrounded by children asking about all the various medallions and continuously pointing out new ones and asking about the hikes that I went on that matched the medallions. I ran out of time before I ran out of questions from the children. Mason was really excited that I was the mystery reader and gave me a big hug when I was leaving his classroom. When Laura, Sophia, and I met Mason in front of the school at the end of his day, he excitedly told Sophia about the hiking poles and the medallions. Suddenly, they both turned to me on the sidewalk and demanded to know why I had never shown them these poles. I started laughing and told them that I never thought they would be interested. Turns out they were very interested and after dinner, I walked out to my truck, grabbed my poles, and we spent the rest of the evening looking at the medallions and talking about many of the hikes.

From that day forward, Mason always helps me attach new medallions and prior to Christmas, he asked me for his own hiking pole. Along with the pole, I ordered several medallions that he earned while hiking with us in Maine and Pennsylvania. He loved this special Christmas gift and several days later, Laura sent a photo of Mason with his new hiking pole adorned with his medallions—his smile in the photo was the proverbial ear to ear version. Now, just like his Pappy Joe, Mason is an established collector and is always excited to earn one on our outdoor adventures.

PHOTOGRAPHING PARK AND FOREST SIGNS

Donna never leaves a park or forest office without snapping a photo of the corresponding sign for her photo books. Obtaining these photographs is always a big motivator for Donna. All are interesting and range from a bulletin board sign to very elaborate ones that come with stone foundations and plenty of timbers. Sometimes obtaining the photographs can be quite challenging because of busy highways with nowhere to pull off to take a quick photo but she always manages—Donna spying a place to park and walking back for a photo is always part of the fun and adventure. One sign comes to mind where it sat on a corner of a highway and a neighborhood street leading to the park entrance. The homes were beautiful, lining the street with manicured lawns, beautiful landscaping, and imposing driveways. I felt like a trespasser after dropping Donna off, reluctantly choosing a driveway to assist in turning my truck around, returning to pick up the intrepid photographer, and backing my truck into another driveway to once again turn around and head to the park (LOL).

I have another story regarding these sometimes-elusive park signs. Duane, Donna's brother, went with us on two of our road trips. He rode his motorcycle on these excursions and his idea was to photograph the signs with him standing next to his bike and the sign appearing in the background. Because the sign locations always varied with a few making it impossible to park the bike (upward/downward slopes, not enough room between sign and highway) he switched tactics and had photos taken with the sign and him wearing his bike helmet. When Donna and I first set out on our quest, my idea was similar to Duane's, only I had the great idea of taking the signs with my truck looming in the photos—the terrain quickly squashed that idea as well! Just saying...sign photos add another element of fun to our adventures and can be a neat motivator to keep the quest on track.

PHOTO BOOKS

Donna continually worked on producing photo books throughout our quest from day one through our last stop at Point State Park.

These books include the park and forest signs just mentioned and so much more. Donna spent countless hours documenting each visit by highlighting so many amazing experiences through her photography; as a result, flipping through any of her five books instantly returns me to many special moments and brings all those positive feelings rushing back. Each book ends with pages devoted to our five favorite parks and why we selected them. This is a very interesting task and exciting to see if there are parks that we both agree on as well as what our rationale is for our selections.

Every time a new book arrives in the mail, we grab a beverage of choice and look back on our latest adventures with both a sense of humor and a sense of awe. When we are finished, we begin itching to start our next road trip—which shows how powerful these books are as motivators for us!

Caution: As this section wraps up, please keep in mind that everyone is motivated by different things so the sky is the limit. Grab onto what suggestions hit your sweet spot and add your own. The key is finding the fun, joy, and encouragement in your chosen motivators as you forge ahead on your quest.

Planning for Success

> *PLEASE KEEP THESE THREE WORDS IN MIND THROUGHOUT YOUR ADVENTURE: FUN, JOY, AND FLEXIBILITY.*

HEALTH CHECK

This is the number one task at hand during the planning process. It does not matter the age of the participants—everyone should make a health check a priority— but having a health check grows in importance as we age. Talking of aging, do not let age stand in your way. Park visits can easily be modified based on age and level of fitness while still enjoying the beautiful natural environments that can be observed from parking areas and picnic groves. At the same time, preparing to launch this quest is a solid inducement to make positive health changes to increase endurance including weight loss, smoking cessation, and exercise. Remember, seek medical advice to both find your current health status and prior to beginning any health-enhancing programs. Always take things slow and easy and do not push yourself beyond your physician's recommendations.

While consulting your physician, take the time to obtain a recommendation on items to be included in your first aid kit for your backpack. Advice from your health provider based on fitness level and any limitations or disabilities, provides the information needed to decide your approach to your park and forest visits. Please keep in mind that much information is available regarding ADA accessibility of Pennsylvania state parks. The PA DCNR states the following: "Many ADA-accessible opportunities are listed under the various recreation pages of individual state parks and state forests. Another tool to find accessible opportunities is DCNR's interactive map, which has a link and filter to search for ADA accessible amenities and recreation opportunities."

TIME

The second step in the planning process is determining a rough estimate of the time needed to invest in completing your quest. One reason to take the time to perform this mental activity is to wrap your mind around the time commitment necessary to complete the quest in order to gauge the impact on your life. The second reason is to assist in planning your road trips. While contemplating the subject of time, here are a few questions for your consideration:

1) Considering your current home life and work life (if not retired), how many days per year are you planning to devote to this quest?

2) How much time will you devote to each park and forest visit? Remember, your visits are for your personal enjoyment. Do you enjoy the excitement of running into the park and forest offices, collecting your stamps, and moving on or are you the type of person that loves learning about new places and bathing in nature?

3) In your time calculations, are you thinking about travel time?

Caution: Please keep these three words in mind throughout your adventure: *fun, joy, and flexibility*. No worries if you fall behind on your timeline—it is just a *rough estimate* and nothing more. If you plan to invest one hour visiting each park, perfect. If you plan on a three-hour visit to each park, great. However, be prepared to deviate from your plan at any time. If you find a special feature or two, indulge yourself and spend more time. For example, one of our big weaknesses is wildflowers and sometimes instead of spending a planned two to three hours at a park, we found ourselves devoting many more hours because of an unexpected bounty of our favorite spring wildflowers. At the same time, if spending three hours is more your visiting style, don't be surprised when researching and planning road trips that a particular park only requires 30 minutes of your time. From our own experiences these are the parks where we plan a snack and a cup of coffee or a picnic lunch. For example, at Mont Alto State Park, Donna and I sat at a picnic table under the roof of the former carousel and enjoyed a picnic lunch before driving off. Another is Hyner View which encompasses six acres and a spectacular view. We enjoyed a fruit snack and our afternoon cup of coffee as we admired the breathtaking view.

RESEARCH

Research, research, and more research—here is our list:

1. <u>Pennsylvania Parks & Forests Foundation</u>
    As mentioned earlier, sign up for the PPFF weekly newsletter—"Take Five Fridays with Pam." This newsletter is written by Pam Metzger,

Membership Coordinator, and each week it is filled with information on various state parks and forests. This is a great read and an ongoing resource for your quest. Also, check out the little park profiles in the PPFF's passport book.

2. PA Department of Conservation and Natural Resources (PA DCNR)

DCNR's website, DCNR.pa.gov, is a wonderful source of information gained through following many links including an amazing interactive state parks and forest map—beware, you can be lost for hours and hours using this tool (it is that good). Also, the site provides a link to the Pennsylvania Campground Reservation System. Do yourself a big favor and open an account for the reservation system. Maintaining an account will save much time in the reservation process and if you are a senior (62+), the software program will automatically add your discount to your invoice when checking out. Plus, it maintains a history of your stays and it will enable you to record your favorite campsites for future visits. The reservation system is efficient, easy, and provides lots of help throughout the process (all unexpected features since many local, state and federal websites appear dated and frustrating to use). For example, you can bring up campsite maps to help with your site selection and many times photos of the exact campsite are available.

A critical item on DCNR's individual park web pages is the e-mail address at each park because it shows where the manager is for that particular park. Not all parks are self-managed and to have your passport stamped, you must travel to the park office that appears in the e-mail address. For example, if you go on the DCNR web pages for Archbald Pothole, Lackawanna, Prompton, and Salt Springs, you will find the same e-mail address under the "Contact Us" section: lackawannasp@pa.gov.

This tells you that all four parks are managed by the administration in place at Lackawanna State Park; therefore, all four stamps will be held at the Lackawanna State Park office. At the same time, some parks that are not self-managed may have a small, outdoor box containing little square papers with a park stamp that can be glued into your passport. Just don't count on this bonus and to obtain an ink passport stamp, you must go to the park that provides management services.

Maps, maps, and more maps are provided by DCNR—a thumbs up to everyone that works tirelessly there for all of us that seek to enjoy Pennsylvania's natural gifts. As mentioned earlier, Pennsylvania State Parks & Forests Recreational Guide & Highway Map is number one on our list since it is so invaluable for anyone undertaking and implementing this quest. Visit the nearest state park office or state forest office to obtain a copy. If not available, a staff member can advise on how to obtain one. This huge map contains a vast amount of needed information. Most importantly, it visually shows the location of every state park and state forest office. This map utilizes a color-keyed system showing the outline of each state park, state forest, state game lands, and federal recreation land in Pennsylvania. All of this is overlaid with major road systems, streams, and rivers. On the reverse side of the map there is a spreadsheet containing 15 columns with the following titles: StatePark/Phone/Electric Vehicle Charging Station (EV)/ Map Coordinates, Cabins, Camping, Other Lodging, Picnicking, Swimming, Boating, Fishing, Hiking, Bicycling, Education Programs, Equestrian Trails, Hunting, Winter Sports, and Sightseeing. This map is pure gold and pure genius—fantastic job, DCNR!

Other great maps produced by the DCNR are individual Park Campground Maps, State Park Recreation Guides, Forest Map and Recreational Guides, and trail maps. We have a complete collection of the

State Park and Forest Guides as well as several Campground Maps. Please be aware that a few of the state park guides cover multiple parks. We always made it a goal to collect as many as possible while we were out and about. Many individual park and forest offices have numerous maps for other parks and forests but we only found the campground maps and trails guides at the corresponding offices. The campground maps are great for navigating to specific campsites and nice to have when walking and biking around campgrounds. Sometimes the campgrounds are so huge that it is comforting to have a map in your back pocket when attempting to return to your tent.

Each state park Recreation Guide includes a park map containing the location of the park office as well as corresponding biking and hiking trails, unique historical sites, streams and lakes, campgrounds, roadways, restrooms, picnic groves, boat launch sites, and state forest and game lands adjoining the park. On the reverse side of the map, one may find park directions, size, history, geological features, and trail descriptions. Thus, these maps are wonderful for planning park visits. However, Donna and I usually did not have park Recreation Guides prior to planning each visit. This gap in information for planning purposes can be remedied somewhat by going on the DCNR website and viewing digital files. However, upon arrival we always tried to obtain printed copies. These guides were always helpful to quickly orient ourselves to our surroundings.

Lesson Learned: When I started writing this book, I was seeking some solitude and spent a few weeks at the Cambria County Library in Johnstown, Pennsylvania, writing. Traversing the rows of books between the stairway and my writing spot, I happened upon a bookshelf that contained row after row of state and federal publications. Guess what I stumbled upon on those shelves? A bunch of state park Recreation Guides! I would advise adding the local library to your research to determine availability.

A State Forest Map and Recreational Guide contains a map of the tracts of land that form the forest. A critical feature of the map is all the roads that exist including hard surface roads, improved gravel roads, unimproved gravel roads, and drivable trails. On the reverse side, topics covered include recreation opportunities, wild and natural areas, and history. The importance of these guides is easily illustrated by an incident that transpired on September 15, 2020, the low point of our park adventures.

On August 27, 2020, we were returning from a really special trip since it included celebrating our 42nd wedding anniversary by hiking up to a beautiful view from a flat rock formation reached through the Flat Rock Trail at Colonel Denning State Park. On this particular road trip, we were camping at Gifford Pinchot State Park, visiting Boyd Big Tree Preserve Conservation Area, Memorial Lake State Park, Swatara State Park, Joseph E. Ibberson Conservation Area, camping at Little Buffalo State Park, visiting Tuscarora State Forest, Big Spring State Park, Fowlers Hollow State Park, Colonel Denning State Park, and Reeds Gap State Park. Anyway, we were coming home that Thursday afternoon and about 10 miles from our house we lost the transmission on our truck with just over 60,000 miles on the speedometer. Unknown to us at the time, this kicked off a series of events that led to September 15, 2020.

With my truck just breaching my 60,000-mile transmission warranty, the manager at the service department at our dealership swung into action. However, it was a long, drawn-out process that finally ended very well thanks to the persistence of our service manager, with the manufacturer covering 95% of the replacement cost. But with another trip locked in and kicking off on September 14, 2020, we had to make alternate transportation plans. With Donna's brother, Duane, following us on his street bike, we folded down the seats on Donna's CR-V, loaded up our gear, and off we went.

We arrived at Raymond B. Winter State Park on the afternoon of the 14th. This park was a bit of a milestone on our quest because we obtained our 61st park stamp and we were now just over halfway to our original goal of 121 state parks. We had a wonderful campsite in this compact, 695-acre park that featured mountain streams, Rapid Run Natural Area, Halfway Lake, and a picturesque hand-laid sandstone dam built by the CCC boys. Our goal for Tuesday, the 15th, was to visit Poe Paddy and Poe Valley State Parks.

This is when the lack of my truck caused major problems. Many times when we are in the wilds of Pennsylvania we have no cell service so we count on my truck's GPS for navigation purposes. Along the way, we lost cell service and Duane's GPS unit on his bike was old and seemed to be leading us in the wrong direction. We pulled into a parking lot to check out our trusty PennDot Transportation Map. We had the map spread out on the hood of the CR-V when this old guy (LOL I was 68 at the time) rolled up in his four-wheel drive vehicle. He asked if there was a problem and we told him of our destination for that day. He said he could save us time by drawing us a map that would easily take us over the mountain and through the heart of Bald Eagle State Forest to our parks. He assured us that the route would not pose problems for the motorcycle or CR-V. He smiled and off he went and off we went.

With Duane in the lead, we found ourselves on a gravel road as we followed our new map. For a period of time all went well but the road began to narrow and the gravel disappeared. Suddenly, it was just mud, large rocks, water hazards and trees moving in from both sides. Now I know how a minnow feels after entering a minnow trap. To the right was a thin screen of trees and behind that was a drop-off down the mountain. To the left was another thin strip of trees with steep rock walls beyond. The road hazards forced me into "white-knuckle" driving mode with too many hazards behind me to attempt to back up. Duane had his own issues keeping his bike upright since his speed was so slow.

As we continued up the mountain, Donna's vehicle got pinstripes on both sides from the intruding tree branches. At the same time, Duane was becoming exhausted because the negligible speed was forcing him to use his legs continuously to keep his bike upright and moving forward. During this ordeal the motorcycle came down hard on both sides without injury to Duane, which was both a miracle and a blessing. To say the least, we were discouraged and angry over the map. The three of us assessed the situation and knew we were in big trouble. No cell phone service and the poor road conditions made us conclude that a normal tow truck rescue would be impossible even if we spent the rest of the day hiking down off the mountain to find a landline somewhere. We decided to stop, have our packed lunches and recover both mentally and physically. Just then, two guys on dirt bikes came down the path (we no longer called it a road), rolled off into the ditch on our left, briefly looked at us, shook their heads, popped back on the path behind the CR-V, and kept rolling down the mountain. All of us agreed they would be entertaining their buddies tonight retelling their encounter!

While we ate lunch, Donna came up with a brilliant idea. She sorted through the maps in her glove compartment, came up with the Bald Eagle Forest Map and Recreational Guide, found the crossroads we were at, and quickly decided on which way to turn. Fortunately, we abandoned the hand-drawn map but Duane's bike came down hard one more time before Donna guided us to an improved gravel road which led to another road and finally to Poe Paddy State Park. It was with much relief and a huge reduction in group anxiety, when we made it to the park office at Poe Valley State Park and a kindly ranger gave us solid directions to reach Pennsylvania Route 45 after we finished exploring his park. The good news is we all ended up safe and not stranded in the middle of Bald Eagle State Forest. On returning home, Duane's motorcycle was declared totaled and Donna traded in her CR-V.

Lesson Learned: This episode really drove home to us the importance of continuing to obtain these paper maps/guides in this digital age, to have the guides specific to the forest you plan to encounter in your vehicle, and to always stay away from roads marked on maps as *drivable trails*. Also, consider the purchase of a Delorme Atlas & Gazetteer for Pennsylvania as well as a portable GPS unit if your vehicle is not equipped with one. We purchased a Delorme after this episode and the map details are amazing.

Opportunity: When visiting each forest district office to pick up the corresponding guide and passport stamp, consider scanning the brochure racks for other good snags. Each forest is a treasure chest filled with numerous recreation choices and the keys to open this treasure are the brochure racks and the staff. Donna and I consider Forbes State Forest our home forest and on our office visits we have discovered numerous amazing trails and scenic spots through 18 separate trail guides as well as by way of some sparkling conversations. Do yourself a favor, find the forest closest to your home, stop by the district office, and explore options through available trail guides and conversations with always welcoming staff. Personnel at both park offices and forest offices are always great resources and really friendly. Forest offices do not have a large influx of tourists compared to park offices, so we always find the staff very excited to see us and anxious to share their knowledge.

3. General Internet Searches

The digital age makes digging up general information to assist your trip planning so simple and fast. Internet searches will help with finding where to obtain groceries near your campsite, determining travel time between state parks, coming up with great places to eat and so much more.

4. Social Media

I am not big on social media but Donna tells me there is a lot of good information to be found there so I would be remiss in not mentioning this source for research purposes. Based on our conversations on this topic, I know this source of research can be very fruitful. People write blogs as they are in the midst of their quests as well as doing so after crossing the finish line. At the same time, many Pennsylvania state parks have local volunteer groups that come together to donate their time and energy to enhance their favorite park. Several maintain a presence on social media to post information about the park and group activities. This provides an opportunity to correspond with people who know a specific park inside and out and enjoy helping others to learn more about it.

Preparing to Hit the Road

FROM DAY TRIPS TO ROAD TRIPS,
IT IS TIME FOR OUR ACTION PLANS.

DAY TRIP ACTION PLANS

Find a nice big table and unfold your Pennsylvania State Parks & Forests Recreation Guide & Highway Map with the map side up as well as your PennDot Pennsylvania Highway Map. Now, on the DCNR map, circle your hometown. Based on this home base, make a list of state parks and forest offices that you can visit on day trips. Once you finish your list, you can begin planning your visits. Since there is no camping on these one-day excursions, you can start your adventures on very short notice.

On day trips, Donna and I always pack a "truck lunch" and complement the picnic items with plenty of water as well as a thermos of coffee for our afternoon break. Consider these day trips your gentle introduction to your quest. You can learn to use the park maps, enjoy collecting your first passport stamps, talk to park and forest personnel, learn from their advice, and possibly tweak the time you plan to spend at each park based on your initial visits.

Caution: My hope with this book is to inspire newbies to indulge themselves in the outdoors by launching their own parks and forests quest. I believe this quest is a great way for young families to have fun in the beautiful outdoors with their kids; at the same time, it is a chance for adults in their sixties, seventies, and beyond to be rewarded by uplifting outdoor adventures while maintaining a pace and physical activity level that dovetails with their abilities. With that in mind, I would ask participants—along with the health check mentioned earlier—to read over my equipment list in a very thoughtful manner. Remember, anticipating challenges and preparing for them is the best way to keep safe and ensure enjoyable experiences.

Lesson Learned: Always grab your passport stamps wherever you find them. When Donna and I picked up our first passport stamp at Laurel Hill State Park on June 1, 2018, we were provided the opportunity to obtain a few more stamps from nearby parks but we declined the offer. The two of us did not want to form a habit of obtaining stamps prior to "earning them" through our visits. Big mistake! Later, we visited both Laurel Ridge and Kooser State Parks and no staff were on hand at either park nor did we find self-service stamp boxes. We had to return to Laurel Hill to obtain those stamps and from that day forward, we never refused a stamp. Also, when you arrive at forest offices check to see if they have any stamps for nearby parks. In most cases, these offices only have the passport stamp for the corresponding forest but occasionally we found forest offices actually had some park stamps.

ROAD TRIP ACTION PLANS

<u>Customizing Your Parks & Forests Map</u>

Donna and I always turned to our DCNR parks and forests map as our main tool for planning and overseeing our progress. Here are some easy steps to follow to customize your copy. First, take a straight edge and use a red pen to draw a line from "J" at the top of your map to "J" at the bottom of your map; next, a line from "S" at the top to "S" at the bottom; lastly, lay your straight edge on the map from "7" on your left to "7" on your right and draw a line from where the straight edge intersects with the "J" line to where it intersects with the "S" line. Now you have successfully created four quadrants—North, South, East, and West.

With the customized map in hand, your quest is no longer so overwhelming—divide and conquer! The "North" encompasses 30 parks and seven forests; the "South" contains 31 parks and five forests; the "East" consists of 36 parks and four forests; and in the "West" there are 27 parks and four forests. See the following tables.

NORTH			
Parks			**Forests**
Hills Creek	Elk	Hyner View	Susquehannock
Mt. Pisgah	Sizerville	Parker Dam	Tioga
Kinzua Bridge	Ole Bull	Susquehanna	Elk
Denton Hill	Worlds End	Simon B. Elliott	Loyalsock
Lyman Run	Sinnemahoning	Ravensburg	Sproul
Patterson	Kettle Creek	Bald Eagle	Tiadaghton
Colton Point	Hyner Run	McCalls Dam	Moshannon
Leonard Harrison	Little Pine	Milton	
Prouty Place	Upper Pine Bottom	Sand Bridge	
Cherry Springs	Bucktail	Raymond B. Winter	

PREPARING TO HIT THE ROAD

SOUTH			
Parks			**Forests**
Black Moshannon	Joseph E. Ibberson	Kings Gap	Bald Eagle
Shikellamy	Little Buffalo	Gifford Pinchot	Rothrock
Poe Paddy	Memorial Lake	Pine Grove Furnace	Tuscarora
Poe Valley	Boyd Big Tree	Susquehanna Riverlands	Michaux
Penn Roosevelt	Trough Creek	Samuel S. Lewis	Buchanan
Reeds Gap	Blue Knob	Cowans Gap	
Prince Gallitzin	Colonel Denning	Caledonia	
Whipple Dam	Fowlers Hollow	Buchanan's Birthplace	
Greenwood Furnace	Big Spring	Mont Alto	
Canoe Creek	Warriors Path	Codorus	
Swatara			

EAST			
Parks			**Forests**
Salt Springs	Hickory Run	Tyler	Pinchot
Vosburg Neck	Big Pocono	French Creek	Delaware
Lackawanna	Lehigh Gorge	Evansburg	Weiser
Prompton	Beltzville	Norristown Farm	William Penn
Archbald Pothole	Tuscarora	Fort Washington	
Varden	Locust Lake	Benjamin Rush	
Ricketts Glen	Jacobsburg	Neshaminy	
Frances Slocum	Delaware Canal	Marsh Creek	
Promised Land	Nockamixon	Ridley Creek	
Goldsboro	Ralph Stover	Big Elk Creek	
Tobyhanna	Washington Crossing	Susquehannock	
Nescopeck	Nolde Forest	White Clay Creek	

WEST			
Parks			**Forests**
Presque Isle	Jennings	Linn Run	Cornplanter
Erie Bluffs	McConnells Mill	Laurel Mountain	Clear Creek
Chapman	Moraine	Laurel Summit	Gallitzin
Pymatuning	Raccoon Creek	Kooser	Forbes
Oil Creek	Allegheny Islands	Laurel Hill	
Bendigo	Yellow Creek	Shawnee	
Maurice K. Goddard	Hillman	Laurel Ridge	
Cook Forest	Point	Ryerson Station	
Clear Creek	Keystone	Ohiopyle	

Caution: We just artificially divided the State of Pennsylvania into four quadrants. Please do not become anal over sticking to these artificial borders. If you are working on your West quadrant but find yourself traveling to Philadelphia for the annual flower show or a sporting event, don't hesitate to grab a few park visits and stamps along the way—never ignore opportunities. Similarly, if you plan a road trip and find that the parks you are planning to visit are in two quadrants, no worries just do it!

Opportunity: I hesitated to introduce this opportunity earlier since I did not want anyone shying away from this quest before becoming more committed. At the same time, some individuals may now be at the point where this huge undertaking is just so overwhelming that they are rapidly losing interest. Hence, this is the perfect time to take stock and provide some alternatives. Based on my earlier thoughts regarding the importance of fun, joy, and flexibility in relationship to the quest, consider reducing its size. How about organizing your quest around all the parks and forests in one quadrant or within 100 miles of your front door, or all the parks with great vistas? Later in the book, I will provide a list of my favorite parks in various categories which can aid in the development of a less extensive quest. Be kind to yourself and flexible in your quest so that the results produce more fun and joy no matter if your quest is focused on all 124 parks and 20 forests or far fewer.

Okay, where to begin road tripping? Well, start with the quadrant that is home to the majority of the parks and forests that you visited through your day trips. Based on this criterion, Donna and I started in the West. For the most part, we worked on the South next, followed by the North and ending in the East. As mentioned earlier, we saved our visits to Allegheny Islands and the Point for the very last. This is the perfect time to select the park or parks where you will complete this amazing quest. Just have fun with your selection and throughout the quest, enjoy anticipating visiting the final park representing your personal finish line.

Hub and Spoke

I recommend road trip planning based on a hub and spoke approach as much as possible. I look at a quadrant on our DCNR map to find a state park with a campground (hub) encircled by other state parks/forest offices (spokes). On the other hand, this is not always an option based on park locations. When park/forest offices line up along an interstate highway/major Pennsylvania state highway or along a river, I plan my road trip based on a more or less point-to-point approach (office A to office Z in a more or less straight line). In these situations, park campgrounds might serve as an overnight place to stay in combination with motels along the route. In conjunction with deciding on a trip plan, I develop a written guide corresponding to the planned road trip. I have selected two of our road trips to illustrate both hub and spoke and point-to-point. These examples also act as templates for your own road trips.

ROAD TRIP 1

It is September and we are visiting nine parks and two forests in the East quadrant using a hub and spoke plan. Our hub will be Promised Land State Park where we will be camping (please note this road trip occurred before former Governor Wolf created Vosburg Neck State Park or it would have been included).

DAY 1
Camping

Driving time from home to the forest office is four hours.

Delaware State Forest District Office - 2174 Route 611, Swiftwater
* 83,518 acres

Driving time to Promised Land State Park from the Delaware State Forest Office is 35 minutes.

Promised Land State Park - 100 Lower Lake Road, Greentown
Make camp
* 3,000-acres with 422-acre Promised Land Lake and 173-acre Lower Lake; surrounded by 12,464 acres of Delaware State Forest
* Masker Museum: interactive look at CCC Boys, wildlife displays, and native plant garden
* 50 miles of trails including Bruce Lake Trail to natural glacial lake and Little Waterfalls Trail—no length noted on either trail

- Pick up two stamps for Promised Land State Park and Varden Conservation Area. Check for information on Varden.

DAY 2

Driving time from Promised Land to Gouldsboro is 30 minutes.

Gouldsboro State Park - Pennsylvania 507, Gouldsboro
- * 2,800 acres and 250-acre Gouldsboro Lake
- * 10 miles of hiking trails

- Stamp held by Tobyhanna State Park.

Driving time from Gouldsboro to Tobyhanna is 25 minutes.

Tobyhanna State Park - 114 Campground Road, Tobyhanna
- * 5,440 acres and 170-acre Tobyhanna Lake
- * 10 miles of trails including 5.1-mile Lakeside Trail that can be used to bike around the lake and Range Trail which is 3.3 miles one way. This trail follows the border of the Black Bear and Bender Swamps Natural Area and passes through several other wetlands and boulder fields created by the last glacial period.

- Pick up three stamps: Tobyhanna State Park, Gouldsboro State Park, and Big Pocono State Park.

Driving time from Tobyhanna to Promised Land is 30 minutes.

DAY 3

Driving time from Promised Land is 28 minutes.

Varden Conservation Area - 1100 Mid Valley Road, Lake Ariel
- * 444 acres; little information on trails—very short trails

- Stamp is held by Promised Land State Park.

Driving time from Varden Conservation Area to Prompton State Park is 21 minutes.

Prompton State Park - West Shore Road, Prompton
- * Prompton State Park provides boat launching and picnicking facilities for the 290-acre Prompton Lake which is operated by the U.S. Army Corps of Engineers
- * 26 miles of hiking trails surround the lake
- * 2,000 acres

- Stamp is held by Lackawanna State Park.

Driving time from Prompton State Park to Archbald Pothole State Park is 28 minutes.

Archbald Pothole State Park - 960 Scranton Carbondale Hwy, Archbald
- * 150 acres; named after Archbald Pothole which formed about 15,000 years ago
- * Part of park is reclaimed strip mine with athletic fields

- Stamp is held by Lackawanna State Park.

Driving time to Promised Land State Park is 43 minutes.

DAY 4

Driving time from Promised Land State Park to Salt Springs State Park is 90 minutes.

Salt Springs State Park - 2305 Salt Springs Road, Montrose
- * 405-acre park which is operated by Friends of Salt Springs which owns land adjacent to the park
- * The focal points of the park are the towering old-growth hemlock trees—many estimated to be more than 300 years old—the rocky gorge cut by Fall Brook with its three waterfalls, and the salt springs

* 15 miles of trails including the Cliff Trail and Hemlock Trail. The Cliff Trail is 1.6 miles and can be reached from the Friends parking lot. The Hemlock Trail is 0.4 miles and access is at the northeast end of the picnic area, past the salt spring. Check out the boardwalk and Penny Rock.

- Stamp held by Lackawanna State Park.

DAY 5
Pack Up Camp

Driving time from Promised Land State Park to Pinchot State Forest Office is 50 minutes.

Pinchot State Forest District Office - 1841 Abington Road, Waverly
* 44,743 acres

Driving time from Pinchot State Forest Office to Lackawanna State Park is three minutes.

Lackawanna State Park - 1839 Abington Road, Waverly
* 1,445 acres and 198-acre Lackawanna Lake
* 18 miles of trails—no information on trails

- Pick up four stamps for Salt Springs State Park, Lackawanna State Park, Prompton State Park, and Archbald Pothole State Park.

Driving time from Lackawanna State Park to Frances Slocum State Park is 37 minutes.

Frances Slocum State Park - 565 Mount Olivet Road, Wyoming
* 1,035 acres and 165-acre, horseshoe-shaped Frances Slocum Lake

* The Patrick Solano Environmental Education Center features exhibits on indigenous people and the ecology of the park
* 14 miles of trails including the 3.2-mile Deer Trail which starts at the environmental education center and passes through diverse habitats

Driving time back home is four hours.

ROAD TRIP 2

It is early April and we are visiting seven parks in the West quadrant using Interstate 79 as the highway corridor providing easy access. We brought our bikes along to take advantage of several beautiful biking trails. On this trip there is only one park with camping, Pymatuning, and we made the decision to use motels since the weather was unsettled and on the cool side.

DAY 1
Motel in Meadville, PA

Presque Isle State Park - 301 Peninsula Drive, Erie

Driving time from home is three hours.

* 13.5-mile paved biking trail along lake, beaches, monuments, and lighthouse
* Tom Ridge Environmental Center
* 3,200-acre peninsula

(We will enjoy lunch at Sara's Restaurant, 25 Peninsula Drive, prior to biking. It is a can't miss experience—open seasonally.)

Erie Bluffs State Park - 11100 West Lake Road, Lake City

Driving time from Presque Isle State Park is 21 minutes.

* 587 acres
* five miles of hiking trails

Driving time from Erie Bluffs to Motel in Meadville is 42 minutes.

DAY 2
Motel in Grove City, PA

Driving time from the Motel in Meadville to Pymatuning is 26 minutes.

Pymatuning State Park - 2660 Williamsfield Road, Jamestown
* 16,893 acres, 17,088-acre lake is the largest in PA
* Buy old bread and feed the carp at the spillway
* 3.25-mile Spillway Trail
* seven miles of hiking trails

Driving time from Pymatuning to Maurice Goddard is 30 minutes.

Maurice Goddard State Park - 684 Lake Wilhelm Road, Sandy Lake
* 2,856 acres and Lake Wilhelm is 1,680 acres
* 12-mile paved biking trail that loops the lake

Driving time from Maurice Goddard to the Motel in Grove City is 22 minutes.

DAY 3

Driving time from Motel in Grove City to Jennings is 21 minutes.

Jennings Environmental Ed. Ctr. - 2951 Prospect Road, Slippery Rock
* 300 acres, 20-acre prairie ecosystem
* five miles of trails

Driving time from Jennings to McConnells Mill is 22 minutes.

McConnells Mill State Park - 1761 McConnells Mill Road, Portersville
- * 2,546 acres in the Slippery Rock Creek Gorge
- * mill and covered bridge
- * 11.2 miles of hiking trails

Driving time from McConnells Mill to Moraine is 10 minutes.

Moraine State Park - 225 Pleasant Valley Road, Portersville
- * 16,725 acres and 3,225-acre Lake Arthur
- * 29.2 miles of hiking trails
- * 14.8-mile Glacier Ridge Trail goes from Moraine State Park to Jennings Environmental Education Center
- * seven-mile paved biking trail

Driving time from Moraine to home is two hours.

Gearing Up for the Quest

I DEDICATE THIS SECTION TO ASSISTING NEWBIES OF ALL AGES TO BEGIN GEARING UP IN ANTICIPATION OF THE BIG DAY WHEN OUTDOOR DREAMING BECOMES REALITY.

I believe many readers of this book are intrigued with the idea of setting out on this quest but have no practical experience enjoying the outdoors or their experience occurred in the 1970s or earlier. I dedicate this section to assisting newbies of all ages to begin gearing up in anticipation of the big day when outdoor dreaming becomes reality. My recommendations are based on personal experiences and none of the suppliers or manufacturers mentioned were consulted about their inclusion. Please use this as a supplement to any input from friends and relatives as well as articles and books that you may have come across on this subject. I am no expert on reviewing outdoor gear but just one person that has used a limited selection of gear over many years and knows what works for me.

One other item to touch on before I start on gear recommendations is where to shop. I am not against buying products from large corporations at times since there are bargains to be found as well as unique products. However, my preference is to shop locally with small businesses. I find the owners and staff are fonts of knowledge pertaining to their products, overwhelm with outstanding customer service, and work hard to serve the communities where they are located.

I admit I am prejudiced regarding small businesses because my dad started one that became a huge part of my life through the age of 27 when

I was forced to negotiate its purchase by one of our suppliers. Typing this sentence, I realize it is time to walk down memory lane again.

My dad started J. B. Supply Company in Pittsburgh on January 22, 1947, which was his 35th birthday. At the time, my dad and mom had three children ranging in age from 11 months to six years old. I would come along almost six years later and my youngest sister would be born 11 years and nine months after the business was started—just 10 months before Dad passed from lung cancer. Dad started this business at 3842 Chartiers Avenue, Pittsburgh 4, PA; next he moved to 2030 Beaver Avenue, Pittsburgh 12, PA; followed by 52 Terminal Way, Pittsburgh 19, PA; and finally to 7095 Babcock Boulevard, Pittsburgh 9, PA. The address for the location on Babcock was later changed from 7095 to 3435. On November 8, 1950, Dad signed a contract with a local general contractor to build a warehouse and office alongside the house. The office opened into the interior of the home on one side and into the warehouse on the other.

When Dad passed away in 1959, Mom took over the business. Looking back at her situation (five kids under 19, no life insurance, taking over her husband's business which served the high-testosterone steel industry) she was a great mom and an amazing business woman way before society was prepared to appreciate women in different roles. In 1974, Mom signed a contract to add a second floor to the old warehouse along with an office and half-bath on the first floor, and a two-story addition onto the front of the warehouse. This was necessitated by a "vendor stocking" contract Paul negotiated with United States Steel Corporation in 1972.

I returned home from attending the University of South Florida and started full-time in the family business in 1972. Later, I began attending early morning and evening classes at La Roche College, located further along Babcock Boulevard from our business location. In 1973, we started operating our own truck—my college friends became drivers—to make deliveries to United States Steel plants and other steel mills including Allegheny Ludlum, Crucible, Dravo, Jones & Laughlin, Shenango, and Wheeling-Pittsburgh.

Since Dad founded the business, the only products our company sold were industrial light bulbs, cast aluminum fixtures, and ballasts. This product line for J. B. Supply became a reality when Dad attended an industrial products show in New York City and met representatives of Radiant Lamp Corporation and the owners of Natale Machine & Tool and immediately realized how these products were perfect for the harsh environment found in the local steel mills. Dad and some of the Natale brothers became the best of friends and when he passed, Andy Natale became our favorite "uncle." Just a quick illustration of how kind and generous Andy Natale was to our family. My brother-in-law, Joe Cuccaro, was a Green Beret and served in many countries around the globe including Germany, Italy, Jordan, South Korea, and Viet Nam. At some point the family was together in Italy and Joe was medivaced to Fort Bliss Army Hospital. Their VW camper was shipped to a port in New Jersey and Andy met Paul there and drove one vehicle back to Pittsburgh while Paul drove the other one. It was a great loss for his family and our family when he suddenly passed.

Speaks Volumes: All across the political spectrum, there are always discussions about reviving manufacturing. No matter what politicians promise, the days of the huge steel mills are long gone but what is critical from the past and what speaks volumes about what we need to do to revive manufacturing is a true story about Natale Machine & Tool. In 1979, a new safety regulation went into effect that required the mills to add an enclosed, glass front on the Circle D 150 Portable floodlights that they bought from us. A purchasing agent from a mill called to discuss the situation and to place an order for several dozen retrofit heads that would meet the new safety specifications. I called Charles at Circle D and Circle D came up with a fix, manufactured several dozen enclosed glass heads with aluminum guards, and shipped them to us in about two weeks. All of this was accomplished without computers and our customer was completely satisfied. To me the "can do" spirit illustrated by Natale is what has been lost and finding this spirit again is what we need to revive manufacturing.

Our relationship with Radiant Lamp Corporation was very good as well but Radiant was bought out by an international manufacturer and the relationship changed. This corporation was focused on developing their own chain of distributors in the fashion of two United States light bulb manufacturers. As a result, my mom was made an offer for the business which she quickly turned down. Each fall, our three suppliers provided pricing for the coming year; in turn, we would add our profit margins and bid on contracts with the mills. In 1978, the lamp manufacturer refused to quote us prices and we had to blindly bid on contracts for the coming year. When we finally received our new pricing from the manufacturer, we quickly realized our business was doomed because of our new mill contracts—losing money on many of the industrial lamps while making a minimal profit on the others.

Paul and I quickly began scrambling as the new year started. Since Paul experienced living in Florida for a portion of his childhood, he always had a desire to move to Florida as an adult but obligations to Mom regarding the family business tied his hands. Similarly, I always had a desire to join the Navy but felt the same obligations as Paul. Our biggest concern was that Mom, despite the urging over the years of Paul, myself, and her accountant, refused to change the ownership form of J. B. Supply from sole proprietorship to a corporation. Paul moved to Florida in June 1979 with the hope that removing his salary would keep the company afloat a bit longer. I began the process of chasing my military dreams.

While we always paid for our inventory from our three suppliers as invoices arrived, in 1979 we began accumulating debt with the lamp manufacturer. In August 1979, the head honcho of the North American subsidiary came to Pittsburgh and we met to begin negotiations. I was at a total disadvantage because Mom stood to lose everything because of the sole proprietorship issue. Bottom line, I had to agree to sign a contract with a non-compete clause in which I agreed to manage their operation in Pittsburgh for five years. In exchange for this contract and the ownership change, the corporation wiped away J.B Supply's debt and provided Mom with a "consulting contract" that would pay her $10,000 per year for 10 years. Her contract would be terminated if I resigned my position with them during the initial five years. My dreams of the Navy ended the day Mom and I signed our contracts.

Over the years, J.B. Supply Company survived and flourished for several reasons. First, Mom had the guts to jump into her husband's business and work 12- to 14-hour days to keep it viable. Second, both Paul and I made the decision to keep our dad's legacy alive, put aside our personal dreams, and support Mom every way we could. Third, Paul and I enjoyed working together, appreciated each other's contributions in meeting challenges as a team, took pride in exceeding customer expectations, and relished the opportunity to experience the freedom of being our own bosses to a point—Mom rarely took issue with our decisions but when she did we were just SOBs (Sons of the Boss). Fourth, everything we did focused on customer service. We knew our product line inside and out. We understood the harsh environments faced by our customers and how critical it was to have the inventory and rapid delivery to support their needs. We maintained strong relationships with our suppliers and knew we could count on them to quickly respond to problems with their products; at the same time, in the case of Natale, we could count on them to design and produce specialty fixtures or accessories expertly and quickly to meet our customer's requirements.

On the down side, running a small business is an all-consuming enterprise and leaves one very vulnerable to unforeseen economic events—there is no corporate safety net. In our case, a large corporation was our demise. However, in hindsight, the loss of her company was a blessing to our mom. If the lamp manufacturer had never acted in a predatory manner, she would have eventually lost all of her assets. Paul, Mom, and myself were blind to the upcoming economic collapse of the steel industry that turned Pittsburgh into a founding member of the Rust Belt. I was working for the international corporation when the steel mills became history and the warehouse was jammed with products that became obsolete overnight. I was forced to liquidate this inventory at huge discounts but the corporation easily survived this economic disaster. With this in mind, sometimes bad news can be good news in disguise, so no matter what area of your life you are addressing, always stay positive.

As you have just read, running a small business has many positives and negatives wrapped around a tremendous amount of hard work and a customer-centric focus. As you read through this equipment list, my advice is to use my recommendations as a jumping off point for further investigation and discussion with the knowledgeable folks at your favorite local outdoor store.

BASIC GEAR

1. Backpack

Donna and I have had many backpacks over the years ranging in size from large, multi-day packs to daypacks. In fact I still see my first one in my mind's eye—multi-day, red in color with an aluminum frame, which I bought in 1970 when I was attending the University of South Florida in Tampa. Donna found the best daypack when we were preparing to hike the Tour du Mont Blanc (TMB) in 2017, an Osprey Sirrus 24. Unfortunately for me, it took her over two years to convince her stubborn husband to buy one and give it a try. My only regret is that I did not listen to her in time for the TMB. I absolutely love my Osprey Stratos 24.

My pack is the most comfortable pack I have ever worn and the reason is that the design takes the weight of my shoulders and transfers it to my hips which is so critical for me and my body mechanics. Coming in as my second favorite aspect of this pack are two pockets on the hipbelt which are very convenient for small items that I can reach and use as I am hiking—amazing what you will find yourself squirreling away in them. Other important reasons for using this pack include the suspension system with a mesh back panel which really keeps the air circulating, lots of attachment points so I can easily stow my hiking poles, a raincover conveniently stored in a external pocket at the bottom of the pack, numerous external zipper pockets, all the internal capacity one needs in a daypack , and it weighs only 2.75 pounds. In full disclosure, I still use my Hyperlite Mountain Gear daypack for my cross-country skiing adventures—not as many adventures as I would like these days because of the impact of global warming on our snow cover during the winter ski seasons in the Laurel Highlands.

2. Gadget Bag (safety gear)

My gadget bag is a small Sea to Summit dry bag. Dry bags are waterproof bags that are great in downpours and kayaking. I have two different types and several sizes of Sea to Summit dry bags. I carry this bag religiously when hiking, biking, skiing, snowshoeing, and kayaking. It is filled with my safety gear and when a dry spot is needed for wallet and phone, they find refuge in my dry bag as well. I emptied my bag on the floor and this is what it currently contains in no particular order: metal signal mirror, LifeStraw Vestergaard, survival credit card multitool by Tuncily, Coghlan's magnesium fire starter, MC-2 SUUNTO compass, elastic bandage wrap (ankles, knees, arms, etc), 102 Woodsman buck knife, MPI outdoors emergency survival bag (2), Coghlan's toilet paper, Coghlan's storm matches (windproof, waterproof), and Ledlenser MH8 headlamp and powercase. Of course, you will not need all the items or even one of these items on any adventure but each provides peace of mind and an opportunity to help others that you run into that are in need. A recent example found me utilizing the multitool when the lock screw on my hiking pole needed tightening. Without this item in my bag, I would have been down to one pole which is a major problem for me.

3. First Aid Kit

Donna is in charge of our first aid kit and carries it in her backpack, bike bag or dry bag. Laura is a Critical Care Nurse and between the two of them, they have created a great first aid kit. I recommend that you talk to a healthcare professional so you can customize a kit to your needs and let personal experiences be your guide as well. For example, a bottle of zinc wound wash was not in our kit until several years ago when I had an accident on the Great Allegheny Passage (GAP). I was happily biking along the trail when a fisherman stepped out of the woods to my left with a very long fishing rod. Quickly swerving to avoid the end of the rod, I hit a soft shoulder, went down, gravel ripping through my clothes, and imbedding into my arm and leg forming quite a road rash. I was a mess on both my right arm and leg. Luckily, we had passed a small town with a drugstore about a mile back and I quickly rode to the pharmacy. The pharmacist suggested that I clean the wounds with a zinc wound wash and the rest is history.

Lesson Learned: By observing Donna, I learned that it is important to record with a permanent marker the expiration date for each medication that is placed in small, sealable, plastic medicine bags in our first aid kit. Each anniversary date of creating the first aid kit and prior to major trips, she methodically goes through each bag and replaces any medications that have expired as she records new expiration dates.

---

4. Boots

Donna loves her Merrell hiking boots and she sticks with that brand. I have no particular brand in mind when I shop for my boots but I always go for boots that are all-leather, mid-height, and waterproof. I would recommend going to a store versus the internet for purchasing because comfort is the key and sometimes the exact same boot coming out of two different boxes can feel different when trying them on. I believe in comfort from the start—if it does not feel right in the store, try another of the same model or another brand. Yes, I believe in breaking in my boots before long days of hiking but all my boots are comfortable from the moment I first try them on or they never make it home from the store. I currently have Grisport Eagle waterproof hiking boots and they are fantastic.

I have enjoyed these so much I might just change my shopping habits and when these wear out, go for another pair.

Lesson Learned: I have had three surgeries on my left ankle, will eventually have surgery on my right, and have had issues with sprains on both ankles. I tried many different supports to stabilize my ankles when hiking but nothing proved satisfactory until I discovered ASO Speed Lacer ankle stabilizers. I have never had another ankle sprain since I first started using them in 2013. I just wish I would have found them sooner! This is an amazing product and if you have ankle issues, I would definitely check them out.

Lesson Learned: Once in a while over many years I would have the unfortunate experience of blisters when hiking, until 2018. Donna and I were preparing for our hike on the TMB and one of the two guides on this hike recommended Injinji hiking socks in their hiking gear list to prevent blisters. So right! I never go hiking without them and I never have experienced blisters since I switched. In fact, I also use Injinji socks for my everyday use. Outstanding socks and I highly recommend them.

---

5. Poles

In my opinion, as we age, poles become essential. Poles take strain off the back, help with balance issues on rough terrain, provide a boost going up steeper grades (like four-wheel drives for humans), and help provide control when going down steeper grades. We both use poles that collapse for travel purposes and for attaching to backpacks when necessary. Our poles are made from carbon fiber and use lever locks. Donna uses Black Diamond poles with Flicklock lever locks and I use Komperdell poles with Powerlock 3.0 lever locks. We are both happy with our choices and the locks work very well over long distances.

Lesson Learned: I started using poles in 2007 when Donna and I completed the Rachel Carson Trail Challenge and Donna started using them several years later. Anyway, we did not find out until 2018, hiking the TMB, that we did not know how to properly hold our hiking pole straps. This makes a big difference (comfort and fatigue) and I urge everyone to not forget to ask for a quick lesson when you purchase your poles.

Lesson Learned: As mentioned earlier I ran into a problem with my locking mechanism becoming loose on one of my poles. Donna's poles require a tiny allen wrench which came with her poles to tighten her locking mechanism. Always carry the tool you need for this purpose in your backpack "gadget bag" because you never know when the need will arise.

---

6. Rain Gear

Gore-Tex is the big name in rain gear and in other waterproof products such as boots and gloves. Some manufacturers produce their own proprietary material as well. All of the materials address and are judged on level of waterproof, breathability, and wind resistance. Along with these factors, I look at weight, packability, pit zips, and the number of zipper pockets. Keep in mind that variance in all seven factors listed above impact prices. Please remember your budget and remember the functionality of the rain gear is not impacted by odd colors, styles from last year, or purchasing them on the bargain rack—always look for bargains. Donna and I have several different name brands when it comes to our rain gear (jackets, pants, gloves) but all have Gore-Tex in common.

Rain gear items are critical purchases so visit your local sports store and seek their advice. Jackets are not just rain gear but important for layering purposes to protect against winds—I use mine in single digit temperatures while cross-country skiing and hiking in cool weather. Cross-country skiing and strenuous hiking generates lots of sweat so pit zips are always on my radar.

Caution: Maintenance is critical when it comes to your rain gear. Check with the manufacturer of your products on how to clean the item to maintain the waterproofing and how to restore the waterproofing (look at label and/or website of manufacturer). Signs of problems are two-fold. If you spray some water on your garment and it beads up and you can shake it off—no issues. However, if the fabric darkens a bit as water seeps into the fabric—there is a problem. Second, if you notice moisture building up on the inside of your garment after use, there is a problem.

---

7. Clothing

Cotton T-shirts are nice around base camp but not when you are out and about doing activities that generate lots of sweat. I am sure you have heard the statement that cotton kills. This is in reference to hypothermia which has caused the death of many people enjoying the outdoors. When cotton becomes wet from sweat, it absorbs the moisture and no longer has insulating properties. Further, wet cotton fabric against your skin has a chilling effect—coupled with falling temperatures, this can lead to hypothermia and death. This is why it is important to wisely choose your base layers as well as your other layers. Look for clothing made from moisture-wicking fabrics. Wool is interesting in that it does wick moisture but retains some of it; however, the surface of the wool fibers remain dry. Again, purchase of these products is critical so I would seek advice from the experts at your local sports store.

8. Orange Gear

Per the DCNR, please be aware that all 20 state forests and 100 of the 124 state parks are open for hunting during the various hunting seasons. Also, there are Pennsylvania state game lands that are adjacent to some state parks. With this in mind, please equip yourself, family members, companions, and pets with orange during the appropriate hunting seasons. Check out orangeaglow.com for reasonably priced gear or your local sports store.

9. Vehicle Gear

Our truck gear includes a tow strap, battery charger with emergency light, rechargeable work light, hand saw, flashlight, phone with an SOS feature, and a few jugs of water.

The tow strap enables us to help others as well as potentially helping ourselves. Once we towed a cross-country skier and his auto back onto the road after his car slipped into a ditch while backing up in a backcountry parking area in Forbes State Forest. On another occasion, we towed a couple onto Pennsylvania Route 30 from a parking area that serves as a trailhead for the Laurel Highlands Hiking Trail. The couple told us that they arrived the day before in early afternoon sunshine and went for a hike on the trail. The weather in the Laurel Highlands has a tendency to change and this day, the sun was replaced by snow as they were hiking back to their vehicle. They attempted several times to drive up the road (somewhat of a steep incline with snow) but could not reach Route 30. It grew dark and with no cell service, they spent an uncomfortable night in their vehicle. When we met our friends (Sue and John) in the parking lot the next morning, the couple in the snowbound car came out and asked for our help. I used my tow strap to pull them out onto Route 30 and away they went. At the same time, having a tow strap is a good safeguard because one day we may find ourselves in a jam and a potential Good Samaritan may not carry a tow strap.

I invested in a GB 70 NOCOBoost HD vehicle battery jumper. It not only jumps batteries but functions as an LED flashlight that has seven modes including an emergency strobe mode, recharging station for USB devices, and power source for 12-volt DC devices such as tire inflators.

My saw is a STIHL PS 90 agricultural saw with a 13-inch blade and sheath. It can take care of four-inch diameter tree limbs. I have it in my truck just in case we are on a forest road and we find an obstacle in our path. I have used it for chores around the yard and it makes short work of limbs that need to be removed.

I know that most of us have cell phones but not everyone is aware of the latest feature on some models. Prior to our trip out West in 2023, our cell phones were ready for an upgrade and I became aware of the "latest and greatest" feature which is satellite SOS. When we upgraded both our iPhones, we made sure this feature was one of the benefits. In an emergency, it would enable us to connect to a satellite to seek help when cell service is not available—perfect safeguard for when we are in areas without cell service. The only time we used this feature was when we were in Yellowstone National Park on June 25, 2023. We pulled into the parking lot at Sylvan Lake as we were drawn to it by the breathtaking view and decided on taking some photos. As soon as we parked, we were approached by a couple that had locked both sets of keys in their truck. Since there was no cell service, no one they talked to prior to our arrival could offer any help. I found the SOS feature very easy to navigate and help was soon on the way.

10. Camp Gear

The biggest part of our camp gear is our tent but also includes a camp stove, grill, rechargeable lantern, collapsible kitchen organizer, collapsible aluminum table, three-season sleeping bags, self-inflating sleeping pad, a portable toilet, and camp chairs.

I will address the tent first since it is the most important part of our base camp. If you are buying a tent to use as a base for exploration and not as a backpacking tent, my suggestion is to always buy a larger tent. For example, for two people, I would buy a four-person tent and for a family of four, I would recommend a six-person tent. The tent capacity listed on marketing material only enables the recommended number of people to sleep together like proverbial sardines. We have learned as we age and when we go camping with kids, more room is always needed. The extra space not only helps with gear such as backpacks but provides more space for times when rain traps everyone in the tent during daylight hours and attention turns to card or board games to provide some entertainment.

A few years ago, we made the big decision to upgrade our tent. We had a popup tent for many years because it is easy to erect and take down.

However, height was limited and we had to crawl into and out of it. Not so much fun as painful knees become problematic as we age. We launched our search for a tent with the necessary headroom to enter and exit standing up as well as to dress and undress without rolling around on the tent floor, unable to rise to the height necessary for these mundane tasks. Again, as you age, be kind to yourself and adapt. After doing our research, we came up with a brand and model we liked. I called the REI store in Pittsburgh and asked if they had the tent in stock and could we erect it at the store before we made any purchasing decision? They said come on down and so we did and failed miserably in our attempt to erect it. Luckily, there was an REI model that we also liked and we found it so much easier to erect which made the buying decision easy. After several years of use, we still love our REI Kingdom 6 tent—it is now replaced by a new version, the Wonderland 6 tent.

Caution: Take time to make a decision on which tent to purchase. Search on the internet and read reviews, talk to other tent campers for their input, and talk to the camping experts at the stores where you are shopping. Once focused on a particular tent, find a store where they encourage the customer to erect the tent model prior to purchasing. Remember, don't believe the marketing hype until you verify the claims by actually making the attempt yourselves.

Lesson Learned: When preparing for your first few camping adventures, I recommend erecting your tent at home prior to packing it for your trip. When arriving at your campsite, the last thing you need is to be the prime entertainment for other campers that arrived before you! This happened to us once when our Kingdom 6 was relatively new and it was not a joyful experience. Plus, knowing beforehand how to quickly and correctly erect your home away from home, makes the experience of establishing your base camp so much faster and less stressful. This good outcome will be appreciated by all participants anytime reaching the state campground requires a long drive or the weather is not ideal.

Our stove is the Coleman Classic two-burner propane camping stove. We use it with a percolator coffee pot, camping teapot, square pancake griddle with folding handle, a rectangular griddle that covers both burners, and a medium-sized pot with lid. I purchased a hose that feeds propane from a propane tank to the stove instead of the small propane bottles.

Our grill is a Weber Q 1000. It is the smallest Weber Q model and is perfect for our camping needs—I also use a larger model for my home grill and it is super. I purchased a propane valve splitter so I can feed propane to both the stove and grill from one propane tank. For our camping trips I purchased a five-pound propane tank instead of lugging our 20-pound tank to our base camp.

Our self-inflating sleeping pad is comfortable but our age makes it much more difficult to roll it into a compact form for stowing in the carrying bag. At the same time, we are finding it more difficult to stand up from a prone position versus potentially swinging our legs off a cot and standing. Recently Donna and I pulled the trigger and bought two foldable camp cots at a 50 percent, end-of-season discount. We have not been camping with them yet so I can't provide a review. As we age, we continue to adapt so that we can maintain our comfort and mobility.

Our camp toilet is a must for me. We try to book tent sites by shower houses but it is nice to have it when I am just too tired to take the walk a few times per night or because of rain. We have a Cleanwaste Go Anywhere portable toilet and love it. The grandkids have also used it when they have gone camping with us.

Lesson Learned: Not sure if it is just me or that folding the portable toilet is just a bit confusing. When you unfold each leg for the first time, observe how it clicks into place so you understand how to reverse the process when you are breaking camp (this advice is applicable to any of your folding camp equipment—chairs, kitchen organizer, cots, etc.). Anyway, I also find that unlatching the toilet legs to fold requires some fairly strong finger pressure which can be difficult at times with my arthritic fingers. Hopefully, a spouse or traveling companion is in better shape and can assist in the process or bring a tool that can provide strong pressure where required. I find the head of needle-nose pliers works well. Worse case scenario, you can leave it as is and transport it home for someone young to fold the legs for storage purposes. Even in the open position, it is fairly compact and this toilet is well worth the effort because it is a fantastic base camp addition, especially for older guys as well as youngsters.

EXTRA FUN IN THE PARKS

Caution: If you plan to carry out either of these activities please obtain your physician's clearance as well as undertake the appropriate training—yes, even bicycle training is a great idea.

11. Kayak

After researching tandem kayaks and based on my plans for using it—flat water only—I decided to go with Liquidlogic's 14.5 Saluda model. My decision-making process included looking at stability, tracking, capacity (holds two adults and a child), impact resistance (rotational molding construction), and seating comfort. Now, I was ready to find the right retailer and confirm my choice by speaking with an expert. For many years I had been aware of 3 Rivers Outdoor Company (3ROC) founded by Christine Iksic. The store is located in the Regent Square neighborhood of Pittsburgh. 3ROC brilliantly engages with the community resulting in it becoming the hub for outdoor enthusiasts that call the city of Pittsburgh home. I had many wonderful conversations with Christine during the purchasing process and she displayed amazing customer service skills. The kayak I settled on had been used by 3ROC as a rental unit and Christine advised me on the rest of the gear—paddles (Aqua Bound Sting Ray Hybrid) and life vests (SOLARIS Mustang Survival-Type III PFD). We have three seasons of use under our belts and the Saluda and corresponding gear have worked very well for us. I have made some other major purchases at 3ROC including some outstanding Yakima gear and always enjoy my visits to the store—all the staff are very friendly and knowledgeable.

Opportunity: As part of their community engagement efforts they offer campfire presentations on many outdoor topics. Check out their 3ROC website for details on this subject as well as their calendar of events (lots of planned outdoor activities). I was provided the opportunity to make a presentation on the completion of our quest which I found very enjoyable. It was not a large crowd that gathered around the campfire but there were both young families and folks my age which made for a fun evening.

To go along with my kayak, I added some other gear. I purchased dry bags and a duffle bag from Sea to Summit. The duffle bag is made of waterproof material and can be carried through hand grips, a single shoulder strap or in backpack mode. It is one tough bag with a huge storage capacity. I keep all my kayak gear in it (no paddles) and when I throw it in the back of my truck, I am ready to roll. I also bought a C-Tug Kayak and Canoe Cart which is simply amazing for moving the kayak from the truck to the launching point and back.

Caution: Please remember to register your unpowered boat or buy a launch permit to be legal in Pennsylvania. As of 2024, the cost of either choice is $24.00 for two years.

12. Bicycles

In 2013, we replaced bicycles we bought in 1992 (which replaced models bought in 1975) with Cannondale Adventure 3 models. Over these many years, we have been very happy with our choice of bikes. This model is a hybrid, meaning it falls between a mountain bike and road bike, having features that are a solid compromise. We bought them for our rail-to-trail riding, which usually means pedaling on gravel surfaces with reasonable grades. Also, these models provide wider seats and an upright rider position with the placement of the handlebars. We find this style to be much more comfortable for older adults like ourselves. I am sure there are newer models and other brands offering a similar type of bike so check them all out and talk to an expert before making a purchase. Along with a hybrid model, I recommend adding a rack for the back with a corresponding bike bag as well as upgrading your bike tubes to models that are more puncture resistant. In our bags, we keep a first aid kit, bike tools, tube repair kit, new tubes, mini-bike pump, rain gear, waterproof bag covers, my gear bag, and snacks/lunches.

Another type of bike to consider is an electric model. These are much heavier because of the battery, propulsion unit, and the beefier frame. To help with the weight issue, I would look for models where the battery can be removed from the frame and loaded separately into your vehicle so it is easier to lift the bike itself onto the bike carrier—check out Yakima for an innovative new bike rack that enables one to roll heavier electric models onto the rack for transportation. Second, decide on the distance (round trip) that you routinely plan on traveling and opt for models that correspond to this distance. For instance, if your trips will not exceed 25 miles, there is no need to look at bikes with heavier batteries and frames that are built for 50 or more miles per charge.

Donna and I are now 68 and 72 respectively and have considered e-bikes but continue using our Adventure 3 bikes; however, an e-bike becomes more tempting every year. For our park explorations and our regular rail-to-trail excursions we find our bikes to still serve our needs. At the same time, as we age, we adapt our biking habits. We rarely bike over 30 miles these days and usually stay around 20 or less. At the same time, we go at a slower pace and plan for either a picnic lunch at our turnaround point or bike to a town, have lunch, and turnaround. If we want to explore more miles in one direction, we will bike with friends and have a vehicle at both ends of our route. Prior to purchasing an e-bike, my recommendation is to rent an e-bike and later, go for a test ride on the bike model you are interested in purchasing. Further, see how loading and unloading goes with the e-bike.

Caution: Please always wear a bike helmet. It only takes a moment for an accident to occur and the protection provided by a helmet is vital for much better outcomes.

Hot Tip: For added bike safety check out Copilot by Velo!

124 Pennsylvania State Parks, Here We Go!

Please keep in mind the beauty within each park can be discovered no matter an individual's physical abilities—just go and soak in the magic.

This section is where I discuss our visits to each of the 124 state parks. Please keep in mind the beauty within each can be discovered no matter an individual's physical abilities—just go and soak in the magic. A few housekeeping notes for this section. The origin of all the park and forest data in this book is traceable to DCNR park guides, maps, brochures, website, and historical and informational placards placed within the parks. I wish to express my thanks on behalf of all of us who visit our Pennsylvania parks and forests for everything the DCNR does on behalf of Pennsylvania taxpayers as good park and forest stewards. I know there are funding limitations and frustration along the way but despite everything, these folks do their best to fulfill their mandates and to interact with us visitors in a very helpful and positive manner. I also want to acknowledge all the volunteers that serve us as well and just say thank you for your service to the parks and forests. Many of our state parks are blessed to have organizations that are entitled, Friends of XYZ Park and that provide many hundreds of hours of volunteer time directed at park improvements. Thank you for your efforts!

The glimpses of our experiences are in no way to be comprehensive views—hopefully these morsels will stimulate the desire to seek out more information and indulge in personal experiences in these natural gems. For example, I mention lakes and streams but for information on fishing such as types of fish found and types of boats that are legal, please check DCNR park maps and website. This holds true for information on hunting in the parks as well. Another example is that I mention campsites in the park but do not discuss other available accommodations such as yurts, cabins, and cottages. For detailed information on what types of accommodations are available please check with the DCNR reservation site. We personally are drawn to the campsites because we find other types of accommodations booked solid for many months in advance—but again, cancellations do happen so check the DCNR site with fingers crossed. Another important aspect of park and forest experiences that I failed to mention in my narratives (despite the fact that this subject is very important to me) is environmental education and interpretation. The reason for this lack of information on my part is that there is so much uncertainty regarding availability based on curtailment during and after COVID, funding issues, and seasonal programming versus year-round. I urge everyone to contact the parks and forest offices prior to their visits to obtain the latest information so kids and adults alike are not disappointed.

As illustrated earlier in this book, I go off the current path at times and merrily run down my personal memory lane so be prepared for more of these activities. When I am out in nature and relaxing, I never know what memory bubble will rise to the surface and pop. In sharing, I am preparing my readers to just go with the flow in the soothing and healing natural surroundings found in our cornucopia of Pennsylvania public lands and be prepared for your personal memory bubbles popping along the way. In my experience, the wonderful memory bubbles are amplified by being in nature while the stressful and painful bubbles that burst are soothed and gently processed by the healing that seems to be found there—being enveloped in nature seems to buttress my emotional wellbeing.

Throughout this five-year quest, I have come up with an ongoing and evolving list of my favorite parks in ten "Best Park" categories and these will be noted under the corresponding parks. These categories include Biking, Family Vacation, Hiking, History, Overall, Overnight, View, Waterfall, Water, and Wildflower (funny, with the latest news from Governor Shapiro, I can soon add Caverns to my list of categories). I would imagine others might have more or fewer categories but the point is that working on such a list really reinforces the joy and fun that one experiences throughout the process. At the end of the park section, I also list my runner-up for each category to add just a bit more spice to the entire list. Donna and I have some agreements and many disagreements between our lists but that is as it should be because selections are very personal and based on what brings us a sense of awe. These selections are not meant to be controversial but to stimulate lots of thought and conversations along the way. My choices grew organically over the five years by using my five senses and I am positive that if I did this quest again, my list of "Best Parks" would evolve differently because that is the nature of the natural world—always changing based on seasons, weather, wildlife, and human intervention.

A wonderful way to record park impressions for later discernment is by listing them based on the five senses:

Hearing—songbirds singing, distinct calls of the hawk and pileated woodpecker, deer running through the underbrush, babbling brook, elk bugling, waves lapping against the kayak, wind blowing, rain tapping on the roof of the tent, crackling of the campfire, roar of the waterfall, thunder.

Sight—mist rising from bottom of a canyon, waterfall tumbling over a ledge and splashing into a pool, a fawn wobbly standing for the first time, a shadow next to a rock formation transforming into a black bear, a bald eagle gliding in a blue sky, hemlocks flocked by a new snowfall, a pink lady slipper in glorious bloom, a meteor flashing by in a field of stars, water lilies kissing the side of our kayak, endless views exposed by a break in a rock formation or from a flat rock at the edge of a cliff, a rattlesnake warming in the sun.

Smell—flowers blooming, fish by a lake or stream, skunk wafting in the woods, pines scenting the air, leaves rotting, air after a storm, onions frying, smoke from a campfire, bacon cooking, coffee perking.

Taste—wintergreen flavor of a birch twig, wild blueberries, wild strawberries, blackberries, currants, bacon and eggs, blueberry-buttermilk pancakes, buckwheat pancakes, omelette with the works, fire-singed corn on the cob.

Touch— pinecone with pine sap, stinging nettle, insect bite, wading in cold water, berry thorns, gently rocking kayak drifting on the breeze, rain and mist on my face, skiing along a trail with snow blurring my vision.

I add a few of my park impressions after each park visit but you will find neither a comprehensive list nor one where all five senses are touched upon. My mind only holds so many thoughts revolving around my senses during park visits and I failed to note many of them in my journal during our quest. Plus, I tried not to be constantly repetitive in my senses sections.

One last item to address is the possibility of developing tunnel vision pertaining to the drives that must be undertaken to reach parks and forests. Easy for those miles and the passing landscapes to become blurs instead of an amazing opportunity to appreciate the bedrock of our state; namely, the small towns that we pass through as we exit the turnpike or interstate and rush towards the objectives of our quest. Consider providing time to slow down and appreciate the towns and people that live in them. One way to do this is by seeking out geocaches as one exits major highways and another is by finding great little places in these towns to enjoy a coffee, snack, or a full meal—avoid chains and indulge in the places where the locals go and enjoy both the atmosphere and the people. Don't want to cook another campfire meal today? Go local and absorb some small town magic.

Thinking about small towns starts my memory bubbles popping and producing memories of my childhood living in the Perrysville area of Pennsylvania. Yikes, it was over a half-mile walk uphill from our house on the corner of Babcock Boulevard and Bernice Street to reach the main drag in Perrysville (Perry Highway/Pennsylvania Route 19). Through my kid eyes, Perrysville was the perfect town with our church, Saint Teresa, my school, the old Saint Teresa Grade School building, many retail stores, and other buildings lining both sides of Perry Highway. When I graduated from Saint Teresa Grade School, I would walk to Perrysville every weekday to catch my school bus that stopped in front of St. Teresa Church and traveled to North Catholic High School. At the time, my high school sat on Troy Hill which overlooked Herr's Island, the Allegheny River, and a portion of Pittsburgh's cityscape—a whole different world from cozy, little Perrysville.

There are just so many memories of Perrysville from when I was a kid—as I move through my memories, I urge Perrysville natives to please ignore my unintentional spelling mistakes and memory lapses involving the names of local stores that have faded into history. First, I will address the place in the town that continues to hold my worst childhood memory. H.P. Brandt Funeral Home has stood at the corner of Jackson Street and Perry Highway since 1937. When my dad died in 1959, his burial service was at this funeral home (I arranged my mom's burial service here as well when she passed in 2003). I never drive by Brandt's without remembering my dad laid out there when I was only a six-year-old. It had such a major impact that I religiously avoided funeral homes and funerals until my Uncle Stanley died in the early 1980s and I was asked to be a pallbearer.

Enough of the sad times, happy bubbles burst with so many joyful, jumbled memories of Perrysville that there is no question why I find little Pennsylvania towns such special places. I loved being taken to Dorings' Shoes which was close to Saint Teresa's Church Rectory. Not only was it fun to be measured for new shoes but each purchase came with a pretzel rod which was a super treat. Close by was the bakery which had great doughnuts, cakes, pies, cookies, breads, and pastries. I remember buying goodies there in the mornings when Paul and I were running the family business in the 1970s. Paul would put on the coffee anticipating my quick return from the bakery with some of our favorite doughnuts and pastries. Mom would join us as I served the goodies and Paul poured his freshly brewed coffee before we both returned to work in the adjoining office and warehouse.

Walking north on Perry Highway past the bakery, there was a butcher shop. Mom would take us there sometimes and I remember the smell of raw meat and the sawdust covering the black-and-white-tiled floor, absorbing any blood from the slabs of beef being cut behind the meat counter. Continuing north, I would cross Lindley Lane and come to Gramatine's Sporting Goods. I always remember it perched there precariously on Perry Highway with what seemed like a cliff just behind the building. I would go there with Paul when he was buying fishing lures and other items like fish eggs for bait and ammunition for his .22 rifle. It was a big store filled with all sorts of things with hunting targets, rifles, and bows making the biggest impressions on me. The last stop in this direction was my favorite, the Dairy Queen. I remember us kids walking up the hill from our little neighborhood on Bernice Street to buy a cone on hot, summer days. One way we earned money for those treats was to find returnable bottles along Babcock Boulevard and in Girty's Run which we redeemed for cash at Myer's Beer Distributor on Babcock Boulevard.

Across Jackson Street from Brandt's sat Heiber's General Store. It was a wooden building that occupied a big swath of property along Jackson Street. I remember the interior was dark and musty, filled with all sorts of manual tools, animal feeds, and other farm-related items. I would go with Paul when he was picking up feed for his rabbits or for chicken wire or other items he needed for his rabbit and aquarium fish businesses. Walking past Brandt's, going south on Perry Highway, one would quickly come to a huge furniture store. I remember going in that store on many occasions with Mom when she was shopping for furniture, lamps, and knick knacks. I remember her buying the desk that I used throughout my high school and college years at this store. Amongst other knick knacks, she bought a colonial militia man that displays the following on its pedestal, "3RD New Jersey 1777" for my bedroom desk and is now displayed in our living room. She also bought a replica of a Spanish galleon which she presented to me on my graduation from Saint Teresa Grade School and sits in our upstairs hallway.

Continue walking south on Perry Highway and one arrived at Wygle's Tailor Shop. The interesting story here is that Paul dated the tailor's daughter when he was attending North Catholic. About a year before he died, Paul told me that she was the love of his life and he tried to find her on the Internet with the hope that she was also single and open to rekindling their teenage romance; unfortunately, his search came up empty. Behind the tailor's, there was a private, little lending library. I have fond memories of checking out a mix of 10 Hardy Boys and Tom Swift books (the limit) and walking home with the big pile of books in my hands.

I always enjoy losing myself in books and this tiny library was such a treasure to me.

Further south on Perry Highway there was a bar and just past the bar, Good Lane came steeply up the hill to meet Perry Highway. Of course, the bar was off-limits and a real mystery to me. In the 1980s, Paul and I shared a lunch and a few beers there on one of his trips back home from St. Petersburg, Florida. Good Lane is where I always ended my uphill trek to Perrysville or began my downhill trek back home since it links to Bernice Street. A portion of Good Lane levels out after its steep decline from Perry Highway and two of Paul's friends lived on Good Lane—Denny, his best friend throughout his life, and Jim. Jim and his family eventually moved to Bradford Woods and Denny, after he retired, moved back to his family home with his wife, Annie. Both Denny and his dad were hard-working roofers and they reroofed my mom's home and the attached warehouse in the 1970s.

Directly across Perry Highway from the entrance to Good Lane was St. Teresa's church, school, and rectory complex. Geri, Paul, Sandy, myself, and Cindy all attended St. Teresa Grade School from the late 1940s through the early 1970s. All of us but Cindy went to the old school, and Sandy, myself, and Cindy all went to the new school (circa 1958) as well. At one point, the number of students became so large that classrooms were installed in the church basement and I spent a portion of my sixth grade there. Again, to accommodate the huge growth in the parish, Mass was held in both the church and the new school auditorium. Some of my classmates left St. Teresa when St. Alexis parish was established further north off of Pennsylvania Route 19.

Bordering the church parking lot was Royston's Pharmacy. This place was like heaven because it had a comic book rack and a soda fountain/

lunch counter. Great place for a pop, milkshakes, burgers, and fries. So many places had soda fountain/lunch counters back in those days but sad to say the overwhelming majority have vanished into history. Royston's was a very special place since it was close to both home and school. Oh my gosh, just one more chance to hang out there would be amazing! I would start from our house, walk up the hill, pop out at top of Good Lane, cross Perry Highway, enter Royston's, take a stroll around the comic book racks, sit down at a stool at the lunch counter, count my coins one more time, and order a burger, fries, and a Coke.

Walking south from Royston's there stood a little deli that sold bread, milk, cold cuts, and some other food items. Each Sunday after Mass our family would make the pilgrimage to buy bread and chipped ham. Yes, the famous Pittsburgh chipped ham. I remember chip ham offered at $0.59 per pound and it would go up in dime increments. This ritual began with Dad and family and continued through the years to my days with J.B. Supply Company. Writing this makes me want to go buy some chipped ham, fresh bread, and dill pickles and simply enjoy the food and my Perrysville memories.

The last significant store in my Perrysville Memory bubbles is Vater's Hardware which stood alone further south on Perry Highway from the deli. Much to my extreme disappointment, the hardware store at this location closed in 2023. My last purchase there was flowers for my Grandfather Brzozowski, Uncle William, and Aunt Fanny's graves located in St. Mary's Cemetery in McKees Rocks. Probably this was in 2022.

I have a boatload of good memories originating with Vater's from when I was a kid to times Paul and I shopped there for hardware items ending in 2002. Since Paul moved to Florida, it was a tradition for Paul and I to vacation together for a week at Mom's and to work in her yard and make home repairs. Over many years, Vater's was not only our source for home repair and yard maintenance items but it was a great variety store. So many of my birthday gifts came from Mom shopping with me at Vater's when I was a kid. My first and only fishing rod and reel were bought there as well as my first baseball glove. The Wilson baseball glove, Pflueger casting reel, and South Bend fishing rod are here at my house and each one bears a "Made in USA" pronouncement. Each time I handle any of them, it acts like a mental time portal and quickly transports me circa 1960s Vater's Hardware and I am shopping with Mom.

The wonderful human portion of Vater's was Shirley. She always ran the cash register and was the sweetest person. Also, Shirley was our family babysitter for many years so there was a wonderful history there as well. Every year when Paul came in for the week and we found ourselves at Vater's, Shirley was always there and excited to see us—when I shopped there without Paul, she always asked about him. I believe Paul had a crush on Shirley from those babysitting days.

I hope this description of Perrysville provides folks with an inkling of how lives interweave and interact in the small town that the locals call home. Likewise, it provides context to what might be hidden in the small towns that all of us see when we are engulfed in our state park quests. Imagine having a cup of coffee in one of these towns, sitting next to someone at a lunch counter, starting a conversation, and discovering just a little history about the man or woman sitting next to you, their thoughts about the town you are in, and just maybe, a wonderful recollection or two about the park or forest you are on the way to visit.

Now, onward to the parks . . .

1. ALLEGHENY ISLANDS

This park consists of 50 acres spread over two islands and seven shoals. This unique park (the only state park where no portion of the park boundaries can be accessed by driving) suffers from noise and visual pollution from both a Pennsylvania Turnpike bridge and a railroad bridge running parallel. Further, the curse of Japanese knotweed is here in abundance. At the same time, there is a striking beauty when kayaking just offshore of the park while observing small, sandy, beaches with sunning turtles, driftwood, cardinal flowers blazing amongst nondescript undergrowth, and trees towering overhead. There will be disappointment if hiking through the interior is on the agenda, much better focusing energy on appreciating the ever-changing relationship between the shorelines and the flowing river. Visuals from two amazing, joy-filled visits come to the foreground of my mind when thinking about this park. These images never fail to bring a smile to my face along with a sense of relaxation and contentment that literally drains the tension from my bones.

Of course, the first visit was the day Donna and I finished our quest. The following mental snapshots vie for my attention: launching our kayak, paddling up stream, stepping foot on the first island, holding hands as we stroll along the beach, finding a Pennsylvania State Park boundary medallion nailed to a tree, Donna finding our first bog violet in 48 years of wildflowering, and observing a huge turtle slide off the beach into the river as we paddle back to our launch site.

My second visit was with Mason—our first kayak trip together. Oh to be young again and see everything through the perspective of young eyes! I must admit, Mason succeeded in turning back my mental clock to the early 1960s as everything we did filled us with joy, wonderment, and amazement. Mason spotted a bald eagle against the blue sky, a motorboat roared by and the two of us rode the kayak like we were on a bucking bronco—laughing all the time, we paddled to a driftwood-like log anchored to the beach and using this natural bridge, Mason deftly headed to landfall. I followed, wading in the river while pulling the kayak onto the beach, Mason used a tree branch to write his name in the sand, we paddled upstream to watch the water roaring over the dam, turned downstream to ease into still waters between two islets, I recorded Mason swimming in the river, we floated downstream munching snacks and talking about the beautiful day and all the fun. As we began our short journey to the dock, I smiled to myself as my mind flipped back memory pages to days gone by where a rickety craft floating on truck inner tubes is in Girty's Run and I'm just a kid again, younger than Mason.

Hearing—water roaring over the dam, turnpike traffic noise; sight—Mason writing his name in the sand, park boundary medallion, blooming bog violet and cardinal flowers, driftwood, turtles sunning on the beach, bald eagle soaring in the cloudless sky; smell—wafting fish smell along the river; touch—bucking bronco time in the kayak, holding Donna's hand as we stroll along the beach, cold river water, pulling the kayak up onto the beach, drifting in the kayak.

2. ARCHBALD POTHOLE

With all the discussions of melting glaciers in recent years, the formation of this pothole through glacier meltwater is very interesting and a good reason to learn more about the Archbald Pothole. Funny, I think many of us plagued by Pennsylvania potholes when driving see the word "pothole" and become turned off. From the main entrance to the park, which was closed because of a structural problem, we drove around to the other entrance that is directly off of Eynon Jermyn Road. We entered the section of the park that was once an active strip mine area that the state has done a marvelous job of transforming. There are paved parking lots, a playground, running trails, and sports fields.

It is a fantastic park for the local community and the Archbald Pothole section of the park provides locals an attraction to boost tourist numbers. Since the main entrance was closed, we looked for a marked path at this location to see if we could walk to the pothole from here but no luck. We spoke to a woman that pulled into a parking space near our truck. She said that to her knowledge there are no trails connecting this recreation area to the pothole area but she loves jogging here.

Sight—wonderful to see what has been created to transform a strip mine site into a beautiful sports complex for the community.

3. BALD EAGLE

This beautiful park opened in 1971 after the U.S. Army Corps of Engineers built Foster Joseph Sayers Dam which created the 1,730-acre lake of the same name. This beautiful lake both sparkles in the sunlight and comes alive at night when the moon is shining. It is definitely the focal point here as it rests at the bottom of Bald Eagle Mountain which has an unbelievable impact on the vista that unfolds from the opposite shore. The gorgeous lake in the foreground and the mountain as the backdrop just makes a picture that is beyond words. Since the dam and reservoir were built as a flood control project, the U.S. Army Corps of Engineers remains in charge of the dam and makes adjustments to the lake-level based on seasons and weather conditions. The lake is well used with features that include multiple boat (unlimited horsepower) launch sites, huge marina (369 slips), fishing, and a 1,200-foot beach for sunbathing and swimming. I really want to come back here someday soon to launch my kayak with Donna. To add to the fun, there are hiking trails and two campgrounds on opposite sides of the lake. The main campground has 94 sites and modern amenities including electric, full hookups, shower/restrooms, drinking water, and sanitary dump station. The other is a primitive campground with 34 rustic tent sites and 34 sites for camping vehicles.

During our visit to Bald Eagle State Park we made the fortuitous decision to stay at the Nature Inn which is located within the park. We first thought about the campground but since it was a short stay and we read such good things about the inn, we were excited to check it out for ourselves. A further stroke of luck was that the only room available for our stay was a small, lakeview suite. Oh my gosh, a second-floor deck, a crystal clear night, full moon, lake, looming dark presence of Bald Eagle Mountain, all combined to produce a view that was spellbinding.

It is a cozy little inn and we found many beautiful views in the daytime as we explored our new environment. It is beautiful, solid construction with wood used throughout which makes sense since it is in the middle of the park and designed to be eco-friendly. We loved the library on the second floor with cupboards filled with board games and puzzles and shelved nature books waiting to be picked up and read. Huge tables and comfortable chairs just asking for our company to explore all the treasures the library has to offer. The tables were perfect for board game purposes and we found ourselves wishing for the presence of Laura, Mason, and Sophia.

Nature Inn, Bald Eagle State Park

Oh my, the breakfast refused to disturb the spell that had overtaken us since our arrival. Blueberry, buttermilk, pancakes with bacon, eggs, fresh fruit and muffins. Hey, I pride myself on my wonderful campsite breakfasts but this really put the pressure on me—I can match or beat most of these items on taste and camping ambiance but fresh fruit and muffins kick it up a notch. My percolator coffee is tops but the quality of coffee at the inn came in a close second and it was endless, just waiting to be poured throughout breakfast. The breakfast area was perfect with huge windows bringing in views to the dining area to further enhance the outstanding breakfast experience.

Outdoors, the wood and stone used in construction blends into the natural landscape that magically flows into the inn's flower beds and walkways. There is a huge patio with solid wood tables and chairs and a huge stone fire pit waiting for another star-filled evening to welcome kids and the kids hiding in all of us, to start working on their campfire marshmallows. Did someone say hungry? Don't worry, there are several barbecue grills just waiting for slabs of beef, chicken, or fish and other fixings necessary to make the meal complete.

Not to be outdone by the inn, the views continued to impress as we made our way around the inn and found trails just waiting for us. We hiked the Butterfly, Skyline, Swamp Oak, and Woapalanne Path trails right from the inn and enjoyed them all immensely. The next morning, after being fueled by another great breakfast, we walked over to the campground and enjoyed hiking the West, Hunter Run, and East Trails before leaving the inn.

The Swamp Oak trail leads to a member of the Pennsylvania Champion Tree Program; namely, the largest swamp white oak tree in Pennsylvania which had a circumference of 18.1 feet when measured in 2016. While we were admiring the tree, we were serenaded by a huge number of croaking frogs which added a nice touch to our experience. The Pennsylvania Forestry Association (PFA) (paforestry.org) is the organization that established the Pennsylvania Champion Tree Program (pabigtrees.com). The PFA is the oldest state organization devoted to forest conservation in the United States. It was founded in Philadelphia in 1886 and the first president was Dr. J.T. Rothrock. This is another great organization that deserves any donations that come their way and a family membership is only $30.00 as of 2024.

The ambiance of the Nature Inn reminds us both of the Trapp Family Lodge in Vermont. No, not the new Trapp lodge but the original family home that was turned into a lodge and was destroyed by fire in December 1980. Donna and I spent our honeymoon there in August 1978. The thought of spending our honeymoon at the Trapp Family Lodge and possibly meeting Maria Von Trapp seemed so romantic to us after both seeing *The Sound of Music* when we were young.

We had the good fortune to meet Maria Von Trapp and she signed our wedding book. We told Maria that we were thinking of her wedding when we were married at the Divine Providence Motherhouse Chapel since many of our teachers/professors at La Roche College became our friends and happened to be nuns and sang at our Wedding Mass. Maria was very sweet to us and I still remember her jumping into her Volkswagen Karmann Ghia and driving through the gravel parking area and scooting onto the paved roadway. She was an amazing lady who really loved people.

Interestingly, Pope John Paul I was elected the day of our wedding, August 26, 1978, and our priest said that our Wedding Mass was the first time he used the name of the new pope. Further, my mom and dad were married on October 16th which is the same day that John Paul II was elected 39 years later in 1978. I was very excited about a Polish pope and August 26th just happens to be the feast day of Our Lady of Częstochowa, a huge feast day in Poland.

The original Trapp Family Lodge was constructed of wood including the shakes that covered the roof. There was a beautiful library with bookcase after bookcase lined with books and in one section, a solid wooden table. Another room on the first floor was filled with plants fed by natural light from numerous windows. This is where the games and puzzles were located. I still remember us playing a board game with a couple from Montreal.

The lodge was built into a side of a hill with an apple orchard above it and in front, there was the largest tree I ever saw until the trees we saw hiking in Mount Rainier National Park. Paths around the lodge led to trails that in the winter months are Nordic ski trails. The Trapp Family Lodge's breakfasts, bag lunches, and dinners were fantastic. The hearty breakfasts fueled our hiking and wildflowering adventures while the bag lunches produced great picnic lunches along the mountain trails. We spent much of our idyllic time together hiking while photographing and documenting the wildflowers that were blooming on the Von Trapp property that August week. Upon returning home, we sent Maria a letter thanking her for her hospitality and providing a list of all the wildflowers we found. In any event, the Nature Inn brought back these sweet memories which just added to the awe we experienced while visiting Bald Eagle State Park.

On a side note, we returned in the winter months to the new Trapp Family Lodge to celebrate our 35th wedding anniversary and to go Nordic skiing—another dream fulfilled. The Trapps's Nordic ski trails are just the best and we had a chance to snowshoe as well. The one disappointment was that the huge, enchanting tree was gone. My favorite photo of our honeymoon shows us holding hands, staring adoringly into each other's eyes, and standing in front of that beautiful tree. In fact, my excitement over the swamp white oak brought back those wonderful, long ago memories of that magnificent tree in Vermont.

Hearing—frogs croaking; sight—sunlight and moonlight on the lake, Bald Eagle Mountain, the Champion swamp white oak, all the colorful butterflies attracted by all the wildflowers around the inn and along the trails, the beautiful beach beckoning to one and all, the wonderful library, nighttime view from our private balcony, reading about the swamp white oak; smell—breakfast arriving at our table including a fresh cup of coffee; taste—all the food included in the breakfasts at the inn; touch—feeling the bark of the Champion swamp white oak.

I am pleased to name **Bald Eagle State Park** as my choice for the ***Best Pennsylvania State Park for an Overnight Stay***. Of course, the Nature Inn has much to do with this selection but I do not want to forget the campgrounds at this park. They are winners as well because of a couple factors. First, both the main campground and rustic campground are small, which I find to be a bonus at any camping site we find ourselves in. Second, I absolutely love that these two campgrounds are separated by the wonderfully huge lake.

4. BELTZVILLE

This park is all about the lake and the amenities adjoining it. There are picnic tables, a playfield, launch sites, seasonal mooring site, boat rentals, fishing, a zoned water-skiing area, and a 525-foot beach for swimming. Also, there are 15 miles of hiking trails with some providing lake views.

We visited the Overlook Rotunda built by the Army Corps of Engineers which provides a great view of the 949-acre Beltzville Lake, the dam itself, and the dry, emergency spillway. We hiked both the upper loop and lower loop of the Sawmill Run Trail.

There are several historical sites along the trail, including a slate quarry from the 1700s and a gristmill raceway. A section of the trail crosses the enormous, dry, spillway of the Beltzville Lake Dam which was the first time we ever experienced hiking across one. It was a really interesting experience to walk across a spillway while imagining the amount of rain needed for it to function.

Hearing—very quiet spring morning; sight—the sparkling lake water from the Overlook on this sunny morning was inspiring, the wide expanse of dry grasses in the emergency spillway, reading the historical and Army Corps of Engineers placards; touch—picking up a piece of slate and holding it for a moment while in the colonial quarry filled me with a sense of awe.

5. BENDIGO

A really delightful, 100-acre community park nestled in a small valley along the East Branch of the Clarion River. We visited in the fall so the swimming pool was closed and there was no activity in the park but us. We walked along the Eagle Trail which runs along the river as it exits the park and goes into state game lands. It was a pretty walk with the changing leaves and views of the river. We returned and walked through the interior park grounds which took us along the river, through picnic grounds, by the swimming pool, basketball courts, and the park office where we turned around and walked back to our truck.

One interesting portion of our visit was reading historical placards by the river which described how the nearby remaining stonework represented the remains from a dam and swimming area that once brought large groups of people to the park for community swimming and picnicking activities. Fun to imagine throngs of people coming here before I was born and having so much fun just enjoying this little park and indulging in the natural surroundings.

Hearing—the flow of water on the river; sight—the picturesque view of the river through the trees and open spaces along the Eagle Trail, reading the historical placards.

6. BENJAMIN RUSH

When we read that the park was within the city limits of Philadelphia, Donna and I were concerned about traffic and overcrowding. However, we timed our arrival to miss the morning rush-hour traffic and found the park virtually empty. We had a pleasant walk and found viewing numerous garden plots to be really entertaining since the crops were very bountiful in August. Our taste buds remained in check because each individual plot is fenced-in and locked. However, there is always hope that a gardener might be in their garden and in the mood to offer some tasty treat. Sadly, we were not that fortunate since no gardeners were hard at work and ready to share their bounty or answer questions from curious park questers like us. Information provided by the DCNR on historical placards reveal that Benjamin Rush was a signer of the Declaration of Independence and known as the "Father of American Psychiatry." Since being outdoors and gardening are pursuits that are said to boost mental wellness, having a giant community garden in the state park that honors Benjamin Rush seems very appropriate.

Along with the gardening plots, large open fields of grasses and wildflowers were in abundance, attracting butterflies and producing a scenic landscape outside the garden fences. A large section of this state park is bounded by Poquessing Creek and it adjoins Poquessing Park in one corner. The creek acts as a natural boundary between Philadelphia and Bucks Counties. There is a hiking and biking trail as well as a trail that leads to the Fairmont Park Trail Connector which is located by the state park and Poquessing Park boundary lines. Also, within the park is a Model Aircraft Flying Field but all was silence during our visit. It is amazing that this 315-acre park just happens to be in the City of Philadelphia. Enjoy!

Hearing—overall quiet solitude, buzz of the bees working in the wildflower-laden fields; sight—amazing vegetable crops waiting to be harvested, beautiful wildflowers in full bloom, tall grasses bending in the breeze, reading the historical placards; smell—sweet smell wafting in the air produced by unknown blooms; taste—yearning to taste a fresh tomato or two warming and plumping in the summer sun; touch—the caress of the breeze on my face as it frequently visits the open expanse of fields.

7. BIG ELK CREEK

This is one of the three new state parks created by former Governor Wolf and announced on September 27, 2022. It is very close to White Clay Creek State Park which is only three miles from Newark, Delaware—just wish Big Creek was established prior to our visit to White Clay! We parked in a lot along Pennsylvania Route 841. The park is on both sides of Big Elk Creek and the trail we hiked follows the one side of the creek, sometimes closely and sometimes with more separation. Walking Springtown Trail provided a serene, scenic view of the creek and surrounding parkland. Views included the sparkling clear waters of the creek, farmland, forests, a stony beach, and ruins of old stone buildings and a stone drainage arch. The trail was very active and Donna and I met two very friendly people who acted as tour guides as we came upon them on an individual basis as we made our way from one trailhead to the other. The trail came to an end at the other trailhead located on Strickersville Road. There is no trail on the other side of the road but per the map, parkland continues to the Pennsylvania-Maryland border which is very close by at this point. We found the newly installed park sign in a parking lot on the opposite side and further along Strickersville Road from the trailhead. Be aware that the park is quite undeveloped at this point in time and there are no restrooms at the trailheads or placards along the trail.

Hearing—babbling of the creek, information from our impromptu trail guides; sight—stone ruins, early spring wildflowers blooming, farmland, picturesque creek, grassland, stony beach.

8. BIG POCONO

The ride up Camelback Road to the summit of Camelback Mountain within the park was somewhat disconcerting since the ever-upward road transverses the Camelback Mountain Resort. Parking at Katrite's Summit House Restaurant, we found it closed (we visited the park in mid-June) but the view was interesting. If one is looking for a pristine wilderness view, it will be a disappointment because of the resort down below. However, if one is staying at the resort in the heart of the winter, the view of the lodge and surrounding countryside would be spectacular.

The summit is located within the park and contains a large parking area, picnic tables, restrooms, hiking trails, and a stone cabin that the previous owner, Henry Cattell, built in 1908. It is still known as the Cattell Cabin today and the DCNR guide states that he kept it unlocked for many years so anyone could use it as needed. The cabin is very picturesque and provides a glimpse into an era where the mountain was undeveloped and had breathtaking views that were, for the most part, untouched by human hands.

We hiked the Indian Trail and North Trail and Lower Loop. There are a good amount of elevation changes but the forest, a scrub oak shrubland, was interesting and the mountain laurel were in full bloom with rhododendron blooms to follow in the coming months. Along with the spectacular mountain laurel blooms and the wind-dwarfed trees, there were some awe-inspiring views to quicken our steps along the trails.

Hearing—the winds causing tree leaves to rustle and limbs to creak; sight—views stretching for miles, spectacular drops into valleys unable to be captured in photographs, an abundance of mountain laurel blooms cascading down the trails, wind-dwarfed trees, huge rock formations.

9. BIG SPRING STATE FOREST PICNIC AREA

This is a very small, 45-acre park which is a trailhead for the Iron Horse Trail. This spot has been a community picnic area since the early 1900s and it was further developed by the CCC in 1936. Along with the old picnic pavilions, restrooms, and outdoor amphitheater with a stone stage, there is a modern, log and stone picnic pavilion complete with fireplaces, wood-fired griddles, and electricity. There are several historical placards showing the huge crowds that once frequented this picnic grove as well as the uncompleted railroad bed and tunnel.

Wow! It was a drizzle- and mist-filled morning visit that made us feel we were stepping back in time to the 1920s. The Tunnel Trail took us on a partially finished railroad bed to an uncompleted railroad tunnel. The failure of the tunnel being dug through Conococheague Mountain led to the bankruptcy of the railroad company and abrupt closure of the entire work site. Interesting to observe different sections of the rail bed from the perspective of the quick shutdown and attempting to understand where the workers were busy building the day it all came to an end. Very old picnic tables seem to date back to the time of the CCC since we never saw that type at any other state park. The oldest buildings and standing-stone-lined trails, along with the moody weather conditions, really produced a time-tunnel of mysteries just waiting for our imaginations to go into overdrive. All and all, a neat little park that owes its survival to the fine people of the Tuscarora State Forest maintenance crews—thanks for your efforts on the behalf of all of us that visit and become enveloped in the mystique of long-passed days.

Hearing—silence, drizzle as it collides with one surface or another; sight—mist and fog producing a dramatic atmosphere, the tall railroad bed that from the side looks like an earthen and rock dam, the imposing entrance to the unfinished tunnel, the old, unique picnic tables, the fairytale look of the stone stage just waiting for the next players to walk across it and begin to perform.

10. BLACK MOSHANNON

Black Moshannon State Park is good-sized with 3,394-acres and it is surrounded, minus some chunks of private land, by 43,000 acres of Moshannon State Forest. The amazing view is of the very dark waters of 250-acre Black Moshannon Lake. The water that fills the lake passes through sphagnum moss-filled bogs which causes the water to darken. It reminds me of the color of some of the waters in Scotland and Ireland that pass through peat bogs. This is a park that cries out for a kayak to explore the lake and see some of the fascinating wildlife and plants. The Bog Trail uses a boardwalk to explore wetlands and a series of panels along this trail has interesting details about what to see and look for when passing through various sections. We also hiked a good chunk of the Moss-Hanne Trail which traverses the Black Moshannon Bog Natural Area. It consists of 1,592 acres of bogs, marshes, swamps and forests. Donna and I spotted and photographed sundews which are tiny, carnivorous plants and immensely enjoyed our fill of blueberries along the way. Hint, we were there on July 19th—yum, yum, yum. There are two boardwalks along this trail but be prepared with waterproof boots, and gaiters would be a good idea as well.

There are many amenities here including four boat launch and mooring areas, a swimming sand beach, boat rentals, picnic tables, picnic pavilions, restrooms, 20 miles of hiking trails, and a 73-site campground. My plan for this park is for us to return in the future and bring along Laura, Mason, Sophia, our tent, and kayak.

Hearing—people frolicking at the beach, the fun and noise that go along with family gatherings at the picnic pavilions; sight—dark, mysterious lake waters, water lilies, swans, sundew, blueberry bushes along the trails; taste—wonderful wild blueberries; touch—the feel of boots sinking into wet spots while hiking.

11. BLUE KNOB

The summit of Blue Knob Mountain is the second highest in Pennsylvania at 3,146 feet and there is a ski resort located there. We visited this 6,128-acre park on July 3rd and found it windy and cooler at the summit area which was refreshing on a hot July afternoon. We hiked on the Three Springs, Mountain View, and Lookout Loop trails which are interconnected. The vistas at Pavia Lookout and Chappell's Field are wonderful and well worth spending time just soaking in the landscapes that unfold from those vantage points. There is a swimming pool and picnic grounds at a lower elevation and a campground with 50 sites at a higher elevation.

Sight—many outstanding views; touch—cool breezes and gusts on the summit.

12. BOYD BIG TREE PRESERVE CONSERVATION AREA

We had a strange visual preamble to this park since our GPS led us through a very industrial section of Harrisburg. We were happy to exit the city and found ourselves on a more scenic road which led us to the entrance where we were greeted by fields containing wildflowers, butterflies, and birds. The parking lot area includes a chestnut tree plantation, an Education Pavilion, restrooms, and trailhead. We sat at the pavilion, enjoyed a hot cup of coffee, and our lunch before hitting the trails. We hiked the Lower Spring Trail since the DNR brochure describes this trail as good for "seeing the heart of the conservation area" as well as a great trail to use for cross-country skiing in the appropriate season.

Returning to our truck, we spent some time looking at the chestnut tree orchard since we had never viewed a chestnut tree before and they were loaded with burrs. The nuts are encased in these burrs which are spiny structures that protect the nuts as they develop. Donna and I took turns getting photographs of us standing in front of some of the trees that are all somewhat obscured by a protective, chain-link fence. The purpose of chestnut orchards such as this one is to develop a blight-resistant replacement for the American chestnut tree. This quintessential forest tree was attacked by a blight starting in New York City in 1904 and was eliminated from all our forests by 1950—two years before I was born. Restoring this tree to forest prominence will have huge aesthetic and economic value and the efforts to accomplish this task are well worth the investment.

Hearing—birds calling out in the forest; sight—American chestnut trees with burrs prominently festooning the branches, birds and butterflies inhabiting the fields of blooming wildflowers; touch—extremely sharp burrs protecting the nuts.

13. BUCHANAN'S BIRTHPLACE

Nice little park (18.5 acres) located along Buck Run within a gap of Tuscarora Mountain. It contains an interesting pyramid-shaped monument to President Buchanan. The park and monument are located where former President James Buchanan was born in 1791. The park contains a parking area with a walking path to the restrooms, picnic tables, a short walking path from Stony Batter Road to the monument, and Buck Run flows through the entire park. The monument is surrounded and protected by an iron railing as requested in the will of Harriet Lane Johnston, the president's niece. The will set the creation of this monument in motion and paid for it along with a monument in Washington, D.C. I highly recommend reading the wonderful, history-filled DCNR Recreation Guide for this park. We checked out the memorial, had a snack at a picnic table and I let my mind drift back to the only day that I was within a few feet of a president.

It was Sunday, October 12, 1962, and we were in for a special day because it was my youngest sister Cindy's birthday and we were going to see President Kennedy. Mom told us that Dad had been on the Board of Directors of Holy Family Institute in Emsworth before he passed and a Sister of the Holy Family of Nazareth, the community in charge of the orphanage, called to tell Mom that President Kennedy would pass by on the way from the airport to downtown Pittsburgh (in later years I found out that Dad was very active in the Polish-American community in Pittsburgh and since the Sisters were from Poland it was natural for Dad to become involved in the orphanage). Sister told my Mom that we could stand with the children from the orphanage and wave and that she believed that the president would stop because of all the nuns and children. Just as predicted, President Kennedy's motorcade came to a stop right where we were standing! I was looking at President Kennedy in "living color" (as the commercial always said) and that fact was shocking to me since the only pictures in my head of the president were in black and white based on images from television and newspapers. As the car idled and he talked to us, I quickly stepped off the sidewalk and touched the side of his car by the trunk area. Immediately, I jumped back onto the sidewalk and waved as his motorcade left. Next came Cindy's party and I was talking up a storm about seeing the president. I was so excited to discover that President Kennedy was a real person and not just a black and white image; however, what most impressed my friends was that I touched his car.

Sight—historical placards, pyramid-shaped monument, Bucks Run.

14. BUCKTAIL STATE PARK NATURAL AREA

In my mind, this is the most unusual park in the entire system. It consists of a 75-mile scenic drive along Pennsylvania Route 120 from Emporium, through Renovo, to Lock Haven. We did not see many pullovers in the most scenic areas but enjoyed the drive just the same. What is most amazing is that the DCNR warns that most of the land within the boundaries of the park is under private ownership.

Sight—viewing scenery as we drove along.

15. CALEDONIA

This 1,125-acre state park is filled with all sorts of history and is located on Pennsylvania Route 30, not far from Chambersburg to the west and Gettysburg to the east. The entire park is within South Mountain which is the end of the Blue Ridge Mountains that roll along from Maryland and Virginia to the south. An iron furnace was established here by Thaddeus Stevens in 1837. He was a congressman during the Civil War and fought for the abolition of slavery. The National Park Service lists the Thaddeus

Stevens' Caledonia Iron Furnace Monument as part of the Network to Freedom program. It appears in the National Park Service interactive map which shows the location of 740 verifiable connections to the Underground Railroad. Unfortunately, the blacksmith shop was closed during our visit because of COVID.

Amenities include two campgrounds, a large swimming pool, picnic tables, pavilions, restrooms, and fishing in the East Branch of the Conococheague, Rocky Mountain Creek, and Carbaugh Run. Further, across Pennsylvania Route 30 from the park office are three historical entities located within the Michaux State Forest or Caledonia State Park; namely, Caledonia Public Golf Course, Totem Pole Playhouse, and Cathedral in the Pines. The golf course was established in 1923 and is the oldest in south central Pennsylvania; the playhouse has been located here since 1952–famous for summer stock productions and the totem pole (the meanings of the totem pole carvings can be found on their website); and the open-air cathedral was started in 1917 and offers Sunday school services in the summer months.

The DCNR provides a booklet at the park that is a self-guided tour of the Thaddeus Stevens Historical Trail. Donna and I completed this trail along with a section of the Appalachian Trail (AT) that runs through the park and crosses Pennsylvania Route 30–we followed the trail into Michaux State Forest before retracing our steps.

Hearing—water flowing from the dam into the race along the Thaddeus Stevens Historical Trail; sight—iron furnace monument, blacksmith shop, totem pole.

16. CANOE CREEK

We visited this park on a beautiful, warm, blue sky, fall day. The 961-acre park includes 155-acre Canoe Lake complete with a swimming beach, boat launches and fishing opportunities. Also, there are picnic tables, restrooms, and the historical Blair Limestone Company kilns. We hiked a loop which had Canoe Lake in the bottom half and consisted of the following trails: Limestone, Moore's Hill, Beaver Pond, Fisherman, and Sugar Loaf. If this loop appeals, use the bridge that crosses Canoe Creek to move from Moore's Hill Trail to Beaver Pond Trail to continue the loop. Check out the kilns as you are leaving the Limestone Trail and hooking onto Moore's Hill Trail.

Sight—sparkling lake, well preserved kilns, historical placards.

17. CHAPMAN

The vast majority of this 862-acre state park is surrounded by the Allegheny National Forest and state game lands which produces beautiful isolation filled with peaceful seclusion. Although Lake Chapman is only 68 acres, it has a swimming beach, boat launches, moorings, and fishing. Along with the lake, amenities include picnic tables, pavilions, restrooms, 91 campsites, and hiking trails, some of which lead into the national forest.

We parked our truck by the park office and hiked the Warming Hut Trail to the warming hut and picnic pavilion 5 where we crossed over Lands Road, turned right along the road to the Lowlands Trail where we crossed a scenic swinging bridge and turned left to continue on the Lowlands Trail to the Nature Trail. We used the Nature Trail to check out the campground and returned to the truck the same way we came. The campground is in a beautiful woodland setting and is a great hub for exploration of both Chapman and the Allegheny National Forest.

When visiting Chapman, I would suggest that this is a great opportunity to check out some of the highlights of the amazing Allegheny National Forest and we did just that before and after visiting Chapman. If nothing else, check out Hearts Content which is very close to Chapman and well worth the drive to see some magnificent old-growth trees.

Sight— beauty of the wilderness, a picturesque, photo-ready swinging bridge.

18. CHERRY SPRINGS

Cherry Springs became the second International Dark Sky Park in the world in 2008. It has restrooms, picnic tables, and a camping area that comes with several restrictions to protect the night sky. We did not visit the park at night but hope to do so sometime in the future. We visited Cherry Hill on a rain-filled spring day and found ourselves to be the only visitors. We hiked the Cherry Springs Working Forest Interpretive Trail (a loop trail) which I estimate is within Susquehannock State Forest for about 75 percent of its length. We also walked around the Astronomy Field, looked at the telescope domes, crossed Pennsylvania Route 44, and walked around the Night Sky Public Viewing Area. Before leaving, we checked out a historical tavern replica built by the CCC which was very interesting. The views of the sky are spectacular and hint at views that await on a clear, moonless, night.

Hearing—gusts of wind blowing through the forest; sight—the wide view of the sky.

19. CLEAR CREEK

This 1,901-acre park is in Clear Creek Valley. Clear Creek flows through the length of the park into the Clarion River which forms a border of the park. The creek and river provide fishing opportunities while an expanded section of Clear Creek includes a beach with swimming opportunities. Along with picnic tables, restrooms, pavilions, and a campground with 53 campsites, there are 25 miles of hiking trails. We hiked on the Clear Creek Trail and the Clear Creek Park Road to form a loop returning to where we parked our truck. Discounting the road experience, the trail twisted and turned through trees, rocks, some running water, and for a time, closely paralleled Clear Creek, which taken all together, made for a delightful, almost magical experience with sunlight filtering through the tree canopy producing all sorts of shadows.

Hearing—flowing water, kayakers shouting to each other on the Clarion River; sight— sunlight filtering through the canopy.

20. CODORUS

We drove to this 3,500-acre state park from Hanover and as a result, we had a wonderful and impressive view of the 1,275-acre Lake Marburg as we crossed over the lake on Pennsylvania Route 216. The lake is interesting because it is a joint project of the Commonwealth of Pennsylvania and Glatfelter Paper Company. The company controls the dam and water usage so the lake can drop over 22 feet during summer. This drastic change in water levels eliminates the possibility of a beach or swimming. Crossing the lake, we made a right turn on Swimming Pool Road and explored that section of the park on foot. Although it was a sunny and hot August day, the area was deserted—the pool was not operating because of COVID. The pool is gigantic and sits on a bluff above the lake. We did some geocaching while in the park which brought us to the Veterans Memorial near the pool as well as the large marina area and picnic pavilions. The park is packed with recreational opportunities including a 193-site campground, hiking trails, mountain biking course, horseback riding area, and numerous boat launch points. It is a very modern, well-appointed park that entices you to stay for days.

Hearing—traffic noise from a busy Pennsylvania Route 216 which runs through the heart of the park; sight—sparkling Lake Marburg, huge swimming pool, spectacular marina filled with numerous sizes and types of boats.

21. COLONEL DENNING

This is a wonderful park that contains within its 273 acres a campground with 49 sites, 3.5-acre fishing and swimming lake, picnic tables, restrooms, and 18 miles of hiking trails. A few of the trails lead into the Tuscarora State Forest, producing even more recreational opportunities. We arrived on our 42nd wedding anniversary with the goal of hiking to Flat Rock in the Tuscarora State Forest. The trailhead is near an informative CCC exhibit which we spent some time reviewing. Flat Rock Trail intersects with the Tuscarora Trail (105 miles in length) which leads to Flat Rock on Blue Mountain. Both trails are steep and very rocky in places—challenging but invigorating and very rewarding when we reached Flat Rock with its stupendous view of the Cumberland Valley. Perfect location for us to share our anniversary gifts with each other, enjoy lunch, and soak in the vista on a sunshine-filled day. When we arrived on the rock, a couple was just leaving and we had a wonderful 30 minutes to ourselves before a hiker arrived as we were packing up to go back down the mountain. The timing could not have been better because she took the perfect anniversary photo for us which found its way to the cover of Donna's corresponding state park book.

Sight—CCC exhibit, Flat Rock, Cumberland Valley vista; touch—Donna and I holding hands as we gaze at the view from Flat Rock on our wedding anniversary.

22. COLTON POINT

One of the two state parks bracketing the Grand Canyon of Pennsylvania; the other is Leonard Harrison State Park. Colton Point is located on the West Rim of the Grand Canyon of Pennsylvania. There is rustic camping, rustic restrooms, picnic tables, and pavilions in the park. We arrived on a cool, rain-shower-filled April morning. We parked at a paved lot and started hiking on the Rim Trail, a mile-long loop filled with overlooks along the canyon rim. On past trips in the fall and summer months we found this trail loaded with tourists, but on this morning we did not see another soul the whole time we were on the trail.

The great experience at this park as well as at Harrison is that for each season of the year, the canyon provides a different, transfixing, face to the world. This spring morning was simply beautiful with foggy mist billowing up the canyon walls from below and at times cloaking Pine Creek only to reveal the canyon walls and creek as we reached the next outlook. Continuing our hike, the trail became more shrouded in white as we made the turn that brought us into the interior of the park. At this point along the trail, the canyon view was replaced by lush forest revealing new green leaves as well as pine needles, all glistening from the rain drops and mist that enveloped us. We were filled with awe as rain increased in intensity as we held hands and made our way back to our truck.

Hearing—only the sounds of nature, rain hitting various surfaces including our rain jackets and rain pants; sight—dream-like atmosphere with fog and mist bellowing up the canyon walls, fog and mist embracing the trails; smell— pines and pine needles; touch—holding each other's hands as we faced the elements together.

23. COOK FOREST

This park is loaded with so much to see and do including 47 miles of hiking trails, 13 miles of the Clarion River, canoe rentals, natural areas, Sawmill Center for the Arts, River and Indian Cabins on the National Register of Historic Places, 210 campsites, picnicking—including tables, restrooms and pavilions, and so much more. Over the years, Donna and I have visited this park several times and she remembers visiting here as a child with her family. We have hiked the Forest Cathedral Natural Area with our children—a perfect opportunity to introduce children to the magnificence of so many old-growth trees.

As a couple, we hiked the Baker Trail for 19 miles ending at the Cook Forest Fire Tower through a "cake walk hike" organized by the Rachel Carson Trails Conservancy—a wonderful organization that has unlocked the great outdoors for so many people. This gave us a great opportunity to view some beautiful scenery along the length of the park including the edge of the Swamp Natural Area and a portion of the Forest Cathedral Natural

Area. I would highly recommend parking a vehicle at each end so this section of the Baker Trail can be explored at a leisurely pace since there is so much to see, enjoy, and embrace. Also, I know the Clarion River Water Trail through the park is highly recommended and it is on our list to eventually explore with our grandkids when we introduce them to the Cathedral. Keep in mind that Cook Forest State Park is a very popular destination so an off-season visit could be more rewarding.

Hearing—silence deep in the park; sight—breathtaking trees in the Cathedral.

24. COWANS GAP

We first visited this park prior to our quest. We find it a convenient location to stretch our legs during travels east to west on the Pennsylvania Turnpike or Pennsylvania Route 30. The Lakeside Trail, which loops around Cowans Gap Lake, is just perfect for this purpose. Cowans Gap with 1,085 acres has numerous amenities that makes it a very busy place in the summer months; however, there is room to roam since it adjoins Buchanan State Forest. The park sits in a valley between Cove Mountain and Tuscarora Mountain, hence the "Gap" attached to the area and its name.

Where to begin? There are two separate campgrounds which provide a total of 201 campsites which I think is quite large for this size park which speaks to its popularity. The lake, at 42 acres, is small but plays "big" with several launch sites, a large swimming beach, beach changing area, concessions for food and boat rentals, and fishing opportunities as well as the aforementioned Lakeside Trail. Picnickers are taken care of with many tables and pavilions along with some CCC-built stone fireplaces. There are 13 miles of hiking trails as well as opportunities for longer hikes with the

110-mile Tuscarora Trail going through the park and the 80-mile Standing Stone Hiking Trail beginning at Cowan Gap Lake where it doubles as a portion of the Lakeside Trail.

Another fun activity is to stop in at the park office and obtain a "Richmond Furnace Camp S-54" brochure. It provides a historical walking tour of the CCC camp that was responsible for so much at the park. The Brightbill Interpretive Center is also worth a visit for both nature displays and CCC photographs and information. When we visited to obtain our stamp, we hiked the Lakeside Trail to the end of the Plessinger Trail and returned the same way to the Lakeside Trail where we turned left to finish that loop. The Plessinger Trail is very scenic since it follows the South Branch of Little Aughwick Creek.

Hearing—laughter and shouts of joy coming from folks on the beach, quiet and soothing stream sounds along the Plessinger Trail; sight—bright sunshine reflecting on the lake waters, beautiful fall leaves, historical CCC photographs in the Interpretive Center.

25. DELAWARE CANAL

This park runs along the 58.9-mile towpath of the Delaware Canal from Bristol to Easton and is designated a National Historic Landmark. The canal itself runs along the Delaware River that separates Pennsylvania from New Jersey. There are two natural areas within the park, namely, Nockamixon Cliffs and 11 State Park River Islands. This is a huge park and there is much to see along the way when biking the towpath including many dips into history. I have developed a three-day itinerary for biking the entire towpath but Donna, Sue, John, and I have yet to pull the trigger on this trip. However, on our visit to obtain our stamp, Donna and I stopped and walked on five sections of the towpath over a two-day period. On the first day we had a wonderful picnic lunch at Lock 21 under a sunshine-filled blue sky. At the same time, during our drives and walks we noted some of the trail damage caused by Hurricane Ida flooding that hit in September 2021.

When planning your visit, I would recommend checking with the park to determine if there is trail damage on your biking route. Talking to a Pennsylvania Park Ranger we learned towpath damage from flooding as well as repair and maintenance are ongoing concerns. The good news is that the Friends of the Delaware Canal is a very organized and proactive non-profit focused entirely on the canal. I would recommend taking a look at their Internet site prior to visiting since it is loaded with great information including events that are scheduled that could be incorporated into trip planning. This is taken directly from their site: "Friends of the Delaware Canal is an independent, non-profit organization working to restore, preserve and improve the Canal and surroundings, providing educational and recreational opportunities and serving as a community and economic asset." Just think, you may love this park so much that someday you may become a member.

Sight—historical structures and placards, flood damage.

26. DENTON HILL

Per DCNR, the ski area at this park has been closed since 2014 but as of 2024, a public-private partnership was working to develop a four-season recreation center. Please check with the park to see what services are available in the future.

On our visit, Donna and I found the park to be a bit on the depressing side of the spectrum with a well-constructed lodge just sitting there and of course, we were the only two there. We hiked up the ski slope and obtained some information on the cross-country skiing trails before we left. With elevations running between 1,800 and 2,400 feet, there might be some good cross-country skiing action in the heart of the winter season.

Hearing—traffic noise from a very busy Pennsylvania Route 6; sight—closed down ski lodge.

27. ELK

Elk State Park contains 3,192 acres which, for the most part, encircle the 1,160-acre East Branch Clarion Reservoir. Swimming is not permitted but there is plenty of boating as well as fishing and with unlimited horsepower motors permitted, water skiing becomes an option. There are picnic tables and restrooms by the only state park boat launch site. The park sits in the mountains and adjoins Elk State Forest but there is no camping within the park or developed hiking trails. The Army Corps of Engineers has property adjoining the park around the dam and maintains a picnic area, playground, restrooms, launch site, and campground.

On our visit in 2020, the reservoir had been partially drained for several years awaiting progress on a major dam repair. We walked out into the dry portion of the lake to view the remains of several building foundations that are normally underwater. It is in a beautiful setting in the mountains and I look forward to seeing it again now that repairs are completed and water levels restored. We met only one person during our time there and she told us about her last ice fishing experience which occurred over 30 years ago. She said it was below zero and she and her family drilled through 30 inches of ice to fish.

Sight—low water in the reservoir providing a unique glimpse of the past exposing foundations that are usually underwater, beautiful backdrop of mountains; touch—walking on some of the foundations.

28. ERIE BLUFFS

A great park to visit to step back in time to experience the shoreline of Lake Erie in its wild state before development gobbled up and transformed so much of it. There are just over five miles of trails and to hike them all, some doubling back must be undertaken but is well worth the effort. Don't forget to hike down to Elk Creek and the beach where there is driftwood and beautiful stones. There are two parking areas, one up in the fields directly off of Pennsylvania Route 5 and the other is at the end of the Elk Creek access road. At the Elk Creek access area there is a picnic pavilion, picnic tables, rustic restroom, and a boat launch. Swimming is not permitted but fishing is available along Elk Creek and where Elk Creek flows into Lake Erie. Next time we come to this little gem, we will launch our kayak in Elk Creek and paddle out into Lake Erie to see the bluffs from the water.

Hearing—waves coming ashore below the bluffs; sight—driftwood and stones along the shore, wonderful view of Lake Erie from a portion of the bluffs; touch—handling some of the smooth rocks on the beach.

29. EVANSBURG

Along with the usual park amenities consisting of picnic tables, pavilions, restrooms, hiking trails, and fishing opportunities (along Skippack Creek which wends its way through the length of the park), there is an interesting array of other amenities. These include an 18-hole golf course, 15 miles of horseback riding trails, and five miles of mountain biking trails. Yes, an amazing combination for any one park but what makes this park unique in the entire park system is the pièce de résistance, a regulation cricket field! Donna and I ran into cricket fields on some of our hiking adventures in Great Britain but in a Pennsylvania state park—wow, unbelievable but true. We had fun checking out the cricket field and taking a selfie standing in front of the "British Officers Cricket Club" that is located across the street from the field.

The Friedt Visitor Center was closed during our visit because of a hornet infestation but looked interesting; we enjoyed walking around Keyser Mill which provided some cool photo opportunities; and we just loved seeing the Eight Arch Bridge. We successfully made it through mud and a huge poison ivy patch (you know poison ivy is bad in this park when the DCNR Recreation Guide includes a paragraph complete with color photographs to warn visitors) to obtain photographs of this wondrous bridge from stream level. Photographs were simply stunning with sunlight in combination with a tree canopy producing amazing shadows on the stone bridge works. Equally gorgeous photographs were produced by the reflections of the stone arches in Skippack Creek. Per the DCNR website, the Eight Arch Bridge "was constructed in 1792. It is the oldest bridge in continuous, heavy use in the nation." From below, trust me, it is readily apparent that this bridge could be in a museum.

Seeing this bridge took my mind on a trip to Acadia National Park and its unbelievably beautiful granite bridges. These 16 unique bridges were built by John D. Rockefeller, Jr. along his amazing 57 miles of carriage roads. Each bridge has a different masonry look but all are steel-reinforced concrete structures faced with granite stone quarried on Acadia island.

Donna and I have visited Acadia National Park numerous times with various members of our family present—over the years all of us have explored the park including Joseph, Laura, Eric, Mason, and Sophia. I think Donna has me beat in the number of visits even though I made it there on a job that took me to Southwest Harbor and the Coast Guard station. Anyway, those bridges are all beautiful but the Eight Arch Bridge built in 1792 bests them all!

Sight—cricket field, British Officers Cricket Club, beautiful exterior of Friedt Visitor Center and gardens, Keyser Mill, reflections of Eight Arch Bridge in Skippack Creek, huge amounts of poison ivy.

30. FORT WASHINGTON

Fort Washington State Park, Valley Forge National Historical Park (first Pennsylvania state park created in 1893 and gifted to the people of the United States in 1976), and Washington Crossing Historic Park are the trifecta of parks in Pennsylvania regarding General George Washington and his Continental Army! The history found in Fort Washington State Park is significant and I quickly linked it in my mind to Valley Forge and General Washington and his army crossing the Delaware River.

Fort Washington State Park is somewhat splintered and Donna and I were confused for a time as we made our way to various sections of the park. The park has four separate sections; namely, Militia Hill Day Use Area, Flourtown Day Use Area, Fort Hill Area Historic Site, and Sandy Run Area (limited access). The day use areas have playfields, picnic tables, picnic pavilions, and restrooms. In the Militia Hill Day Use Area we checked out the Hawk Watch observation decks, walked up and down Militia Hill, and had our lunch at a pavilion. We briefly checked out the Flourtown Day Use Area before driving to the Fort Hill Area Historic Site. The road on this site was blocked by a downed tree so we parked with the tree in front of our truck and explored the site through the historical placards. We could just feel the history oozing out of the ground here as we stood where the temporary fort was built by troops of the Continental Army in November 1777.

Thinking about the Revolutionary War while standing on Fort Hill, I quickly understood the domino effect of history when thinking about the actions honored by these parks in our state. In my mind the first domino fell when General Washington and his troops successfully crossed the Delaware and defeated Hessian forces in the Battle of Trenton. After the unsuccessful battle in Germantown, General Washington and his troops built a temporary fort on Fort Hill in Whitemarsh Valley. They stayed here from November 2, 1777 to December 11, 1777. The general and his approximately 12,000 troops made a stand against British troops maneuvering against them, resulting in the British withdrawal back to Philadelphia which, to me, represents the fall of the second domino. From here, General Washington and his troops marched to Valley Forge and successfully wintered there which represents the fall of the third domino.

Without these dominos falling in the favor of the Continental Army, I believe the Revolutionary War would have ended successfully for the British and not the Americans. Please take all of these thoughts with a huge grain of salt because I am neither a military analyst nor a Revolutionary War historian, just a guy moved by the moments I spent on Fort Hill. Thinking of Fort Hill, I think it deserves more love from state funding sources as well as more interest from common folks interested in United States history.

Sight—historical views from Militia Hill and Fort Hill; touch—treading on history walking up and down Militia Hill and around Fort Hill.

31. FOWLERS HOLLOW

This is a small, 104-acre park in a narrow valley that was once the location of a sawmill. Fowler Hollow Run flows through the length of the park and is open for fishing; there are 18 shady campsites, restrooms, a few picnic tables, and several trails come through the park from Tuscarora State Forest which brackets the park. We obtained a DCNR trail guide there that shows some of these trails and forest roads. We hiked a portion of the Beaston Trail into the Tuscarora State Forest before retracing our steps. This trail can be used for hiking, horseback riding, and snowmobiling. I would recommend checking with staff members when picking up the Tuscarora State Forest map to see if they have more detailed trail maps if you plan to use this park as a jumping off point for any of these forest trails. Donna and I took a selfie standing by what looks like a giant stone barbecue fireplace. If memory serves me correctly, it is the remains of a boiler that was used to power the sawmill.

Hearing—quiet solitude; sight—our rain-filled arrival, in a narrow valley with a large tree canopy, produced an overpowering gloom.

32. FRANCES SLOCUM

This 1,035-acre park is loaded with amenities. To begin with, there is the 165-acre, horseshoe-shaped Frances Slocum Lake where it is all about boating and fishing with two boat launches, two mooring areas, a boat rentals concession, and a fishing pier. Other amenities include picnic tables and picnic pavilions, restrooms, a swimming pool with snack bar, a campground with 100 campsites, over 13 miles of hiking trails, and five miles of mountain biking trails. This is a really delightful park with an interesting history and inspiring hiking trails.

In 1778, a group of Delaware Native Americans captured a five-year-old girl named Frances Slocum and they spent the first night in a rock shelter located within the park. Donna and I hiked the Frances Slocum Trail to view the rock shelter before having lunch sitting at a picnic table with a view of the lake.

After our lunch, we jumped on the Deer Trail by our picnic site and quickly found our dessert, bunches of grapes growing by Francis Slocum Lake. No, these were not small, sour, wild grapes but super sweet Concord grapes which happen to be my favorites! Donna had to drag me away or we would never have finished our hike. The Deer Trail was a joy since it led us through a marshy section at the end of one prong of the lake using huge concrete stepping stones—a very picturesque setting that just happens to be on the cover of the park's Hiking Trail Information and Guidelines brochure. The photo produces great expectations and the reality of the trail does not disappoint. Speaking of not disappointing, this brochure is wonderful with great trail photos and trail information. In combination with the trail map within the DCNR Recreation Guide, we were perfectly oriented on our hike. After the photo opportunities with the stepping stones, we followed the Deer Trail along the lake to where we could jump on the Upper Deer Trail which took us through some beautiful fieldstone walls before dropping down onto the Deer Trail at the point where we quickly returned to the land of the Concord grapes. Yes, yum, yum, yum!

Sight—rock shelter stirs the imagination, stepping stones are a wonderful scene setter, fieldstone walls so stoic-like and picturesque; taste—Concord grapes so unexpected and delicious; touch—all those plump Concord grapes in my hand just waiting to hit my tastebuds.

33. FRENCH CREEK

This is a huge, 7,916-acre park that seems even bigger since it has shared boundaries with Crow's Nest Preserve, State Games Lane #43, Birdsboro Preserve, and Hopewell Furnace National Historic Site. Further, it is at the heart of Hopewell Big Woods which consists of 73,000 acres, making it the largest contiguous forest in the southeastern part of Pennsylvania. There are two lakes in the park, 22-acre Scotts Run and 68-acre Hopewell. Boating and fishing are permitted on both lakes but no swimming. There are boat launches and boat moorings at both lakes and boat rentals are available at Hopewell Lake along with a fishing pier. There is a huge pool overlooking Hopewell Lake and the setting with the lake spreading out below is really breathtaking. Unfortunately, the pool was closed because of COVID which was painful because we were there in summer heat. There are picnic tables, restrooms, over 35 miles of hiking trails, more than 20 miles of mountain biking trails, the 140-mile Horse-Shoe Trail which passes through the park and is open to horseback riders as well as hikers, and a beautiful, wooded campground with 200 sites.

We camped here for four nights since French Creek was one of our hub parks. The campground was great and we had a perfect site to break in our new, six-person tent. It was so wonderful to have room to stand to change our clothes and to walk in and out instead of crawling. Finally, our knees took down their picket signs protesting unfair work conditions! My orthopedic surgeon will need to forget that extra trip to Hawaii too!

We used several trails to explore both lakes, swimming pool area, and Hopewell Furnace National Historic Site. A looping section of the Lenape Trail took us from our campground to Hopewell Furnace and back. We both really enjoyed the trail and highly recommend it. Hopewell Furnace is a must-see when visiting French Creek. It is an amazing trip back in time with unbelievable buildings, exhibits, and history that keeps folks interested and entertained throughout their visits.

Hearing—some traffic noise from Pennsylvania Route 345 drifting into our campsite at night; sight—mesmerizing view from a hill overlooking the huge swimming pool with Hopewell Lake as backdrop.

34. GIFFORD PINCHOT

This 2,338-acre park with 340-acre Pinchot Lake is easily accessible from Harrisburg by way of Interstate 83 (Exit 32) which easily justifies the huge campground containing 289 campsites. Pinchot Lake must attract lots of attention from folks in Harrisburg and beyond with three launch sites, 286 moorings, fishing including a fishing pier, boat rentals, and a swimming beach. Add to this mix of amenities with a trail open to bikers, disc golfing, horseback riding trails, 18 miles of hiking trails, and plenty of support for picnickers including picnic tables, picnic pavilions, restrooms, grills, playgrounds, ball field, volleyball court, and horseshoe pits. We visited in the heart of the summer during COVID so the park was fairly empty but normally I would guess this place is a real zoo with many, many happy folks coming and going on both day trips and overnights.

We camped here overnight and found the campground to be very nice and Pinchot Lake was very accessible from our campsite since the Lakeside Trail goes through the campground as a portion of the loop the trail forms around the lake. We enjoyed our before-dinner hike on a portion of this trail and were delighted by some awesome views. Normally, I am sure we would have had lots of company but with COVID, crowding was not an issue.

There was so much work involved in establishing camp for one night and breaking it down the next morning but this park was well worth the effort. I made fresh corn on the cob, hotdogs, and onions and potato slices for dinner that evening. On leaving, Donna said I was really hitting my stride with my outdoor chef skills between dinner last night and my outstanding breakfast this morning which consisted of scratch blueberry-buttermilk pancakes, bacon, over-easy eggs, scratch oatmeal, and coffee. I think it was cooking the corn in the husk long enough to develop some charring as well as using my favorite spices on the potato and onion dish that did the trick, as well as the blueberries and buttermilk!

Hearing—virtually no traffic noise; sight—sunshine striking the waters of Pinchot Lake; taste—love the charred corn on the cob, blueberry-buttermilk pancakes from scratch along with all the sides and a cup of fresh coffee.

35. GOULDSBORO

This large park with 2,800 acres adjoins both Tobyhanna State Park and Tobyhanna Army Depot. Along with wooded picnic areas, a picnic pavilion, and restrooms, there is 250-acre Gouldsboro Lake. The lake has a swimming beach, 50 moorings, a boat launch, boat rentals, and a fishing pier. Although there is no campground, one can be found at Tobyhanna State Park.

We sat at a picnic table overlooking the beach and ate lunch, enjoying the lake view. Afterwards, we briefly walked on the beach before accessing the Frank Gantz Trail which we hiked on for approximately a mile before retracing our steps to the parking lot and our truck. This trail connects Gouldsboro and Tobyhanna State Parks and is 3.2 miles in length. The Frank Gantz trail meanders around a portion of Gouldsboro Lake before it crosses Tobyhanna Road, skirts the Black Bear & Bender Swamps Natural Area, and leads to the Lakeside Trail of Tobyhanna State Park. A right turn where the trail crosses Tobyhanna Road, leads to Tobyhanna Army Depot.

Sight—swimming beach from our picnic table.

36. GREENWOOD FURNACE

This 423-acre park and six-acre Greenwood Lake create a perfect community park with the historical district as a fascinating bonus. This park has everything needed for family gatherings as well as for overnight visits. There are picnic tables, picnic pavilions, restrooms, snack bar, playground, horseshoe pits, volleyball courts, ball field, swimming beach, fishing, small boat launch site, and 51-site campground. At the same time, there is a huge amount of history here regarding the community that formed around the iron furnace that operated from 1834 to 1904. Amazingly, one of the four furnaces remains along with several buildings. Per the DCNR website, tours are available of the historical district but none were available because of COVID. However, there are many historical placards which we took full advantage of during our visit.

We hiked a portion of the Standing Stone Hiking Trail which goes through the park and is 80 miles in length. Other trails lead into the surrounding Rothrock State Forest as well and thus provide plenty of room to roam beyond the 423 acres within the park. Pennsylvania Route 305 cuts though the entire length of the park but did not appear as a busy traffic artery during our visit.

Sight—historical buildings, furnace, historical placards.

37. HICKORY RUN

This is a giant of a park with 15,990 acres of land, more than 40 miles of hiking trails, a 380-site campground, two lakes (no boating)—Sand Spring Lake, a small 14-acre swimming lake close to the campground and Hickory Run Lake, a very small fishing lake—miles and miles of fishing streams, three natural areas—Boulder Field, Mud Swamp, and Mud Run—a picnic area with tables, pavilions, restrooms, and playground, Hawk Falls, and a beautiful visitor center/park office. The park is so big with so much to see that the first stop must be the visitor center/park office for information. The building is new, beautiful, energy-efficient and contains 2,400 square feet of exhibits. Be sure to pick up the park map, other brochures of interest, and especially, a sheet entitled, "Driving Directions to Popular

Destinations from Visitor Center"—I guarantee you will be using it throughout your visit.

We visited both the Boulder Field Natural Area and Hawk Falls. The Boulder Field is a National Natural Landmark and is a wonderful place to both see and walk through. We shared a picnic lunch at a shaded picnic table at the edge of the Boulder Field after we experienced the fun of making our way through a section of the boulders. We found walking through and over the boulders to be challenging but doable. Shade at our picnic table was very welcoming because in full sunlight the boulders became a heat sink and without shade in the Boulder Field itself, it was very, very hot making our way through the boulders. Remember to take plenty of water with you when you enter the field.

The hike from the parking lot along Pennsylvania Route 534 to Hawk Falls is a bit challenging at times but very scenic. The only negative is that a bridge on the Pennsylvania Turnpike carries the turnpike over Route 534 in close proximity to Hawk Falls and the constant traffic on the bridge produces quite a lot of noise pollution. This noise is so incongruent with Hawk Run, Hawk Falls, and the overall scenic setting that it quickly becomes very distracting and mars the experience of seeing the 25-foot waterfall. Although nothing can be done about the noise pollution, a visit to Hawk Falls is still a must.

We ended our visit on a high note by hiking the Shades of Death Trail. We jumped on the trail by the park office and hiked downhill to a chapel. This trail follows Sand Spring Run through a gorge filled with hemlocks, rhododendrons, and rock formations. The scenery is gorgeous and includes several small waterfalls, footbridges, ponds, 15-foot high Stametz Dam falls, and a stone staircase that wends the trail through two large boulders. Outstanding! This is a park we plan to return to and camp for a few days.

Hearing—traffic noise by Hawk Falls; sight—Hawk Falls, Boulder Field, stone staircase, Stametz Dam Falls; touch—feel of sun beating down and heat radiating off of boulders in Boulder Field.

38. HILLMAN

Hillman State Park is basically undeveloped and the only park in the system that is a state game lands, in this case, number 342. It is an old coal-mining site so very extensive reclamation was undertaken and completed prior to opening it to the public. There are 34.2 miles of trails that can be used for hiking, mountain biking, and horseback riding. For no real reason, we selected the Haul Trail to hike on before leaving the park for the long ride home. Much to our surprise, it turned out to be a great choice because we were rewarded by finding a wildflower in full bloom that escaped our observation for all the years we have been wildflowering, namely, spotted wintergreen. We found numerous examples on this trail to our delight and we celebrated with hot cups of coffee from our thermos when we returned to the truck.

Hearing—quiet place to hike; sight—spotted wintergreen in full bloom.

39. HILLS CREEK

This 407-acre park and 137-acre Hills Creek Lake combine together to make a neat destination for family vacations. The lake has 30 moorings in three areas, two launch sites, boat rentals, a swimming beach with snack bar, and fishing pier. The park has five miles of hiking trails, two picnic areas with tables, pavilions, and restrooms, and a campground with 85 sites.

We hiked along Hills Creek Lake for a time on the Lake Side Trail which is a three-mile loop around the lake. Part of the Lake Side Trail is also a tiny segment (1.5 miles) of the Mid State Trail which is 327 miles in length. Down by the lake, we picked up a DCNR "Common Birds" checklist brochure for this park that is divided into Forests, Fields, Grassy Areas, and Wetlands/Water habitats; further, each of these categories is divided into three seasons. Very interesting brochure and not for the first time on this quest, we both wished we had a workable knowledge of birds.

Hearing—quiet, peaceful, environment; sight—the views of the lake from the Lake Side Trail were beautiful and enticing.

40. HYNER RUN

This small, 180-acre park is surrounded by Sproul State Forest land which produces a wonderful wilderness-style environment. In my park descriptions, I have labeled several of our state parks as wonderful community parks and Hyner Run fits this profile. It has two large picnic pavilions, holding 82 and 96 people respectively, which are perfect for family gatherings or taken together, a wonderful venue for a community or company party. In addition, a large swimming pool and wading pool are open in the summer months. Individual families find plenty of space for their picnics as well with approximately 150 picnic tables spread over a seven-acre picnic area that includes restrooms and plenty of parking spaces. There are other attractions including Hyner Run for fishing and exploration by kids being kids, a neat little campground with 30 sites, and there is a trailhead for the 81-mile Donut Hole Trail system. As a bonus, Hyner View Road is right by the park entrance and leads up to the spectacular Hyner View State Park.

We checked out the stone fireplace in Pavilion No.1 since it once heated the recreation hall in the CCC camp that once existed here. The CCC boys were responsible for the original development of this park including the original plantation of red and white pine trees that are found here. We hiked on the Long Fork Loop of the Donut Hole Trail for over an hour and it is a beautiful trail that sucks you into the forest as if by magic. When we returned to our truck, we easily made our way to Hyner View State Park.

Sight—forest everywhere, the massive stone fireplace makes one ponder the CCC boys.

41. HYNER VIEW

This six-acre park is all about the view and history unless you are a member of the hang gliding community which adds the additional perspective of this being a spectacular launch point from the wooden platform where the steps end and open sky begins. During our visit, a hang glider buff arrived and began unloading his equipment.

The viewing and launch area sits at 1,940 feet and down below, the West Branch of the Susquehanna River sits at 640 feet so this spectacular and entrancing view encompasses a 1,300-foot drop. The view to the left, right, and center from the viewing platform is just beyond words.

The View, Hyner View State Park

Along with the obvious, this little park contains some historical features—a wall, a statue, and a monument. The stone viewing wall, which acts as a magnet when one pulls in and parks, was built by the CCC in the 1930s. A wonderful, bronze, life-size statue of one of the CCC boys and a visual symbol of all the boys from around the United States, was dedicated on September 18, 2012. Joseph Wiedemer donated the funds to honor his long-time friends who served with the CCC. Donna took a photo with the statue in the foreground and the wall, USA flag flying high, and a glimpse of the view all in the background, which made an outstanding composition. The memorial is dedicated to Pennsylvania fire wardens who have kept our forests safe since 1915. It was erected in 1965 by the Forest Inspectors Association to honor 50 years of service. This simple and moving memorial primarily consists of a huge, somewhat obelisk-like stone with a plaque honoring the fire wardens' devotion to the state forests. On both sides of this stone are a total of 20 smaller stones that were taken from each of the

20 Pennsylvania state forests. A beautiful and touching memorial to all those that have served.

We passed up a picnic table for our lunch and let the view draw us to the wall where we stood and ate while once again being captivated by the stunning and mesmerizing view. We were really blessed with perfect weather and we found that time mysteriously slipped by as the landscape captured us in its embrace. When Duane, Donna, and I finally tore ourselves away from the view, our conversation focused on whether or not we would see another park view to top this one. Duane accompanied us on two trips during our quest but at this point, Donna and I had been on this journey for 16 months and nothing had compared to what unfolded at Hyner View. Although the three of us speculated about the future, none of us could declare this as the ultimate view since so much was ahead of us. Although Duane would soon leave the quest behind for other pursuits, Donna and I had the privilege to continue these adventures which led to many other amazing views but nothing topped this one. I am pleased to name **Hyner View State Park** as my choice for the *Pennsylvania State Park with the Best View*.

Hearing—rush of the wind in the wide open space; sight—astonishingly beautiful views complemented by gorgeous weather, flow of the West Branch of the Susquehanna River, hang gliding launch platform beckoning one and all to give the sport a try, historical wall and viewing platform, USA flag majestically flying in the breeze, CCC boys statue, Pennsylvania fire wardens memorial; touch—cool breeze cooling us on a hot July day.

42. JACOBSBURG ENVIRONMENTAL EDUCATION CENTER

This park consists of 1,168 acres with amenities that include 18 miles of hiking trails with most open to horseback riders, picnic facilities including tables, a pavilion, and restrooms, and fishing available in Bushkill Creek that meanders through a large section of the acreage. At the same time, it is both an environmental education center and historical site. The environmental center serves school students ranging from pre-schoolers to college students as well as the local community and park visitors. The Jacobsburg National Historic District is here and both the John Joseph Henry Estate and the Pennsylvania Longrifle Museum are located within the Boulton Historic Site.

We arrived at the park in the middle of a thunderstorm bringing massive amounts of rain to the park. Seeking shelter, we found the visitor center and environmental education exhibits closed.

However, the Passport to History weekend was in full swing so other buildings normally closed were open for the festivities. We toured the Longrifle Museum as well as the Henry Mansion. Both were staffed by members of the Jacobsburg Historical Society. We bought raffle tickets for a Pennsylvania long rifle on our tour of the museum but we had no luck. The rifle was beautiful and would have looked great above our fireplace mantle.

Both the exterior and interior of the mansion were beautiful and the contents were incredible since five generations of the Henrys lived there and when the last survivor passed in 1989, her will bequeathed the mansion and unbelievable contents to the Jacobsburg Historical Society. Donna and I would love to visit the mansion during the Christmas holidays since it is decorated in a Victorian manner and the staff said it was well worth making a special trip to experience it.

Hearing—very interesting presentations by the Jacobsburg Historical Society staff, roar of the thunderstorm and the pounding of the rain; sight—so many examples of the Pennsylvania long rifle, mansion contents including typewriters, clothing, and furnishings, historical placards.

43. JENNINGS ENVIRONMENTAL EDUCATION CENTER

This is a 300-acre park focused on educating students ranging from preschoolers to college students. Public programs are also hosted along with teacher professional development programs. The highlight of the park is the 20-acre prairie ecosystem which contains many prairie-specific plants led by the blazing star along with serving as a refuge for the endangered eastern massasauga rattlesnake. There are also five miles of hiking trails, picnic tables, restrooms, and a beautiful visitors center that contains educational exhibits, space for lectures, and a nature gift shop. Moraine State Park acreage abuts the Jennings acreage and the Glacier Ridge Trail (14.8 miles) connects the two parks. Please be aware that this trail is also designated as a portion of the 4,600-mile North Country National Scenic Trail.

We have visited this park many times over the years, have hiked all the trails, and have seen the blazing star and many other wildflowers in full bloom. Donna remembers visiting this prairie-park when she was young and we visited with our own kids and hope to bring our grandkids in the future—yes, this place is that worthwhile. As a heads up, the blazing star blooms in July and early August.

We really love the fact that as part of their mission to educate the public, Jennings' staff publish a double-sided sheet entitled, "What's Blooming?" for each month during the flowering season. One side shows small photos of the blooms and the other is a flower list with a key that reveals where to look for the blooms as follows: **G** In the native plant gardens, **WL** In wetland areas, **F** In forested or shady areas, **P** In the prairie, **S** In sunny, disturbed areas along a trail or road, and **PE** In the prairie expansion. Also, an asterisk is used to designate invasive or non-native wildflowers. Grab a sheet when you visit and see how many you can find! We have never seen the elusive massasauga rattlesnake but we are always hopeful.

Sight—wildflowers in bloom, educational placards, handouts entitled, "What's Blooming?"

44. JOSEPH E. IBBERSON CONSERVATION AREA

This park contains 803 acres with several interconnected hiking trails. The 1.1-mile Evergreen Trail and 0.9-mile Old Saw Mill Trail are recommended for cross-country skiing when weather permits. The AT runs across the width of the park and can be reached by means of the three-mile Victoria Trail. The Victoria Trail continues past the AT and enters State Game Lands 211 which abuts a section of the conservation area and ends at a parking lot on Pennsylvania Route 325.

    The main entrance of the park sits on Back Road. As we drove on Back Road I remember lots of cornfields and when we turned into the park entrance road, there were more cornfields as we drove to the parking lot. At the parking lot, there are restrooms, a pavilion for education purposes and trailheads. The trail system is well blazed and we hiked the Evergreen and Pine trails which we used to form somewhat of a double loop (while backtracking a bit) which began and ended at the parking lot. The conservation land is very forested, beautiful, and peaceful.

Sight—cornfield; taste—we poured hot coffee when we returned to the pavilion by the parking lot.

45. KETTLE CREEK

This 1,793-acre park is in a valley with about half of the park boundaries bordering Sproul State Forest. Kettle Creek runs through the length of the park and flows into the 167-acre Kettle Creek Reservoir which is formed by the Alvin R. Bush Flood Control Dam. Kettle Creek continues flowing downstream past the dam which is controlled by the Army Corps of Engineers. Fishing is available in the reservoir as well as Kettle Creek. At the Lower Campground, Kettle Creek forms the seven-acre Kettle Creek Lake as a result of a small CCC-built dam and this is known as a nice fishing spot. Once Kettle Creek flows past the CCC dam, water quality is diminished by mine drainage.

In addition to fishing, other park amenities include a trailhead for a 22-mile horseback riding trail, two miles of hiking trails within the park which lead to many miles of trails in Sproul State Forest, volleyball and softball fields, picnicking areas featuring tables, a pavilion, restrooms, and playgrounds, and a boat launch site and moorings. There are two campgrounds, the Upper Campground with 27 sites overlooking the reservoir and the Lower Campground with 41 sites along Kettle Creek in Sproul State Forest below the reservoir dam.

We drove through Kettle Creek State Park on Pennsylvania State Route 4001 which is very scenic. On this foggy April morning we found a very, very quiet park. Only two fishermen and a few Canadian geese were on the waters of the reservoir, which made for a peaceful experience. We stopped at the boat launch and mooring area, grabbed some photos and afterwards, we stopped by the park office. We continued on Route 4001 past the Upper Campground and stopped to view the Alvin R. Bush Flood Control Dam before reaching the Lower Campground. We parked and checked out the little Kettle Creek Lake and the CCC dam that spans Kettle Creek at this point before driving out of the park.

Hearing—fog-shrouded hush; sight—picturesque, foggy morning.

46. KEYSTONE

This 1,200-acre park is a great community park which we have visited many times over the years. Visits have included hiking, kayaking, beaching and swimming, and going on first-day (January 1st) hikes which are planned at numerous parks annually. We have hiked on all the trails over the years. Some lower sections of McCune Trail can be wet so have your waterproof boots on when hiking this 0.5-mile trail which leads to Strawcutter and Davis Run trails. We always enjoy lake loop trails and Lakeside Trail is no exception. This 2.2-mile trail is a combination of park roads and walkways open to both hikers and bikers. Kayaking is enjoyable in the 78-acre Keystone Lake and the lake provides a fishing pier, launch and mooring sites, and a swimming beach. There are two campgrounds totaling approximately 100 sites as well as picnic areas, pavilions, restrooms, a ball field, and visitor center.

Hearing—busy community park during the summer months, the Davis Run Trail provides peaceful sounds of nature; sight—the Lakeside Trail provides picturesque views.

47. KINGS GAP ENVIRONMENTAL EDUCATION CENTER

This is a large park on South Mountain consisting of 2,531 acres of forest with a portion of the park bordering Michaux State Forest. The heart of the park is the Cameron-Masland Mansion and mansion grounds. The mansion grounds include the mansion garden, a carriage house, education building and several other buildings. The mansion is available for meetings, retreats, weddings, and individual overnight stays. The Environmental Education Center offers programs for students ranging from preschoolers to college-level as well as teacher training and programs for the general public. There are 20 miles of hiking trails (more in Michaux State Forest), picnic tables, picnic pavilions, restrooms, and an orienteering course.

The beautiful, winding, four-mile road in the heart of the forest that takes visitors up the mountain to the mansion grounds is wondrous to experience. The mansion itself is imposing with a stupendous view of the Cumberland Valley. The long drive up to the mansion, the mansion and accompanying grounds, and the incredible views blend together in the mind's eye to create a magical place that overwhelms the senses—at least that was my experience. It was all just so unexpected and awe-inspiring. During our explorations, we walked to the back of the mansion and found The View, walked through the garden that was in full November retreat, and hiked the 0.6-mile Woodland Ecology Trail and the 1.3-mile Maple Hollow Trail to form a loop.

We picked up a brochure on the garden and found it to be very detailed with a cornucopia of information that promises so much in the warmer months as wildflowers, herbs, shade plants, trees, shrubs and vines all come to life and present different faces throughout the growing seasons. At the same time, we found a flyer touting the availability of mansion bedrooms for overnight stays (minimum two days) from May through mid-November. We plan on returning to stay a few days to really explore everything that Kings Gap has to offer during the spring or summer months.

Sight—the beauty of the forest displayed around each curve in the road, view of the Cumberland Valley from on high, the mansion.

48. KINZUA BRIDGE

We have visited this 339-acre park several times over the years.

I dreamed of taking a train ride with Donna over the bridge just as her parents did many, many, years ago. Unfortunately, my dream came to an end when a tornado hit on July 21, 2003 and destroyed a large portion of the bridge. July 21st is an unhappy, dreaded day in my life since my dad passed that day in 1959 from lung cancer. Now, each time I think of this park, it reminds me of not only the loss of a historical bridge but the loss of my dad.

On a much happier note, I must say that turning the remainder of the Kinzua Bridge into a walkway and observation deck in 2011 and building the beautiful visitor center in 2016 upgraded this park beyond words from its pre-tornado days. It is a great boon to tourism and the local economy as well as a wonderful way to preserve history while bringing it to life through exhibits. During our visit to obtain our passport stamp, we had a wonderful picnic lunch and afterwards explored everything the park had to offer including the two miles of hiking trails.

We enjoyed the visitor center's exhibits and gift shop where I was able to purchase a medallion for my hiking pole. The skywalk and viewing platform provided amazing views but I would suggest it is not the best place to go for those with acrophobia. We enjoyed taking the 0.4-mile Kinzua Creek Trail to the debris field way down below but one needs to be aware it is a very steep, shadeless, 0.4-mile hike back up to the visitor center so have plenty of water and be physically prepared. This trail provides an opportunity to observe the power of a tornado by seeing the twisted steel girders. Remember, be safe, observe the signs, and stay out of the dangerous debris field. Standing on the valley floor provides an excellent perspective for viewing the people on the observation deck and understanding how high you find yourself when walking out to check out the view.

Once we were back in the upper section of the park, we hiked the 1.6-mile General Kane Trail which is a loop starting and ending at the overflow parking lot. As a bonus we walked for a short period of time on the Knox & Kane Rail Trail that also has a trailhead at the overflow parking lot. Currently, it is a 7.5-mile, crushed limestone trail but eventually it will be 73.8 miles in length which will make for a wonderful biking experience. The great news is that the entire 73.8-mile corridor is owned by the Headwaters Charitable Trust so this trail will eventually become reality as enthusiasm, dedication, and donations move it forward.

Sight—views from walkway and observation deck, debris field and observation deck from the valley floor.

49. KOOSER

This cozy, 250-acre park sits in the Laurel Highlands at about 2,600 feet. Pennsylvania State Route 31 forms the border of one side of Kooser Park and on the other side of this major artery sits Forbes State Forest. Before 2012, this little park was very busy during the summers. Amenities include a nice campground with 47 sites, a healthy trout stream in the form of Kooser Run which flows through the length of the park, a wonderful beach on four-acre Kooser Lake, picnic area with restrooms and pavilions, short but scenic trails that can be used for hiking and cross-country skiing, and easy access from Pittsburgh through the Donegal Exit of the Pennsylvania Turnpike.

Prior to 2012, when we traveled on Route 31 in June through August, the huge Kooser parking lot that parallels the highway and Kooser Lake was jammed with vehicles. At the same time, we would hear the shouts of the beach goers and swimmers having a blast. It reminded me of my days as a college student at the University of South Florida in 1971 and my spring break adventure at Daytona Beach. The other enjoyable memories of years gone by at Kooser revolve around cross-country skiing. Several times we followed Hidden Valley cross-country trails to the ski trails at Kooser or vice versa and always found the snowy scenery along the Kooser Park trails to be outstanding.

The park still has everything that makes it wonderful except for swimming and great snowfalls during the winter months. Swimming was shut down in May of 2012 because of unsafe conditions caused by a buildup of sediments and algae blooms. It is so sad to drive the same route in the summer heat to see an empty parking lot and no joyful, happy noise emanating from the beach and lake. Looking back at our photos of our last visit, the beach was deserted and this was on July 19, 2018 which was pre-COVID. On that visit, we hiked the one-mile Kincora Trail and the 0.5-mile Tree Army Trail which were scenic and empty. We spotted a few fishermen along Kooser Run enjoying the solitude which is how my new memories of Kooser will always be headlined unless somehow the water quality situation can be rectified.

Sight—empty beach and parking lots.

50. LACKAWANNA

I would imagine this 1,445-acre park is well-loved by folks from the Wilkes-Barre/Scranton area. It is loaded with amenities including 198-acre Lackawanna Lake, picnic grounds, hiking, biking, horseback riding, and cross-country skiing trails, swimming pool, and campground. Lackawanna Lake is not open for swimming but is served by a boat rental concession, fishing pier, several boat launches, and a limited number of mooring sites. Picnickers are supported by picnic tables, pavilions, and restrooms. The campground has 112 campsites that provide easy access to the swimming pool and lake.

    Entering the park on Pennsylvania Route 438 and making a left turn onto Pennsylvania Route 407 to reach the park office provided beautiful views of Lackawanna Lake sparkling like a gemstone in the bright sunshine. When we stopped by the park office to collect our three passport stamps, the ranger on duty suggested we hike a series of interconnecting trails from the office to the dam and back to gain a flavor of the park. The views of the lake on the way out were wonderful as were trails on the way back that included us meandering through the forest.

Not for the first time, my mind spun various scenarios where Donna and I had more time to spend at some of the more expansive parks visited on our quest but if we gave into any of my musings, we would still be out on the road attempting to complete our park visits. When these thoughts cropped up, I had a desire to find some magical solution where I was suddenly 30 years younger and had all the time in the world to explore this vast bounty of natural beauty.

Sight—sparkling lake waters, sunshine pouring through the tree canopy and producing amazing shadowing effects.

51. LAUREL HILL

Oh yes, Laurel Hill State Park, where our quest began! This is a large park with 4,062 acres and shares a border with Forbes State Forest, providing more room to roam. Laurel Hill Lake (63 acres) comes equipped with a great swimming beach, changing rooms, food concession, boat rentals, boat launch sites, boat moorings, fishing pier, picnic tables, pavilions, restrooms, volleyball court, playground, and an extensive beach parking area. We have enjoyed many wonderful experiences here in the past 47+ years including beaching, boating, picnicking, hiking, and touring.

There are two experiences that are unique to this park. First, is exploring an amazingly intact CCC camp. This opportunity is provided by park staff once or twice a year and is a "walking back in time" experience that should not be missed. Throughout the tour of the camp, an understanding of the CCC boys' experiences when not working to create magic in the forests becomes tangible and heartfelt. Second, is climbing to the top of an observation tower that has a great view but was once unavailable to the public since it was on private property. Fortunately, it is now part of the park and a newly completed trail provides a path to hike to the tower instead of driving which can be quite challenging without written directions—we know this from personal experiences. In fact, even with the driving directions in hand, a wrong turn or two is not out of the ordinary but the view is well worth the effort of hiking or driving.

We have really enjoyed camping in this large campground with 264 campsites. Usually, I find such a large campground outside my comfort zone but this one is nicely divided into many separate sections. Our favorite camping experience was with Laura, Mason, and Sophia. It was our first camping experience with the grandkids so naturally, Donna and I spent a whole day touring campsites to find the perfect one as well as a few others to serve as backups. LOL, our first choice was booked but our second choice was available and we had a blast. Since it was much further from the restrooms, my portable toilet and shelter served for the late night needs of both myself and the grandkids.

A path from the cabin section of the campground forms a link to other trails that brought the five of us to Mill Run Dam built by the CCC which produces an amazing waterfall-like effect that is stunning (a sneak peek is available in the DCNR Laurel Hill Recreation Guide). Along with seeing the dam, the other can't-miss hike we took with the grandkids is the Hemlock Trail which loops through the Hemlock Trail Natural Area containing many old-growth hemlocks. We all had a good time, linking hands to see if we could encircle some of the really huge trees we encountered. Unfortunately, a dangerous windstorm hit several years ago and there are not as many of the old-growth trees still standing.

One point to bring up before ending this discussion on Laurel Hill State Park is the Laurel Hill Creek Water Trail. Laurel Hill Creek flows through a section of the park and provides the water for Laurel Hill Lake before it continues flowing past the dam. Anyway, a brochure on this water trail is available at the park and shows a six-mile water trail along Laurel Hill Creek, beginning at the boat launch site located in Picnic Area #1 within the park and ending just past Kings Covered Bridge. This looks like a fun kayaking adventure and we hope to undertake it in the future.

Hearing—roaring of the waterfall at Mill Run Dam; sight—water flowing over Mill Run Dam, scenic stream side views; smell—campfire, fresh coffee brewing outside the tent; touch—running my hand along the side of a CCC structure and feeling the history.

52. LAUREL MOUNTAIN

This 493-acre park is devoted to downhill skiing. This ski resort was built by General Richard Mellon in 1939 for his private use and donated to Pennsylvania in 1964. Since we have moved to this area in 1988, it has been an on again, off again, and on again resort that is now in the capable hands of Vail Resorts. Donna and I have hiked and cross-country skied to the park several times over the years but have never gone downhill skiing.

Hearing—quiet and peaceful when we have hiked and skied over to the park from Forbes State Forest.

53. LAUREL RIDGE

This 13,625-acre park is in fragments that extend from the Conemaugh Gorge near Johnstown to where it meets Forbes State Forest and State Games Lands #111 close to Pennsylvania Route 653 where a Cross-Country

Ski Area sits within the park (great place to ski). The main attraction is that it serves as a backbone of the Laurel Highlands Hiking Trail (LHHT). This amazing 70-mile hiking trail begins in Ohiopyle State Park, wends through Laurel Ridge State Park fragments as well as state game lands, other state parks, a state forest, and ends at the Laurel Ridge Park segment that borders Route 56 and the Stonycreek River. Laurel Ridge State Park serves its purpose well and the LHHT continues to thrive year after year aided by beautiful, forested ridges and valleys as well as eight camping areas. Each camping area includes five Adirondack shelters with fireplaces as well as tent sites. The common area includes men's and women's vault toilets, stainless-steel kitchen sink with pumping-action water supply, and stacks of firewood. We used one of the Adirondack shelters many years ago and found it to be very comfortable. Like in the other state parks, the shelters and tent sites must be reserved and a fee paid. Yes, the park rangers do come around in the evenings to check to see that everyone is safe and fees have been paid.

Considering it is so close to Pittsburgh, what continuously surprises me is that unlike some parks in the system, it is not being overwhelmed by park visitors. When I am out and about in the region—Pittsburgh, Ligonier and Johnstown—many people I have interacted with do not even know the LHHT exists. In my mind, it is like a proverbial phantom trail or Flying Dutchman trail that only a small number of people know about and enjoy. Before moving to the Laurel Highlands in 1988, Sue, John, Donna, and I hiked the entire LHHT in segments with a program organized by the Western Pennsylvania Conservancy (a great organization that invested the money in partnership with the State of Pennsylvania to purchase the land needed to make this trail a reality). Living in Pittsburgh pre-1988, it was a wonderful, eye-opening experience to be exposed to all the natural

Snowshoeing on LHHT near Milepost 56, Laurel Ridge State Park

wonders along such a lengthy trail. Donna purchased patches corresponding to each segment of the LHHT, mounted and framed them together, and hung it on our family room wall as a memento of our experiences with this trail. We still have the LHHT guide produced by the Pennsylvania Chapter of the Sierra Club that was given to us by Sue and John as a Christmas gift in 1984. It is a great reference and it comes off the shelf of our bookcase at least once a year—super gift and we are filled with gratitude each time we pick it up.

Since we moved to Laurel Hill Mountain in 1988, a major trailhead off of Pennsylvania Route 271 on Laurel Hill Mountain is only five minutes by car from our home. Also, we can walk out our front door, access a utility (water) line cut, and hike out to the LHHT. When this water line connecting water sources in Johnstown to Ligonier was installed in 2012, it went right through our front yard. Over the years, we have hiked, Nordic skied, and snowshoed sections of the LHHT on a consistent basis. For the past several years, with the increasingly mild winter weather, we have been hiking in all four seasons. We love the LHHT and continue to form great memories with our grandkids.

Since the LHHT could not exist without Laurel Ridge State Park, I am pleased to name **Laurel Ridge State Park** as my choice for the ***Best Pennsylvania State Park for Hiking***.

Hearing—large sections of the parkland are filled with serene sounds of nature; sight—beautiful, awe-inspiring views during all four seasons, numerous wildflowers in full bloom, mountain laurel and wild azalea blooming in large swaths, rock formations that take your breath away when cross-country skiing; taste—eating wild blueberries along the trail; touch—the feel of my cross-country skis as I travel across the ridge tops or rapidly go downhill into valleys, the feel of skiing around trees and rock formations, moving forward in deep snow with my snowshoes.

54. LAUREL SUMMIT

This is a six-acre picnic park that sits at 2,739 feet so it is a cooler spot for a picnic when heat waves come along in the summer months. Amenities include a picnic pavilion, picnic tables scattered about the area, and restrooms. More importantly, this little park is the trailhead for Spruce Flats Bog and Wolf Rocks trails. It is no exaggeration to say we hike both trails on an annual basis. I will write about these trails when discussing Forbes State Forest. Donna and I have also used this parking area as an unofficial trailhead for a portion of the LHHT and Fish Run Trail. The LHHT is very close to where Linn Run Road and Laurel Summit Road come together by the entrance to the park.

Hearing— very busy parking area on a seasonal basis; sight—quaint picnic pavilion; smell—well-used restrooms.

55. LEHIGH GORGE

This 6,107-acre park follows the Lehigh River and steep walls of the gorge from Francis E. Walter Dam to Jim Thorpe. The 26-mile Lehigh Gorge Trail is of rails-to-trails style construction and parallels the historical remains of the Lehigh Canal, the Lehigh River, and an operating train line. This trail is multi-purpose in nature, open to hikers, bikers, and cross-country skiers. It is very picturesque with heavily wooded slopes, thick understory, rock outcroppings, boulders, and the well-known Buttermilk

Falls. There are three access points, beginning with the White Haven Access Area, followed by the Rockport Access Area, and ending with the Glen Onoko Access Area. I begin with White Haven because the trail is slightly downhill all the way to Jim Thorpe so biking one way from the White Haven Access Area is the best choice for recreational bikers. There are boat launch sites at each access point as well as restrooms. Along with biking, kayaking is very popular with snowmobiling a popular option in the park when snow permits.

During our quest, we first visited Lehigh Gorge during the spring of 2021. We used the White Haven Access Area and biked on the Lehigh Gorge Trail for a total round trip of 10 miles. The highlights of our little excursion included checking out the ruins of Locks 24 and 28 as well as the Tannery Historic Site. We enjoyed our biking experience so much that we decided to plan another trip to bike the entire trail.

During the summer of 2021, we stayed in Jim Thorpe which is a beautiful and lively little town with great restaurants. We were lucky to find a rental that provided off-road parking, decent accommodations, and budget prices in this wonderful tourist town during the busiest tourist season. All the locals we encountered were very friendly and we rode the Lehigh Gorge Scenic Railway from downtown Jim Thorpe to White Haven.

There was a neat historical narration during the train ride, our conductor was lots of fun, and the ride was a perfect way to begin our morning. When our bikes were unloaded we picked up our pre-ordered lunches at a local deli before starting towards Jim Thorpe. There were five of us on this adventure, Donna and myself as well as her brothers Don and Duane, and Don's wife, Dee. We stopped at some beautiful spots along the way including Buttermilk Falls, an abandoned railroad tunnel, canal lock ruins, and rock outcrops. Even with a stop for our delicious lunches, the 26 miles seemed to quickly vanish under our bike wheels.

Hearing—train wheels moving and whistles blowing, Buttermilk Falls, shouts of kayakers, peaceful biking moments; sight— beauty of the gorge walls, Buttermilk Falls, light at end of the abandoned railroad tunnel, bike train chugging along through the gorge just like a miniature railroad scene, a black rat snake sunning on the side of the trail; taste—yummy deli lunches; touch—warming ourselves on a massive boulder projecting off the side of the trail and directly over the Lehigh River.

56. LEONARD HARRISON

This 585-acre park is located on the east rim of the Grand Canyon of Pennsylvania. It has a campground with 26 campsites, numerous picnic tables with some being covered as well as a picnic pavilion, restrooms, and a visitor center that is worth checking out. Our visit occurred on the same day we tackled Colton Point State Park. The difference was amazing for two reasons. One, the weather improved with the rain slowing down and the fog and mist in the canyon beginning to clear. Two, there were visitors on this side of the canyon so the solitude and the "just the two of us" vibe vanished. There is another statue dedicated to the efforts of the CCC boys located in this park and makes one think about how much we all owe their efforts. As we made our way along the Overlook Trail, the rain returned with a sudden ferocity that sent all the other visitors running for shelter. We remained in our waterproofs and relished the view of the ever-changing landscape of the canyon from our perch at Otter View.

Before continuing, our use of two trails here on other occasions needs to be addressed, one hiking and one biking. The Turkey Path Trail is found in both this park and Colton Point. In each case, this path descends to the bottom of Pine Creek Gorge, a one-mile descent in Leonard Harrison (very picturesque with wooden steps and waterfalls on sections) and 1.5 miles in Colton Point (wonderful 70-foot, cascading waterfall about one-third of the way down). We parked and started on Colton Point's Turkey Path and since there is no foot bridge across Pine Creek, at the end of our descent, we removed our boots and socks, rolled up our pant legs, and waded across Pine Creek, crossing the Pine Creek Trail, and ascending the Turkey Path Trail to the rim in Leonard Harrison where we had our bag lunches at a picnic table. After our lunch, we resumed our hike, eventually completing our rim-to-rim-to-rim hike at Colton Point. We undertook this enjoyable hike with a group of our extended family members. During the following year, once again on vacation, Donna handed out T-shirts with the "Rim to Rim to Rim in the Pennsylvania Grand Canyon" slogan on each. These were a big hit and worn proudly by everyone that followed us on the Turkey Trail a year earlier.

Caution: Placards ask hikers to be aware of rattlesnakes on this trail. If spotted, admire but give them a wide berth. On the topic of rattlesnakes, we have run into these beautiful creatures many times over the years on both state park and state forest land but never have had any issues. In my mind awareness (no matter the trail) as well as staying calm when one is encountered are critical attributes.

Caution: The Turkey Path Trail can be very challenging and not the place for inexperienced hikers to begin their hiking adventures.

The biking trail is the Pine Creek Trail, a rails-to-trails that runs for 62 miles along Pine Creek and is on the same side of the canyon as Leonard Harrison State Park which it traverses for one mile. It runs from Wellsboro Junction to Jersey Shore. By the way, Wellsboro is a great town to explore with many reminders of a long past era—several great places to stay there if camping is not an option. Another fantastic option is Rough Cut Lodge on Pennsylvania Route 6 near Colton Point State Park. We stayed there twice when visiting the Grand Canyon of Pennsylvania. The Log Cabin Inn Restaurant on Route 6 between the Lodge and Colton Point is a perfect stop for a can't-miss meal—walleye, in season, is my favorite.

One summer weekend, we biked all 62 miles with our friends, Sue and John. We completed our ride by transporting our bikes to a trailhead and biking a section of the trail to where our other vehicle was parked, loaded our bikes, and drove back to the beginning to collect the other vehicle and repeated this process until we were finished. This is a wonderful rails-to-trails bike trail that is very isolated for the most part, producing a tranquil environment that enhances the beauty that is found throughout the ride. Highlights included spotting a bald eagle overhead and a timber rattlesnake sunning itself on the side of the trail.

Caution: This trail is very remote much of the way, without many access points and little or no cell service. Therefore, prepare with the thought that this is a "help yourself trail" with food, plenty of water, bike tubes and or patch kit, air pump, bike tools, a first aid kit, and waterproofs.

Hearing—chatter and tangible excitement of tourists on the Overlook Trail, quiet times on the Turkey and Pine Creek Trails dominated by the sounds of nature, listening to the rain pelt our waterproofs and the foliage; sight—the canyon from Otter View, mile after mile of viewing Pine Creek in all of its manifestations as well as the magnificent canyon walls from our bikes, the imposing CCC statue.

57. LINN RUN

This 612-acre park is a mountainous beauty with gorgeous Linn Run flowing through it. There are two picture-perfect picnic areas with restrooms, namely, Adams Falls and Grove Run. Adams Falls Picnic Area is accessed by a picturesque wooden bridge and has a picnic pavilion and at Grove Run there is always a line of folks to access the ice-cold spring water flowing out of a pipe 24/7. There is no campground but there is a cabin colony of nine rustic cabins and one modern cabin which are open year-round. Fishing is highly prized on Linn Run and this stream is just a pretty spot to go fishing to lose oneself in nature. There are only 3.15 miles of hiking trails but a section of the park borders Forbes State Forest so plenty of room for your hiking legs to roam.

Donna and I call Linn Run our "go-to park" since moving to the Laurel Highlands in 1988 because it contains the trailhead for our favorite trail, namely, Grove Run Trail. We hike this trail in all four seasons and love the spring since we find wildflowers right by the trail and we love to just meander, spotting wildflowers, obtaining numerous photos, and returning several weeks during the season to make sure we spot them all—red and white trilliums, several shades of hepatica, bloodroot, and so many others. Grove Run is a loop trail that remains in the park for a very short time before it jumps into Forbes State Forest. It is very scenic with steep climbs and descents, waterfalls, stream crossings, and handling the four-mile loop at a good pace provides an outstanding workout filled with plenty of zen time. We also use Grove Run Trail to access other amazing trails in Forbes State Forest so it represents a cornucopia of pleasurable hiking. I will discuss these trails further when discussing Forbes State Forest.

Along with Grove Run, I recommend hiking the Adams Falls Trail as well as the Flat Rock Trail. Grab a look at Adams Falls in the spring or after a summer rainstorm to enjoy a more robust waterfall. This trail is only a one-mile loop but it is very rocky with some amazing boulders. Flat Rock Trail leads to a flat rock, naturally, and provides a close-up of Linn Run which is a gorgeous stream that reminds me of some of the streams we hiked along in Smoky Mountains National Park. Pick a spot along the run and you have found a wonderful place for a backpack picnic or to settle in with a good book. Just be aware this area can often become overcrowded during hot summer days.

Hearing—roaring Linn Run in the spring, kids yelling and screaming with joy splashing in Linn Run, quiet moments along Grove Run Trail; sight—the flowing magic of Linn Run in full roar bounding from rock to rock over fallen logs with mini-waterfalls, rays of the sun making Grove Run glisten like a million diamonds flowing speedily along miniature canyon walls, springs flowing over rock ledges along the Grove Run Trail, numerous wildflowers in full bloom along Grove Run Trail.

58. LITTLE BUFFALO

This 923-acre park is a fantastic family vacation destination. Where do I begin? There are 10 miles of hiking trails, picnic grounds, playgrounds, and a large swimming pool equipped with water slides, spray towers, food concession, restrooms, and changing rooms. The 83-acre Holman Lake is open for fishing but no swimming; however, there are boat launches, boat rentals, boat moorings, restrooms, fishing pier, and some picnic tables. The campground is really sweet with 46 sites and a recreation hall close to the entrance that is available as a rental to serve family reunions, weddings, parties, and meetings.

On top of all these amenities, just like a cherry on top of an ice cream sundae, there is the Little Buffalo Historic District which is on the National Register of Historic Places. This is a jammed-packed district with Shoaff's Mill—an operating gristmill from approximately 1835, Blue Ball Tavern Museum—earliest record of operation is 1773, Sulphur Springs Cemetery—burials from 1845 to 1944, Clays Covered Bridge—built in 1890, and Newport & Sherman's Valley Railroad's Way Car 12—the last car from the railroad that ran at this location from 1890 to 1937. Added to these family-pleasing ingredients are two super-charged brochures designed to introduce the wonders of Little Buffalo to youngsters. One is entitled, "Little Buffalo Quest" and the other is "Little Buffalo State Park Discover E! Activity Book." The activity book is 32 pages in length and is both entertaining and educational.

We have camped in this park twice. We love everything about it and during our quest we celebrated our 42nd wedding anniversary here. The campground is super compact with a new shower/restroom facility that is outstanding. During our first stay, our campsite was #40 in a loop of 40 sites. It is flat as a pancake and tucked away into a little hillock that made it a private little spot for us and our pop-up tent. As a happy bonus, it was listed as a non-electric site but to our surprise, it had an electric hook-up. Mike and Karen were fantastic camp hosts and they have been returning annually so keep an eye out for them. We used the trail system to explore

Shoaff's Mill, Little Buffalo State Park

the entire historic district but both the gristmill and tavern were closed during our stay, as was the swimming pool, because of COVID.

Our second camping trip brought us to campsite #1 which is next to the camp host trailer. It is a huge, flat site that we enjoyed immensely. We revisited some areas of the park and again we found the gristmill, tavern, and pool closed. COVID was gone but the gristmill and tavern are only open on weekends and the pool was closed since it was too late in the season. However, we still had two great adventures here in 2024. First, we kayaked two days in a row on Holman Lake. It is a peaceful lake during the week and we took photos of lots and lots of turtles which we later shared with Mason and Sophia. Our other adventure was hiking through the 10-acre Box Huckleberry Natural Area which is about 12 minutes from the park. The most difficult aspect was finding a place wide enough on the side of Huckleberry Road to safely park my truck since there is no parking lot serving this natural area. There were no self-guided brochures at the site but we did enjoy seeing the rare box huckleberry.

Donna and I just loved this park after our first visit and after our second visit, I find it easy to say that **Little Buffalo State Park** is my selection for the ***Best Pennsylvania State Park for a Family Vacation.***

Hearing—splash of our paddles on the lake; sight—lake shoreline from our kayak, Blue Ball Tavern, Shoaff's Mill, Clays Covered Bridge, Way Car 12, Mill Race; smell—campfire; touch—sensation of drifting in our kayak during a stiff breeze.

59. LITTLE PINE

The majority of this 2,158-acre park is surrounded by Tiadaghton State Forest and is nestled in a valley surrounded by mountains. Little Pine Creek runs through the length of the park and a dam constructed in 1950 forms Little Pine Lake. This is another park with great amenities including four picnic groves within the park as well as a Lower Picnic Area that is separated from the main section of the park, Little Pine Lake provides fishing, boat rentals, boat launch, moorings, and swimming beach, and there are 14 miles of hiking trails within the park as well as others that go into forest land.

There are several other recreational opportunities, some fairly unique to note including a shooting range, archery range, fishing along Little Pine Creek, bald eagle nesting area, the 250-mile Mid State Trail goes through the park, and the 5.5-mile Lake Shore Trail provides an excellent cross-country skiing venue when the weather cooperates. A bonus is that Happy Acres Resort is directly across from the park and their restaurant, bar, general store, and ice cream parlor are all open to the public. Also, the resort provides many forms of accommodations which are great options when planning a Little Pine State Park family vacation. Biking is another wonderful opportunity to keep in mind because an access point for the 62-mile Pine Creek Trail is only four miles away.

Little Pine was a hub on one of our quest road trips so we camped there for four days. The campground has 88 campsites with some along Little Pine Creek and it is filled with many beautiful trees. We enjoyed our time here and the large flat patch of site #074 provided room for our two tents since Duane was with us on this trip. Although we were very busy visiting other parks at the end of our spokes, one day we carved out some time to explore a bit of our hub park. We decided to go on a hike while Duane checked out the Eagle Watch Area where he spotted a bald eagle. Donna and I hiked Spike Buck Hollow Trail to where it intersected with the Mid State Trail.

Oh my gosh, the park Recreation Guide warns visitors about the steepness of Buck Hollow and the need to be in good physical condition—not an understatement, we found it to be truly challenging! The day was hot and humid and it really was an energy-sapping, steep ascent. We were overjoyed to see the Mid State Trail sign so we could briefly rest, refresh with water and snacks, and begin our descent. We took a selfie at the intersection of the trails and it captured our exhaustion rather well (it is in Donna's corresponding photo book). Keeping the amenities of this park in mind along with all that Happy Acres Resort has to offer, the combination is beckoning to us to plan a trip with Laura, Mason, and Sophia if we can ever tear ourselves away from our annual national park trips.

Hearing—murmur of the water flowing from the dam provides gentle background music for us campground denizens; sight—beautiful campground area comes into view crossing the bridge across Little Pine Creek, dam looms behind the back of the campground; touch—high humidity producing lots of sweat climbing up Spike Buck Hollow Trail.

60. LOCUST LAKE

This 1,772-acre park is a great camping park and is close to an Interstate 81 exit. The campground map provides a better overall view of the park grounds compared to the park Recreation Guide that covers both this park and Tuscarora State Park. However, both information sources together provide all the information necessary for a successful park visit. The campground is colossal with 282 campsites and is divided into four distinct sections. Two sections have campsites located close to the 52-acre Locust Lake. The one accessed directly from the camp entrance is closest to the camp store (source of ice cream), boat rentals, boat moorings, and one of two boat launches, while the other is reached by driving across the breast of the dam. The swimming beach is located on a portion of the lake where Locust Creek flows into it. Everything around the lake is pulled together by a 1.3-mile paved bike trail that encircles the lake by utilizing the roadway that crosses the dam.

Locust Lake was a hub on one of our quest road trips and we stayed there for five days. Without a doubt, this is a perfect family park as illustrated by families biking and walking across the breast of the dam, families fishing together, some kids and parents playing tag football in a field near the camp store, and still others walking along the park road eating ice cream cones on their way to campsites at higher elevations.

To reach our campsite, we drove across the breast of the dam which is fun in itself and proceeded up the hill, passing other campsite loop entrances until it came to a 'T' and we made a left turn into the final loop. Our site, #189, sat right behind the shower house/restroom which was very convenient. One day, Donna and I rode our bikes all the way downhill, reached the bike trail, hung a left, and continued to the trailhead for the Oak Loop, Oak/Hemlock, and Oak/Ridge trails.

We parked and locked our bikes around a tree just off the bike trail and hiked all three of the Oak trails—very scenic and contained some fun geocaches. From there, we continued to circle Locust Lake, stopping at the camp store for ice cream, crossing the dam, and huffing and puffing our way back up the hill to our campsite. Just too much fun and dreams of another trip with the grandkids—not sure we will ever find the time for all these return trips but we can still dream.

Hearing—lots of laughter and other sounds of joy echoing across the lake from the swimming beach, insect noises in the campground at night provide an enjoyable bedtime chorus; sight—view of the lake from the breast of the dam, some beautiful scenery along the Oak trails; smells—the smell of bacon as I prepare breakfast sends my taste buds on a wonderful journey of anticipation; taste—camping breakfasts and dinners are always yummy.

61. LYMAN RUN

If 45-acre Lyman Run Lake did not exist, I would call this 595-acre park simply a trailhead park with a picnic grove, but the lake adds another dimension. There is fishing in the lake and in Lyman Run which runs the length of the park. The amenities at the lake include a boat launch, boat rentals, and swimming beach with snack concession, changing area, restrooms, and showers. There are two campgrounds in separate areas of the park with a total of 35 campsites. Two trailheads are found here for two diverse trails. The 3.8-mile Lyman Run Trail runs the length of the park and connects to the 85-mile Susquehannock Trail System which is a loop trail. The other trailhead is for the 43-mile Susquehannock ATV Trail and it is located in a parking lot on Lyman Run Road just east of the park office.

The drive to reach this park and the park itself reveals a beautifully forested area which is no surprise since about 98% of the park boundaries border the Susquehannock State Forest. We parked by the park office and followed the Lyman Run Trail across the spillway and breast of the dam for a short distance along the lake. At this point the winds started to howl, the sky darkened, we turned around, retraced our steps, and reached our truck just as the rain pelted us with vigor.

Hearing—wind howling through the trees; sight—rain sweeping in, lake waters becoming agitated by the approaching storm.

62. MARSH CREEK

The 1,784-acre park and 535-acre Marsh Creek Lake are an amazing combination. This park makes you feel good just because it exists. One minute we were driving in a neighborhood of large, high-end homes and the next minute we found ourselves in a beautiful state park and instantly felt at peace. Such a wonderful gift to all of us that this land is protected and cannot fall victim to land developers looking to make tons of money. It is difficult to put into words our amazement to see this sparkling lake unfolding before us with numerous sailboats skimming along the lake waters—like a fairytale come alive.

There is no swimming in Marsh Creek Lake but a swimming pool is available to cool off during those hot summer months. There are two launch sites and mooring areas, East and West. The East Launch area is impressive with a food concession, restrooms, a large boat rental concession that rents five types of watercraft including sailboats as well as offering lake tours, trailheads for the Park Road Trail and Red Trail, and huge parking lot. The West Launch offers parking areas that accept horse trailers, restrooms, and an equestrian concession to service a large selection of horseback riding trails within the park. The 6.07-mile Yellow Trail consisting of interlocking loops is recommended for mountain biking and is served by a parking area near the dam.

We parked our truck at the East Launch parking area and hiked the 1.5-mile Red Trail that follows the lake shore for an extended period of time before entering the woods and looping back to the East Launch parking area. It was near sunset and the lake views were spectacular with those beautiful sailboats everywhere. It was a wonderful end to our day as we sat at a picnic table enjoying coffee before we continued our drive.

Sight—spectacular lake views with numerous sailboats, beautiful lake and shoreline views along the Red Trail; taste—cup of coffee from our trusty thermos really hit the spot.

63. MAURICE K. GODDARD

This 2,856-acre park has no swimming or camping but it does have the 1,680-acre Lake Wilhelm which is a wonderful recreational asset for so many other reasons. The 240-acre portion of the lake that is on the western side of Interstate 79 falls within State Game Lands #270 and includes three boat launch sites. There are four boat launches in the park including a marina which includes a large parking area, 241 slips, boat rental concession, fishing pier, and a fueling station. All four launching sites include restrooms, picnic tables, and picnic pavilion. For bikers, there is the 12-mile John C. Oliver Multi-Purpose Loop Trail that forms a paved loop around a large portion of the lake. The Goddard-McKeever Hiking Trail is 2.84 miles long and connects the park to McKeever Environmental Learning Center.

During our visit while on our quest, Donna and I biked the entire loop by starting and ending near the park office. The trail has some beautiful lake views as well as scenic looks at field and forest habitats. Along the way, we stopped at a picnic table by the dam and enjoyed our bag lunches. Please keep in mind that there are some steeper sections of the trail so be careful while enjoying the landscape. Funny, all those years ago we visited McKeever Environmental Learning Center while completing our practicum at La Roche University but did not visit the park next door. Years later we biked the loop trail with our kids but did not visit the park again until we were on our quest. Now it is on our radar not only for the great biking trail but because we want to kayak in Lake Wilhelm.

Hearing—serene sections along the loop trail; sight— sunny day livening the lake waters.

64. MCCALLS DAM

McCalls Dam is no longer there but this eight-acre picnic park is very peaceful as it is within Bald Eagle State Forest. White Deer Creek flows along the edge of the park which adds to the beautiful landscape you can enjoy from the scattered picnic tables. I remember this park for the coffee. Donna and I are in the habit of having afternoon coffee between 3 and 4 PM but sometimes we ignore our habits which happened during this visit.

When we first started out on our quest, we always joked about a coffee shop being around the next bend of the trail or the next bend in the road. Of course, in reality only on very few occasions did we find a coffee shop in a small town at the right time of day and unlike hiking in Europe, we never ran into a coffee shop on the trail. I know this sounds simple but it took us a few day trips to come up with the idea of bringing the coffee with us. After that eureka moment, when the timing was right, we carried coffee in our backpacks and found a convenient log on the next bend in the trail to enjoy our coffee between 3 and 4 PM. Usually, our coffee break time found us at the truck where we enjoyed our coffee tailgating or sitting at a picnic table at a park we were visiting. The joys of coffee! At McCalls Dam, we were running late for our lunch stop so at 2:00 PM we granted ourselves a dispensation and enjoyed the magical smells and tastes of our coffees with our lunch while soaking in the scenery and the wonderful sounds of White Deer Creek. The joys of nature with a hot cup of coffee in hand!

Hearing—relaxing sounds of Deer Creek flowing by; sight—following the short park trail into the forest and crossing and recrossing a picturesque wooden bridge; smell—scent of pine in the air, opening our thermos and releasing the magic coffee aroma.

65. MCCONNELLS MILL

As mentioned at the beginning of this book, McConnells Mill is part of my childhood family experiences as well as the first state park Donna and I visited while dating. We also enjoyed picnics there with our friends and later, with Joseph and Laura when they were kids. Writing this sentence, I realize that we need to introduce Mason and Sophia to this amazing landscape. As a kid, what amazed me the most was the rock formations and the rushing water—it was a natural environment that I never experienced before. Plus, the drive down to the mill was just magic to me since the road partially led our car under a rock overhang which made me think of a photograph I saw of a national park out west.

The park's 2,546 acres are located in Slippery Rock Creek Gorge which is a National Natural Landmark. Along with the McConnells Mill Covered Bridge (National Historic Landmark) and gristmill, there is the Kildoo Picnic Area which actually has a relatively flat area containing a pavilion, numerous picnic tables, restrooms, playground, and play field.

The Stairs Trail descends into the gorge from Kildoo Picnic Area, popping out by the bridge and mill. A very rugged hiking trail, whitewater boating (two boat launches), climbing and rappelling, and fishing are all great choices for recreation but swimming is not permitted and there are no camping facilities.

Over the years, we have hiked the Slippery Rock Gorge Trail and the Kildoo Trail with Sue and John. The Kildoo Trail uses the covered bridge and Eckert Bridge to cross Slippery Rock Creek twice to form a three-mile loop. This is the go-to trail for many park visitors and can be quite busy. To leave the crowds behind, at Eckert Bridge jump on the 6.2-mile (one-way) Slippery Rock Gorge Trail which rewards the hiker with unbelievable scenery and a real escape into the gorge. With Sue and John, we crossed the covered bridge and turned left on the Kildoo Trail, picked up the Slippery Rock Gorge Trail, and turned around at the Hells Hollow Parking Lot. This round-trip hike is a very strenuous, 15.4 miles with steep ascents and descents along the way. At our ages now, we will only hike this 7.7-mile route in one direction and set up a vehicle shuttle system to return.

Caution: Please only attempt the Slippery Rock Gorge Trail with the proper gear, lots of water, food, and with the secure knowledge that it is within your physical abilities. Even the Kildoo Trail requires the proper gear, water, snacks, and a decent amount of stamina to complete.

During our quest visit, we parked by the mill, walked across the covered bridge and jumped on the Kildoo Trail and completed the loop back to the mill. We spotted several spring wildflowers along the way and this hike brought back the memory of us finding a cucumber root in bloom for the first time during one of our early visits together.

Hearing—roaring water in Slippery Rock Creek, machinery of the gristmill, shouts of joy of kayakers on the creek; touch—ice-cold creek water, heat radiating from a substantial boulder projecting into the creek which we used as an impromptu picnic table along the Kildoo Trail.

66. MEMORIAL LAKE

The main feature of this 231-acre park is 85-acre Memorial Lake. Amenities include picnic pavilions, picnic tables, boat rentals, two launch sites, a fishing pier, and restrooms. Swimming is prohibited and there are no camping facilities. Fort Indiantown Gap National Guard Training Center surrounds the park and the lake was established in 1945 as a memorial to Pennsylvania National Guard soldiers who served in World War I and World War II.

There are two miles of trails here and we walked along the Overlook and Lakeside trails before retracing our steps and returning to our truck. The Overlook Trail traverses the breast of the dam and spillway. This vantage point is a great place for photos of the lake. During our walk, we heard several explosions in the distance coming from the training center. There were a few joggers using the trail and one family picnicking but no activity on the lake itself. Walking the trail brought back memories of reading in the local newspaper about Fort Indiantown Gap functioning as a refugee camp after the fall of Saigon for many Vietnamese and Cambodian refugees.

Hearing—explosions emanating from the training center.

67. MILTON

This is an 82-acre island park in the West Branch of the Susquehanna River. It is reached by using Pennsylvania Route 642, which crosses over the island and uses exit and entrance ramps for island traffic. The northern half contains picnic tables, drinking water, restrooms and soccer fields. On the other hand, the southern half remains in an undeveloped, natural state. We hiked on the exterior section of the South Trail which offers looks at the river environment and shoreline. We combined our hike on the South Trail with the Mid Trail to form a loop so we could begin and end with the parking area where our truck was located. The Mid Trail skirts the playfield, restrooms, picnic tables, and soccer fields to its north and parking lots to its south. Just prior to picking up the Mid Trail, we walked down to the boat launch area that sits on the east side of the island and checked it out.

Sight—beautiful natural areas on the southern portion of the island.

68. MONT ALTO

This small, 23-acre park became the oldest state park in Pennsylvania when Valley Forge State Park was presented to the United States in 1976. A passenger/freight train brought tourists to a park that was established at this location in 1875 as a commercial endeavor. When it became a state park in 1902, some amenities were added including a carousel and swimming pool. The natural environment remains intact as the park shares a border with Michaux State Forest on three sides while the remaining border is shared with the Mont Alto campus of Penn State University.

Today, the only part of the carousel remaining is the roof, which now covers a picnic pavilion, and the swimming pool is long gone. Just behind the picnic pavilion, a picturesque wooden bridge crosses Antietam Creek. The creek flows the length of the park and is open for fishing. Pennsylvania Route 233 also travels through the length of the park and there was sporadic traffic on the roadway during our visit. Across Route 233, there is a large parking lot with a trailhead for Oak Knob Trail which crosses from the park into Michaux State Forest. This trail is listed as both a hiking trail and a snowmobile trail so that explains the large parking lot which is needed to handle pickup trucks hauling snowmobile trailers.

Sitting under the roof of the old carousel, enjoying lunch, soaking in the peaceful surroundings, my mind drifted to the town of West View and old West View Park. My first memories of West View go back to when my dad would take me with him to do his business banking and package shipping. The bank sat in a small shopping center which was across the street from an Islay's and the Gerard Theater. The post office was around the corner from the shopping center, just across the street from the street car tracks and West View Park.

First stop was always the bank where the tellers were always friendly to me and many times I walked out with a treat. Next came the post office which was home to Red, the postman.

He was always friendly and Dad and Red always spent some time talking during and after Dad mailed out his packages. When Dad finished at the bank and post office, we often stopped at Islay's and Dad would treat me to a Klondike bar. The first time he gave me one, he demonstrated how to bless it before eating it by carving a small cross into the layer of chocolate. From that day forward, I followed my dad's example and I taught Joseph and Laura the same blessing when they were little kids.

Funny, the Islay's store in West View is still operating even though the chain closed in the 1970s. I imagine one can still order the chipped ham, huge dill pickles, and skyscraper cones there as well as Klondikes. I love the taste of anything sour so when my dad would order chipped ham and Swiss cheese I would beg for those pickles.

Many memories come to mind when thinking of the Gerard Theater. Us neighborhood kids would go to the Gerard once in a while as a group. We would usually walk from our neighborhood to Perrysville and walk along Perry Highway to reach West View. Sometimes, we would go through our woods up to Laurel Gardens and walk down the hill to Rochester Road. There was a fruit market on the corner of Rochester and Glenmore where we crossed Rochester Road and walked up Glenmore Avenue to make our way to the Gerard. One fun thing about the Gerard was that it had a crying room. I remember going to the movies with Mom and Cindy and ending up in the crying room because Cindy would not stop crying. The movie we went to see that day was *The Great Imposter*. I also remember going to see The *Blob* and *Gorgo* with the kids. As an adult, Donna and I went to West View to shop for an aquarium for our first home at Tiny's which was located in part of the building that was once the theater.

At the corner of Perry Highway and Center Avenue there was a large drugstore where we sometimes ate after coming back from Pittsburgh on the streetcar. Mom would call Paul to pick us up when we finished. The drugstore had great counter service with all the good food kids love. Other times we just entered the store so Mom could use a pay phone to call Paul and if we were lucky, Mom would treat us to a Coca-Cola or even a milkshake while she had a cup of coffee.

The biggest draw in West View for us kids was West View Park. It was one of the original Pittsburgh trolley amusement parks and was around from 1906 to 1977. Some kids grew up with Kennywood Park memories, another trolley park, but for others like me, it was all about West View Park. Our grade school picnics were at West View Park and we had family outings there as well. I always remember walking through the tunnel that connected the parking lot to the park. We would scream with all the other kids with echoes bouncing in all directions. Unlike most parks today, you did not pay to enter West View Park, instead tickets were purchased for the rides with signs listing how many tickets were needed for each specific ride. Tickets were discounted for our school picnic when purchased at school. If you ran out, regularly priced tickets were available at the park—a marketing incentive to buy more ticket packets at school. I also remember going with neighborhood kids to the park just to buy the best pizza ever! It was so good and one slice of heaven only cost 10 cents. Today, based on inflation, the cost for a slice would be about one dollar so still a good deal.

My favorite ride was the carousel! Yes, the carousel, which is why I started walking down this memory lane in the first place, because of the carousel pavilion at Mont Alto and the fact that Mont Alto Park was served by a railway similar to West View Park being served by a trolley. I loved kiddieland and my favorite ride there was the helicopters. My favorites at the main park were the turtles, bumper cars, house of mirrors, and the haunted house. I did not go often in high school and never made it there with Donna. Danceland was a special place for my older siblings—many famous singers and bands performed there over the years. I really miss the park but what I miss the most is the pizza! Oh well, enough of my musings and back to our quest.

Hearing—flow of Antietam Creek; sight— picturesque wooden bridge over Antietam Creek, roof and footprint of carousel.

69. MORAINE

This is an enormous, 16,725-acre park with its land encircling the huge, 3,225-acre Lake Arthur. I will not even attempt to describe all that can be found in this park but will suggest the DCNR Recreation Guide deserves a lengthy review. Suffice it to say, boaters will find all their needs met including rental opportunities and fuel, fishing is big with bait available for purchase, swimmers and sunbathers have two beaches, picnickers find numerous picnic tables, pavilions, and restrooms, bikers have a seven-mile paved trail as well as six miles of mountain biking trails, hikers find trails for day hikes and backpacking, and horseback riders find 20 miles of trails. Also, other seasonal recreational opportunities are found here including windsurfing, cross-country skiing, and snowmobiling. The one thing that continuously amazes me is that there are no campgrounds within the park; however, there are private ones that serve park visitors. Considering all the park amenities and the easy access to Pittsburgh by means of Interstate 79, I believe that a huge state park campground would be a great addition to the park amenities and tap into a big market.

Paul loved to fish here before he moved to Florida. His three favorite spots were Glade Run, Moraine, and Pymatuning. I went with him a few times on his fishing trips to Moraine and Glade Run but never made it to Pymatuning. Donna and I explored Moraine many times as a couple and later with Joseph and Laura. We continue to enjoy using the paved bike trail which is 14 miles out and back. Please be aware that there are some steeper sections and sharp curves along the way because this is not simply a flat, lakeside path. We have never hiked the 14.6-mile Glacier Trail from Moraine State Park to Jennings Environmental Education Center which would require a car shuttle. Both hiking this trail and kayaking are on my wish list. We biked 14 miles in the sunshine during our visit to obtain our passport stamp. As always, we find biking here not as easy as those days long ago when our kids were young; however, the ride continues to be enjoyable despite those steeper sections.

During my high school years, I remember news articles in the Pittsburgh papers regarding the reclamation efforts and dam work pertaining to the creation of a new park near Pittsburgh. Our family members, like so many folks around Pittsburgh, were filled with anticipation. I still remember returning to Pittsburgh from attending the University of South Florida to work in our family business in 1972 and going to Moraine State Park for the first time. The drive across Lake Arthur on Pennsylvania Route 422 and seeing the expanse of the lake made me feel like I was back in Florida. Those were the days!

Sight—wonderful and numerous lake views, spectacular view of Lake Arthur on a sunny day crossing the bridge on Pennsylvania Route 422.

70. MT. PISGAH

This 1,302-acre park sits at the base of Mt. Pisgah. Water from Mill Creek fills 75-acre Stephen Foster Lake which is surrounded by the park. The park boundaries are adjacent to both State Game Lands 289 and Mt. Pisgah County Park. Although there is no swimming in the lake, there is fishing, boat rentals, launch site, and moorings. There is a beautiful swimming pool on a hill with beautiful views of the surroundings along with picnic areas including pavilions and restrooms. There are 11 miles of hiking trails with a flyer available at the park office that lists all twelve trails. The longest is the Oh! Susanna Trail which is 2.55 miles in length and forms a loop around the lake.

We decided to hike the Oh! Susanna Trail since the sun was shining and the lake was sparkling. There were several placards along the trail which included information on Stephen Foster. This famous composer was once a nearby resident, hence, the name of the lake, and the trail itself bears the name of one of his famous compositions. After hiking we had our lunch at a picnic table by the pool so we could enjoy the wonderful views.

When we visited the park office, the ranger on duty encouraged us to visit the adjacent Mt. Pisgah County Park. Leaving the park on Pisgah Road, we headed in the direction of East Troy. As instructed, we made the first right turn off of Pisgah Road and onto Wilcox Road which steeply ascended and came to an end within the park. After parking our truck, we found a beautiful vista along with a statue of Chief Wetona. The information provided on Chief Wetona was both inspiring and tragic in nature. He is definitely a historical figure that I would like to learn more about. Donna and I loved his statue, the viewing rock where he meditated, and the gorgeous views. Wow! We were very happy that we followed the ranger's advice and did not miss this opportunity. If I was in charge of planning lunch during another visit, I would select a picnic table here, and save the picnic table at the state park for afternoon coffee.

Sight—historical placards, sunshine twinkling on every movement of the lake waters; taste—views from our picnic table enhanced the taste of our bag lunches like a secret spice.

71. NESCOPECK

This 3,550-acre park is surrounded by State Game Lands 187 and includes nine-acre Lake Frances. Nescopeck Creek flows through the length of the park unencumbered by a dam and provides excellent fishing. Lake Frances is not open for swimming but does provide fishing opportunities. There are 19 miles of hiking trails that provide ample opportunity to explore this vast, undeveloped acreage in habitats that include Nescopeck Creek and other streams, forests, fields, and wetlands. Some of the trails are open for cross-country skiing and snowshoeing when snow coverage cooperates. With little in the way of amenities except for restrooms, a wonderful and architecturally pleasing Environmental Education Center, and an accompanying Nature Discovery Area focused on children, this fantastic park is all about the natural environment. With the large amount of undeveloped land including the state game lands, a wonderful quiet prevails along with a sense of solitude so one can easily become lost in a personal, meditative state.

We hiked the Nescopeck, Red Rock, Woodland Way, and Lake Trails. This enabled us to check out the beauty found along and within the meandering Nescopeck Creek as well as the wetlands, dense woods, and lake shoreline. The flow of water around and amongst boulders and downed trees and shaded by dense forest, beckoned us to sit on the bank, and watch all the beauty that unfolded before us while we listened to the water flowing down the stream. Since Donna and I started chasing wildflowers during our college years, our focus has leaned towards the magical spring wildflowers. However, in our retirement years we are making up for lost time by expending more of our efforts on summer and fall wildflowers while not forgetting our spring favorites. During our early summer visit to Nescopeck, our flower identification efforts were in overdrive. We identified and photographed white water lily, northern blue flag iris, whorled loosestrife, narrowleaf cow wheat, sheep laurel, Maryland black-snakeroot, fly poison, partridgeberry, and ghost pipes. A truly magical park!

Hearing—sweet sounds of Nescopeck Creek; sight—riffles, pools, and runs along Nescopeck Creek with dense woods lining the banks, abundance of wildflowers in bloom.

72. NESHAMINY

This amazing 339-acre park is very close to Philadelphia as well as Interstate 95. The park itself is divided into two distinct sections by Neshaminy Creek which flows into the Delaware River at this point and both portions of the park also border the Delaware River. The two sections of the park are not connected by a bridge so some driving (under two miles) is necessary to travel from one section to the other. The largest section contains picnic grounds, a huge swimming pool with a spray park, 4.4 miles of hiking trails, and a community theater, The Playmasters. Across the Neshaminy River, the smaller section is all about boating with a 16-pier marina (317 slips), dry storage, boat trailer parking, two boat launching sites, and fishing.

Donna and I decided to explore the park by using some of the hiking trails. We parked in Lot-2 and walked along East Walk to Lot-4 and made our way along the road to the River Walk Trail. Thanks to the educational placards we were able to explore the Delaware Estuary. According to the DCNR, tides cause the river to rise and fall here by seven feet and our visit was during a time when the river was lower. The scenery was gorgeous with driftwood, sandy beaches, stony beaches, trees, bushes, and wildflowers in bloom. We eventually hooked onto the Locust Lane Trail to go back to Lot-4 and from there we walked the Eagles Forest Trail which is a loop through the woods sponsored by the Philadelphia Eagles football team. From there we made our way back to the truck by using the South Walk, Playground Road, and Logan trails.

At our truck, we grabbed our coffee and snacks and walked over to a picnic table. We talked about the fascinating tidal rise and fall (116 miles from the ocean) as well as the great work done by the Eagles football team in conjunction with the DCNR. As our conversation tailed off, my mind drifted to another football team, the Pittsburgh Steelers. I know that over the years the players, coaches and ownership have undertaken many amazing charitable programs as well as providing funds, time, enthusiasm, and name recognition to so many charitable organizations serving the Pittsburgh region. However, I am not aware of any undertaking comparable to the Philadelphia Eagles Forest at Neshaminy. Emerald View Park, which can be seen from Acrisure Stadium and Hays Woods (Pittsburgh's newest park) near the UPMC Rooney Sports Complex, would both be worthy beneficiaries of such an endeavor by the Steelers. I know that I would love to hike a trail or two with a Steelers connection and be willing to help in such an undertaking along with so many other Steelers fans.

Sitting at that picnic table, sipping my coffee with Donna, memory bubbles quickly popped. I was eleven when Paul took me to my first Steelers game on November 24, 1963 and I went to my last Steelers game, again with Paul, on February 1, 2009. Weeks prior to my first Steelers game, Paul talked to me about the Bears and how I would have the chance to see my football hero, Mike Ditka, at Forbes Field. Ditka was a star at Pitt and was in some classes there with our sister, Geri.

I was really excited about the game but two events dented my enthusiasm. The first seemed really bad at the time but turned out to be nothing compared to the second event. The week before the big game, Vince Lombardi and his Green Bay Packers lost to George Halas and his Chicago Bears. The Bears wiped out Green Bay 26-7 and those monsters were coming to Forbes Field in a week! The second event was the assassination of President Kennedy—my president, gone. We prayed for the life of President Kennedy at St. Teresa Grade School where I was in grade six. Our principal, Sister Eileen, announced on the PA system that President Kennedy had been shot and told us to kneel and pray.

All the sad news was everywhere at once but Sunday came, the games were not cancelled, Paul had the tickets, and Mom said to go. Feeling lost, we attended Mass at St. Alphonsus Catholic Church in Wexford. The Mass time at St. Alphonsus was the earliest in our area so Paul drove there so we could arrive early in Oakland to find parking. We arrived in Oakland, Paul found parking, and we walked to Forbes Field. The seats were good because none of the steel pillars blocked our view.

We forgot the terrible news and focused on the game with our Steelers getting a field goal in the 4th Quarter to take a 17-14 lead. Paul and I were amazed that we had the lead but fate came calling in the form of my favorite player, Mike Ditka. I was very excited to see him on the field during the game but his amazing play in the 4th Quarter enabled Chicago to gain a tie with a field goal. Ditka caught a pass from Bill Wade and started running—it was Ditka at his best as he broke Steelers tackle after tackle before running out of gas short of a touchdown but the play was good for 63 yards. It was a strange day with the death of President Kennedy on our minds, the news that Lee Harvey Oswald was shot dead, and the game ending in a tie because of Mike Ditka, but it was a day I would never forget. At the start of the next season, it felt great to know that the Steelers tied the Champions of Football in 1963 and almost beat them while Paul and I watched. Many years later, I realized how controversial Pete Rozelle's decision was to play football that Sunday but I am still glad I was at the game with Paul and saw Ditka play well and the Steelers earn a tie against the tough Chicago Bears.

My last Steelers game with Paul came about when my best friend, Aaron Miller, talked to me and our friend Chuck about going to the Super Bowl. We both gave a thumbs up and I called Paul and our favorite cousin, George, and they both were good to go as well. Aaron found five tickets at a reasonable price and planning went into high gear when the Ravens lost to our Steelers. We purchased the tickets and bought a $100 parking pass. Next, I visited George's Song Shop in Johnstown which is the oldest record store in the United States and I bought two Steelers cds to play on the way to the game to make the miles fly by.

We left Johnstown in a snowstorm—glad my truck is an AWD model. We swung by Frederick, Maryland to pick up George and continued driving south. When we reached the "South of the Border" complex, we stopped to buy food and gas, take some photos, tell stories about other trips that included this stop, laughed a lot, and jumped back in the truck. We drove straight through to Paul's home in St. Petersburg, Florida by rotating drivers along the route—we crashed on his living room floor for the night. I was so happy to see Paul and my nieces before the big game.

On Saturday, the five of us enjoyed bumming around the stadium area and looking at all that the NFL had to offer us. Another night on the floor and we woke up to Super Bowl Sunday. We arrived early to find a good parking space in the reserved area. It was one big party with Steelers and

Cardinals fans mixing together prior to the game. We had a blast and were happy that we arrived many hours before the gates opened. A Cardinals fan from Canada stopped by and asked us if we could please store his video camera in our truck because he was told that he could not take it into the stadium and he was parked far away from the stadium gates. I said no problem and that we would wait for him after the game, which we did. It was a nice, peaceful atmosphere—nothing like I have seen when the old Browns and Raiders came to town to play the Black & Gold or at a Pitt-West Virginia game.

There was a set of two tickets and a set of three. Paul and I sat together using the two and George, Aaron and Chuck used the three. I wish we could have all sat together but I was just so happy that Paul and I were together. We had such a wonderful time and a honeymoon couple from Pittsburgh sat to the right of us. We jumped off to a 10-point lead but suddenly it was 10-7 and the Cardinals were driving for another score at the end of the half. Paul and I were very nervous but the next thing we knew lightning struck in the form of James Harrison. He intercepted Kurt Warner and ran 100 yards for the touchdown—a Super Bowl record! Reminded me a bit of Ditka's play in the 1963 game. Anyway, James made it into the end zone before collapsing on the turf and being given oxygen to recover. The stadium erupted and Paul and I went nuts. An amazing swing in fortunes and the Steelers went into the locker room leading 17-7.

The scoring in the second half was mostly on the Cardinals' side of the ball, including a safety. The big blow against the Steelers came late in the game. Again, just like in my first Steelers game back in 1963, my favorite player on the opposing team and a former Pitt Star, Larry Fitzgerald, scored on a 64-yard play to give the Cardinals a 23-20 lead with two minutes and 37 seconds on the game clock. The husband part of the honeymoon couple buried his head in his hands and never saw what happened next—sad and funny at the same time. Later, I found out that Joseph, back in Pittsburgh, told Donna not to worry because he knew the Steelers would score. Donna was happy to see that he was correct as usual with his predictions.

Here we go Steelers!!! Things started badly—with the ball on our own 22, a holding penalty took the ball back to the 12 with 88 yards needed for a touchdown. Paul and I were anxious but hopeful as the clock continued to tick. Here we go Steelers!!!!! Ben connected with a series of passes and a huge play arrived when Ben threw a short pass to Santonio and he turned it into a 40-yard play to the Cardinals' six-yard line. Here we go Steelers!!!!!! On second and goal, Ben hit Santonio in the corner of the end zone—TOUCHDOWN! Paul and I were hugging each other and the honeymooner looked up after the play—at least their honeymoon was saved thanks to Big Ben and Santonio even if the new husband missed the play of a lifetime. With 29 seconds remaining, the Cardinals moved the ball to the Steelers' 44 with the help of Larry Fitzgerald. I remember Paul and I were just on fire as we screamed, DEFENSE, DEFENSE, DEFENSE and splat, Woodley sacked Warner, the ball came out and Keisel recovered for the Black & Gold!! Here we go Steelers!!! The rest of the evening is a blur. The five of us were just so excited but exhausted as we returned to Paul's and left for home the next morning.

With the Super Bowl retreating in my mind, Donna and I returned to our truck after another wonderful park sojourn.

Hearing—COVID hush even though we were there in August; sight—wide spectrum of scenery along the Delaware River and Neshaminy Creek, estuary placards, flat-topped goldenrod and autumn clematis in bloom; touch—smoothness of the river rocks and driftwood, sand underfoot.

73. NOCKAMIXON

This 5,289-acre park and 1,450-acre Lake Nockamixon form an amazing recreational opportunity for people residing in Allentown, Bethlehem, and Philadelphia. The DCNR map shows a specific parking area for buses which I believe indicates that many school districts take advantage of the environmental education programs here. The lake is loaded with amenities including six launching areas, a marina with a capacity of 648 boats, 120-space dry storage, boat rental concession, fishing pier, and windsurfing. Other amenities within the park include a huge swimming pool complex with a half-acre pool, hiking trails, two-mile paved biking trail, 10-mile mountain biking system, horseback riding, picnicking including some pavilions, and disc golf. Depending on seasonal weather conditions, cross-country skiing, ice skating, ice fishing, and sledding are possibilities. Unfortunately, there is no camping but there are 10 rental cabins.

Donna and I were glad that we visited in the spring since this park must be jammed in the summer months. We parked at the impressive marina area after visiting the park office and walked on the paved bike trail to the Old Mill Trail which is a 5.6-mile loop. There were beautiful views of the lake, the waterfall and pond were picturesque, and the millstone and historical placard were interesting. We hiked along the Old Mill Trail for 1.5 miles before retracing our steps back to the truck. Along the way we identified bloodroot, trout lily, spring beauty, Virginia saxifrage, lesser celandine, and northern spicebush.

Hearing—waterfall, hush throughout our visit thanks to the springtime; sight—blue skies, shimmering lake waters, waterfall, glorious blooms of the bloodroot and trout lily; touch—ice cold mill pond water.

74. NOLDE FOREST ENVIRONMENTAL EDUCATION CENTER

Per DCNR's Recreation Guide, Jacob Nolde bought this acreage in the early 1900s and at that time, there was a single White Pine growing on the property. Jacob was inspired by this tree and hired an Austrian forester to create the forest we see today. Many, many years later, this beautiful forest, consisting of over 665 acres, became the home of the first environmental center operated by the Bureau of State Parks.

The mansion is beautiful from the outside with some whimsical details but it was closed because of COVID. Not sure if any of the interior can normally be viewed because it is the location of staff offices. A separate building serves as the environmental education center. There are 10 miles of trails that intertwine throughout the park and can easily be used to form longer or shorter loops. We hiked the Watershed and the Boulevard trails to form a loop which included crossings of Punch Run. The park is heavily forested and the trails we selected provided an enjoyable look at the dense woods interspersed with a stream, wooden bridges, and wooden walkways. On the way out, we drove on Pennsylvania Route 625 and stopped at the sawmill on the edge of Nolde Woods. It is very picturesque with Angelica Creek flowing along the mill and small picnic area. We sat at a picnic table, enjoyed lunch, and were delighted by the scenery at this cozy spot.

Hearing—zen-like, peaceful environment in the woods; sight—Tudor-style mansion with cute exterior touches for the Nolde children, the sawmill along with Angelica Creek produce a perfect scenic spot.

75. NORRISTOWN FARM PARK

A very interesting and unique 690-acre park that is six miles from Philadelphia. In 1992 the property was leased by DCNR to the Montgomery County Division of Parks. There are eight miles of paved roads/trails that are open to bikes. Fishing is available in a farm pond as well as two streams. Along with 15 historical buildings and fields that have been farmed since colonial times, there are picnic tables and picnic pavilions. Reading about this park, Donna and I thought it would be situated amongst other farms but we failed to think of its proximity to Philadelphia. We found the borders of the parkland to be a mix of an urban Norristown and suburbs filled with ribbons of grass surrounding gleaming, glass and metal commercial developments. I am sure that this undeveloped land represents a paradise for local families during evenings and weekends as well as for workers from nearby businesses enjoying a quick sandwich or stroll during their lunch breaks.

Since the use of automobiles is limited to parking areas near the park office and outer perimeter, the easiest way to explore this park is through biking on the paved roads/trails that weave throughout the property. Be warned, there are some very steep grades to conquer along the way so be prepared to shift gears in time to make it up some of the more challenging ones. We spent several hours biking 6.5 miles and stopping at many of the historical buildings. We really enjoyed the Millennium Grove of Historic Trees planted in 2000. This was a nationwide initiative that produced seedlings from 21 parent trees with historical links.

We arrived at this park in a convoluted manner that took us through a section of Norristown that reminded me of McKees Rocks. After we finished biking and loading our bikes, we sat at a picnic table and enjoyed some coffee on a cool, spring day as I let my mind drift to McKees Rocks.

I always remember McKees Rocks to be a tough, shopworn town, filled with gritty people striving to create a better future for their families with a sense of pride and hope. Maybe this memory is colored by my dad and his siblings growing up there and listening to stories about the Rocks from my Uncle Mitchell, Uncle Stanley, and Uncle Walter. I do return there at least once a year for cemetery duty and despite occasionally reading of the continuing violence plaguing this little town, I still feel positive energy when I am there. My cemetery chores consist of going to St. Mary's Cemetery to weed and plant flowers on my Grandfather Brzozowski's grave along with my Aunt Fanny and Uncle William's grave. According to their joint gravestone, my Aunt Fanny died in 1915 and Uncle William in 1920, neither living beyond childhood. My grandfather died October 17, 1938 as a result of a stroke.

During one of my visits, the October 17, 1938 date on his gravestone just jumped out at me. My dad married my mom on October 16, 1939 which must have provided some emotional turmoil for my dad since it was the day before the first anniversary of his dad's passing. I remember my dad bringing Paul and me to this cemetery in the fall of 1958. I have a strong memory of the three of us standing together on the hilltop and seeing nothing but massive clouds of smoke which in later life I realized was air pollution from the surrounding steel mills. After visiting the graves, Dad treated us to ice cream at the local ice cream shop and from there we stopped at Mancini's Bakery for a loaf of their delicious Italian bread.

The lack of a view from that hilltop did not strike home with me until my brother, Paul, and I visited St. Mary's for the first time since that day in 1958. The view of the city of Pittsburgh that unfolded from that same hilltop just blew our minds. Our return had to be sometime in the early 1990s since I was living in Johnstown by that point. The changing views really reflect how Pittsburgh's air has improved through evolving environmental laws and the eventual demise of the steel mills which led to a mass exodus from the region which included Paul, myself and our families. I realize there continue to be major issues with the air quality in Pittsburgh but it has come a long way from the bad old days. The major issue is that it is the hidden pollution that is causing the major health issues now and since it is not visible, it is difficult to rally public support for more investment in cleaning the air we breathe.

Once I finish my chores at the graves, I usually indulge in some nostalgia and reprise my first and only visit to the cemetery with Dad. First, I drive by the ice cream shop which is still going strong at 1238 Chartiers Avenue. Next, I turn left onto Broadway which I remember as the main drag when I was a kid. Mancini's Bakery is located at 601 Woodward Avenue—coming from the direction of the ice cream shop it is a right turn off of Broadway.

Mancini's has been around since 1926. The basic bread is a wonderful Italian loaf and has a long history in our family. I remember Dad telling us that as a kid, he would walk from his parents' home at 1141 Dohrman Street to pick up a loaf of bread at Mancini's. He was born in 1912 so that would mean that his first opportunity to do this would have been when he was 14. Any time we were in the Rocks, a trip to Mancini's was part of the plan. When Dad died in 1959, trips to McKees Rocks ended along with our stops for the best bread anyone could buy. However, we had another connection to Mancini's; namely, my dad's brother and my godfather, Uncle Stanley and his wife, Aunt Helen. They lived close to the Rocks and when they visited, they always brought us loaves of Mancini's bread. Not only the super delicious bread, but my Aunt Helen would bring one of her fresh-baked apple pies. They always joked about trading the bread and pie for our well water since they always arrived with empty water jugs to fill. We loved our well water and so did they!

Meanwhile, back to Mancini's where I usually go wild with my purchases. Mancini's product line has increased by leaps and bounds and everything is fantastic. A case in point, after buying three loaves of bread including two Italian—one for Laura and her family and one cranberry walnut to split—I added a bag of mini-pizza shells to the haul. I drove back onto Broadway and to the location of our old family home in the Rocks. It was sold in the 1960s by my dad's brother, my Uncle Mitchell, and was replaced by an apartment building. Uncle Mitchell did not let anyone know that it was sold and as luck would have it, Paul was in the area and happened upon a truck being loaded with the furnishings from the home. Paul bought a few things right off the truck and that was the end of our family history in the West Park section of McKees Rocks. A sad ending to our physical link to our past. Dad, Mom, Uncle Stanley, and Aunt Helen lived there after their marriages for a period of time before they saved enough money to buy their own homes. I know that my three oldest siblings—Geri, born in 1940; Paul, born in 1942; and Sandy, born in 1946—all lived in that house prior to the family moving to Ross Township. Our home in Ross Township was located on Babcock Boulevard which was zoned commercial so my dad was able to build his office and warehouse as an attachment to the home they bought and that is where J. B. Supply remained until it came to an end.

I do not have many memories of visiting the family homestead on Dohrman Street but one constantly surfaces when I am in the Rocks and drive by the apartment building where the house once sat. I do remember it was only a couple minute walk from the house to the school and football field which remain as the Sto-Rox Junior-Senior High School and football field. When I was young, Dad would take us to the fireworks at West Park and we would park at the house and walk over to the field. These fireworks were amazing because much of the action occurred right on the field. I remember displays of tanks and battleships outlined in fireworks. The tanks and battleships would fire cannons at their counterparts in the form of fireworks. It was really cool and I never have seen such fireworks displays since that experience at West Park. I also remember that the grand finale was so intense that us kids ran back to the house, holding our hands over our ears. Thinking about loud bangs, my Uncle Walter told me that his older brothers, including my dad, would celebrate the New Year by going into the back yard with their rifles and firing rounds into the air. Those days are long gone!

My final act along this memory lane was driving back onto Broadway, making a left onto Tunnel Way and driving through the Stowe Tunnel to Pennsylvania Route 51. This tunnel seemed so much longer when I was a kid and it always seemed like it was the secret entrance into another world, namely, the Rocks. Going through the tunnel when my dad was with us always meant joy and fun because it was not only the way to bread and ice cream but also my Uncle Stanley and Aunt Helen's house where a fun picnic and Max, the dog, awaited our arrival. Too many times those visits ended with my dad and his brothers arguing but the food (including my aunt's apple pie) and soft drinks were always wonderful. In those days, soft drinks were a special treat and not something you enjoyed on a weekly or even monthly basis.

Caution: Using the park address, our GPS brought us to Norristown State Hospital. We continued to follow our GPS and soon found ourselves stopped at a gate. The gate had a sign posted that provided the correct driving directions to the park entrance. Viewing this sign, we realized that we were not the first nor would we be the last to make this mistake. On the DCNR web page for the park, there are driving directions so please read the latest driving information when planning your visit.

Hearing—park perimeter traffic, quiet spots where modern life recedes; sight—picturesque buildings, historical trees such as the John F. Kennedy Post Oak.

76. OHIOPYLE

This 20,500-acre park is a giant playpen for kids and adults alike. The Laurel Highlands Trail begins here, the Great Allegheny Passage (GAP) biking trail comes through the park, there are beautiful waterfalls, natural water slides, both tame and wild rafting on the Youghiogheny River and much more. This gem of a park is the perfect spot for a vacation so the campground with 246 sites is a wonderful amenity. Another great facet of the park is that the community of Ohiopyle is surrounded by the park so no need to go far to find places to eat, have ice cream, rent bikes, arrange for rafting trips, and so forth. The only complication is that the little town of Ohiopyle and Ohiopyle State Park are the epicenter for so many great outdoor activities that seasonal crowds of joyful, enthusiastic participants can overwhelm both the town and some portions of the park. However, with so many trails waiting to be explored, an escape from crowds does not pose a problem.

This is a park we visit several times a year and throughout all four seasons. In the summer and fall, biking the GAP from Ohiopyle to Confluence is stunning. We have stopped at River's Edge Cafe in Confluence for lunch many times. It is just off the bike trail and reached by means of a bike/pedestrian bridge that crosses the Youghiogheny River from the GAP. The Cafe is very charming, the food is top notch, and B & B rooms are available. After lunch, we usually bike to the heart of this little town by the use of another pedestrian/bike bridge to check out the bicycle shop and other retailers. Also, in the summer and fall, we enjoy hikes up to Baughman Rock and back. Baughman/Sugarloaf Loop Trail begins with the Baughman Trail which is just off of the GAP near the railroad station/visitor center. We have completed this trail with our friends, Sue and John, many times—the woods, rock formations, and the vista provide a beautiful plunge into nature. Visiting in winter and seeing Ohiopyle Falls garbed in winter ice never fails to produce moments of awe.

Spring is for the Great Gorge Trail. We check it out each spring to ensure we don't miss the spectacular spring wildflower display. On our very first hike on this beautiful trail we found the best spring wildflower display that we have had the pleasure of experiencing excluding our spring adventures at Smoky Mountain National Park. The wildflowers along the Gorge Trail are just so beautiful and magical that I cannot find the words to adequately describe the experience. We identified 30 different wildflowers that day and the thousands of white trilliums in full bloom were dazzling. Also, we briefly left the trail, walked across a vehicle bridge surfaced with metal grating to reach the Cucumber Falls parking area, and checked out Cucumber Falls. Well worth the quick detour since it produced a spectacular display boosted by spring rains.

Yellow Lady Slippers, Ohiopyle State Park

This park is so vast and offers so many recreational opportunities that I recommend reviewing the corresponding DCNR Recreation Guide in great detail. A few of the nuts and bolts include 79 miles of hiking trails, 27 miles of the GAP, 25.2 miles of mountain biking trails, and 11.6 miles of horseback riding trails. Also, there are areas to fish, well-equipped picnicking areas, rock climbing spots, and winter sports venues for snowmobiling, cross-country skiing, and sledding. Other can't-miss opportunities include the Environmental Education and Interpretation Center which is a fantastic place to visit for both children and adults; as well as hiking trails within the 100-acre Ferncliff Peninsula National Natural Landmark.

We visited Ohiopyle State Park to pick up our passport stamp in the winter. It was on a cold February day but we were rewarded with wonderful views of icy Ohiopyle Falls. With the lack of snow on the ground, we hiked Ferncliff Peninsula which gave us more opportunities to check out Ohiopyle Falls as well as the ice-fringed rocks lining the Youghiogheny River. A joyful winter escape with the icy views substituting for the snow that was missing from the landscape.

Based on our experiences with spring wildflowers on the Great Gorge Trail for several years running, I am happy to name **Ohiopyle State Park** as my choice for the ***Best Pennsylvania State Park for Wildflowers***.

Caution: For many years a pedestrian bridge has been missing on the Great Gorge Trail and spring water levels usually prevent a potential stream crossing at this point which would involve stepping gingerly from rock to rock through the stream. To avoid a potential fall, wet feet, or a soaking, please hike this trail in two segments.

Hearing—Ohiopyle Falls, Meadow Run Waterslides, shouts of excitement from whitewater rafters; sight—miles of wildflowers in bloom, pink lady slippers and yellow lady slippers in full bloom, Ohiopyle Falls, Baughman Rock vista.

77. OIL CREEK

History abounds in this 6,250-acre park and it all revolves around the early oil industry as Oil Creek Valley is where the first commercial oil well was established in 1859. This history is on full display within the park including two historical tableaus and the Train Station Visitor Center at Petroleum Center. Also, the Drake Well Museum and Park is adjacent to the section of Oil Creek State Park nearest to Titusville. Oil Creek flows through the length of the park, providing fishing and boating (kayaking, canoeing) opportunities. Day use areas provide restrooms, pavilions, and picnic tables for picnickers.

In addition, there are wonderful venues for hikers, bikers, and cross-country skiers. The 36-mile Gerald Hiking Trail offers hikers a challenging loop trail through the entire park and the adjacent Drake Well Museum and Park property. There are four waterfalls along the path and two overnight camp sites. Each camping area has six Adirondack shelters, tent sites, and restrooms. A point-to-point, 9.7-mile paved bike trail traverses the majority of the park and is served by restrooms, picnic tables, benches, rain shelters, and historical placards. The Oil Creek Gorge and Oil Creek itself provide outstanding scenery for bikers using this trail. The cross-country ski area has 11.5 miles of groomed trails with a warming hut, restrooms, and parking lot. There is a fee-based ski pass for this area but the bike trail is also available for cross-country skiing without fees.

Many, many years ago, we biked 19.4 miles on the paved trail in the fall and enjoyed the experience immensely—highly recommend taking bikes when visiting this park. We visited the park in a rainstorm to obtain our passport stamp and spent our time at the Train Station Visitor Center in Petroleum Center. A year later, we experienced a perfect fall day here and traveled on the Oil Creek and Titusville Railroad through the length of the park. We boarded in Titusville, reached Rynd Farm Station, and returned to Titusville. The scenery with all the spectacular leaf colors set ablaze by sunshine made for an amazing train ride.

Hearing—train whistle, water tumbling along Oil Creek; sight—museum exhibits, colorful leaves becoming a riot of colors through the magic of the fall sunshine.

78. OLE BULL

This little park consisting of 132 acres really has a lot going on. Kettle Creek flows through its length providing both fishing and swimming opportunities that includes a swimming beach. There is significant history with a monument to Ole Bull within the park gifted by the people of Norway to commemorate his attempt to establish a Norwegian settlement here in the 1850s. A picnicking area along Kettle Creek provides four pavilions, picnic tables, restrooms, and a playground. There are trails that provide plenty of room to roam since many cross into Susquehannock State Forest which almost totally surrounds the park. Winter guests are served as well with the campground and restrooms remaining open, parking by a snowmobile trailhead that provides access to the surrounding state forest, and groomed cross-country ski trails.

Donna and I hiked up the Castle Vista Trail to look at the foundation of Ole Bull's home, a portion of the Daugherty Loop Trail, and the Beaver Haven Nature Trail which briefly entered Susquehannock State Forest. We also took photographs of ourselves at the impressive Ole Bull's monument that was installed in 2002. We were provided much food for thought when we viewed an interesting sign erected in the park that reads, "YOU CAN'T TEACH A CHILD TO BE AN ENVIRONMENTALIST BUT, IF YOU TEACH A CHILD TO FISH THAT CHILD WILL BECOME AN ENVIRONMENTALIST." – IN MEMORY OF DR. JOSEPH 'DOC' SCISLY.

Hearing—soothing sounds of Kettle Creek; sight—monument, picturesque stone foundations, sign to honor Joseph Scisly.

79. PARKER DAM

This 968-acre park and 20-acre Parker Lake provide a wonderful setting for family vacations, community gatherings, and family reunions. It is surrounded by Moshannon State Forest which helps provide a sense of tranquility and the parkland acts as a trailhead for hikers seeking to meander through the state forest. One of these trails is the 73-mile Quehanna Trail which provides many adventures for backpackers. Amenities include fishing, boat rentals, a swimming beach with a food concession, geocaching and orienteering, mountain biking, and hiking. Picnicking is a very strong component here with many picnic tables, seven picnic pavilions, and restrooms. Each pavilion holds approximately 75 people so perfect for community gatherings and family reunions. There is a nice campground with 107 sites that serves the park as well. There are 17 cabins that remain open year-round to service winter visitors attracted by many recreational opportunities including ice fishing, sledding, cross-country skiing, snowshoeing, and snowmobiling.

Donna and I hiked the Log Slide Trail which is a 0.4-mile section of the Quehanna Trail within the park and we continued along the trail into Moshannon State Forest for a few miles before retracing our steps. The Log Slide section of the Quehanna Trail displays a reproduction of a log slide as well as historical lumbering tools from the days when this was a logging area which ended in 1911. We also hiked a section of the Laurel Run Trail that runs along one side of the 20-acre Parker Lake, crosses large stones strung across the water flowing from the dam, and follows Laurel Run to the edge of the park bordered by Tyler Road. Laurel Run flows through the length of the park and is responsible for filling Parker Lake. We had hoped to check out the CCC Museum which is within a building constructed by the CCC but it was closed because of COVID.

Sight—picturesque boardwalk along Parker Lake, endearing CCC construction that lifts the veil of time to another era.

80. PATTERSON

This tiny, 10-acre park is surrounded by Susquehannock State Forest and split in half by Pennsylvania Route 44. It is close to Cherry Hill State Park which makes it an alternative if Cherry Hill has no room for an overnight stay. Be aware of the following in considering camping here: primitive campsites that are not screened from Route 44, rustic restrooms, and there are no reservations for campsites so be prepared to leave payment in the envelope. The good news is the sites do have lantern posts, fire rings, and picnic tables. Other amenities include two small picnic pavilions where reservations are accepted and the park serves as a trailhead for the Susquehannock Trail System (STS) that runs through it. We hiked a bit of the STS before retracing our steps back to our truck.

Hearing—traffic noise from occasional vehicles; sight—beautiful, natural landscape along the STS, two rustic and picturesque pavilions.

81. PENN-ROOSEVELT

Because of road closures, we reached this isolated park by taking a gravel road for 12 miles from Greenwood Furnace State Park. Penn-Roosevelt is only 41 acres but is surrounded by an 80,000-acre chunk of Rothrock State Forest. Penn-Roosevelt Lake is listed at 3.5 acres on several sites but in reality, it is more like a small pond with much of the lake now appearing to be a wetland. There are 18 rustic campsites served by rustic restrooms and made available on a first come, first serve basis. There is one picnic pavilion and some picnic tables scattered about. We hiked a small portion of the Mid State Trail which goes through the park and into the state forest. This is a historical spot since there are a few remnants of the African-American CCC camp that was once located here. While exploring the area we viewed a fireplace from those camp days.

Donna just loved this park because of the overwhelming sense of isolation that it produced when we visited. I think camping here would be an amazing experience with the total lack of road noise and the dark sky at night. It was just us in the park as we hiked and made for a wonderful spot to briefly decompress from the realities of our technology-laden society. I cannot fathom what a week here would be like!

Hearing—tranquility abounds with the sounds of nature; sight—foggy patches driving towards the park produced a sense of timelessness, vast woods on both sides of the road called out to be explored.

82. PINE GROVE FURNACE

This 696-acre park is packed with many opportunities for visitors. Swimming, beaches and snack bars are found at 1.7-acre Fuller Lake and 25-acre Laurel Lake. Fishing is available at both lakes as well as Mountain Creek. There is no boating on Fuller Lake but there is a boat launch, boat rentals, and 85 mooring spaces on Laurel Lake. There is a campground with 70 sites and a camp store is located away from the campground but by the section of the Appalachian Trail (AT) within the park. There are approximately four miles of hiking trails within the park and some lead into the Michaux State Forest that surrounds the park including the AT. The AT reaches its midpoint here and there is an Appalachian Trail Museum celebrating everything about the AT. Other amenities include a two-mile biking trail and picnic tables as well as three pavilions. History is a big theme with Pine Grove Furnace operating here from 1764 to 1895. Pine Grove Iron Works is on the list of the National Register of Historic Places with some structures still standing. The CCC also left its mark on the park.

We visited during COVID and missed out on the AT Museum as well as the camp store. Donna and I hiked up the very steep Pole Steeple Trail to the Pole Steeple Overlook which was well worth the effort. The view of the park and forest was spectacular as was the rock outcrop forming the overlook. After a short break, we continued up the trail to where it intersected with the AT. At that point, we hiked on the AT for a short time before turning around, retracing our steps, and returning to the parking lot. From there we walked on the Bike Trail to the dam at Laurel Lake and ended our visit by driving over to Fuller Lake and checking out the beach there.

Hearing—relaxing sounds of water flowing over the dam at Laurel Lake; sight—view from Pole Steeple Overlook, the Furnace, Paymasters Cabin.

83. POE PADDY

This 23-acre park is surrounded by Bald Eagle State Forest. Yes, this is the forest we struggled through on the drivable trail when we were heading towards this park and Poe Valley State Park (all described in detail within the *Research* section in Chapter 3). There is no paved road leading here but we did find out that well-maintained gravel roads are excellent and bear no resemblance to drivable trails! Excellent trout fishing is the huge draw with Big Poe Creek dividing the park in two while forming a confluence with Penns Creek that is bordering the park on one side and Bald Eagle State Forest on the other. Camping consists of five Adirondack shelters, 32 campsites, restrooms, and drinking water. Showers and a sanitary dump station can be found at nearby Poe Valley State Park. Other amenities include a boat launch on Penns Creek and two pavilions for picnicking. For us, we were looking forward to walking through the 250-foot Paddy Mountain Railroad Tunnel which the Mid State Trail uses as it passes through the park. The 2.7-mile Penns Creek Path also uses the tunnel and provides a crushed stone, rails-to-trails experience. Both the Mid State Trail and Penns Creek Path share this converted rail bed until near the end of the Penns Creek Path where the Mid State Trail branches off to the left.

To say the least, we were exhausted and mentally spent by the time we made our way through Bald Eagle State Forest to the parking lot at Poe Paddy. However, we decided that this tunnel was not to be missed so we walked on Poe Paddy Drive/Mid State Trail in the direction of the tunnel when fate intervened in the form of a dog. Shortly after we walked over the bridge that spans Big Poe Creek, a cute little dog with a collar joined us. We were not sure if the dog was lost from afar, left its owners at the parking lot, or belonged at a campsite. The camping areas near us were quiet so we turned around and walked back to the parking lot with our new companion at our heels.

Only Donna's CR-V and Duane's motorcycle were parked in the lot. We provided the dog with some water and waited for the owners to turn up. Luckily for all concerned, dog and owners had a joyful reunion about 30 minutes later. At this point, we made the decision to pull the plug on the walk to the tunnel. We realized that we were just too tired to go on exploring here since we knew Poe Valley State Park was waiting for us and afterwards, our campsite at Raymond B. Winter State Park.

Hearing—a hush prevails surrounded by the vastness of Bald Eagle State Forest; sight—picturesque streams.

84. POE VALLEY

We drove into the park on Poe Valley Road after leaving Poe Paddy State Park. This 620-acre park is surrounded by Bald Eagle State Forest and the fact that gravel roads must be used prior to reaching a paved road near the park, makes it feel like a really hidden gem. Amenities include a campground with 45 campsites, fishing on 25-acre Poe Lake, a boat launch, boat rentals, a swimming beach, a food and drink concession, and a picnicking area with picnic tables, pavilions, playground, and restrooms.

Duane, Donna, and I checked out the beach and hiked the Nature Trail that is a loop starting and ending at the park office. We spent some time talking to the ranger, gaining the necessary information to eventually find our way to Pennsylvania Route 45. Hopefully we will return to this park for a more leisurely visit that will include launching our kayak on Poe Lake and enjoying the beautiful beach. At the same time, we would include a stop at nearby Poe Paddy State Park to finally walk through the restored train tunnel on the Mid State Trail. By the way, the directions of the ranger were perfect and we had plenty of daylight back at our campsite at Raymond B. Winter State Park to make a great meal and enjoy the campfire as the three of us talked about our crazy day.

Hearing—reassuring words of the park ranger providing us with directions to Route 45; sight—beckoning sand beach seemingly carved out of the forest; vast woods.

85. POINT

I wrote about Point State Park extensively in the beginning of this book since we ended our quest here. However, it is time to take another look at this amazing, historic, 35-acre park. First, the downtown section of Pittsburgh is known as the "Golden Triangle" and the park is at the tip of the triangle. The triangle is formed by the Monongahela and Allegheny Rivers coming together to form the Ohio River. This land was a very strategic location for a fort and the critical history that occurred here with Native Americans, French, and British can be discovered by touring the Heinz History Center's Fort Pitt Museum which is right next to the Fort Pitt Block House. The Block House is the last remaining portion of Fort Pitt and it was constructed in 1764. Of importance to folks on the quest, the Fort Pitt Museum staff have the passport stamps for both Point State Park and Allegheny Islands State Park.

Point State Park is crowned by a magnificent fountain which shoots up to 150 feet in the air, depending on wind conditions. While viewing the fountain in operation can be mesmerizing, the views from the park shorelines of trains, tugboats, large sight-seeing boats, the inclines going up and down Mount Washington, and cityscapes including baseball and football stadiums can all be just as mesmerizing. On top of all that action, the Great Allegheny Passage begins at the fountain and in combination with C & O Canal Towpath can be used by bike riders and hikers to go all the way to Washington, DC. Wait, there is more! A pedestrian walkway/bridge is attached to the Fort Duquesne Bridge and can be used to cross over the Allegheny River from Point State Park to Pittsburgh's North Side/North Shore. This route regularly is taken by locals, tourists, and very large numbers of Pitt and Steeler fans when their teams are playing at the football stadium. Along with all of this action, fishing awaits in the park along the Monongahela and Allegheny River shorelines as well as boat cleats so boaters can moor their boats at the park during the day. Yes, never a dull minute in this park!

Before moving on, there are just a few more items to mention. The Fort Pitt Block House together with the Forks of the Ohio River are listed as a National Historic Landmark. This speaks volumes regarding the history that is encompassed by this magnificent public space. I think if I had the gift of painting, I could spend my whole artistic career capturing the past and the ever-evolving present that can be found within its boundaries. Anyway, a few shirt pocket notes before I move on. Yes, there are restrooms and a snack bar within the park. However, a big staple at Pennsylvania State Parks is missing from the scene, namely, picnic tables. Drifting back in time, I remember having picnics here on blankets but really can't visualize ever sitting at a picnic table. I am not 100 percent sure that my memory is correct regarding no picnic tables in the past or if picnic tables once were part of the landscape. However, I do believe the former is the correct answer.

Hearing—the setting provides lots of sounds that blend together to form an interesting soundtrack to our visits; sight—so much to see in all directions, the blockhouse, the fountain, the rivers coming together; touch—breezes, sunshine.

86. PRESQUE ISLE

This 3,200-acre peninsula-park on Lake Erie enables Pennsylvania citizens to enjoy a great beach vacation without leaving their home state. Presque Isle State Park is so amazing that it is a National Natural Landmark. There are 11 beaches, a marina, several launch points, a pond with numerous boat-landing locations, a lighthouse, hiking trails, 13.5-mile paved, multi-purpose trail, the Tom Ridge Environmental Center, and so much more. However, there is no park campground. This is another park with so many moving parts that studying its Pennsylvania Recreation Guide is essential. Most importantly, focus on one fact, everything here revolves around Lake Erie and all the recreational opportunities it represents.

Perry Monument, Presque Isle State Park

During our visit to obtain our passport stamp, we toured the Environmental Center and went biking on the multi-purpose trail. This was not our first experience biking here and it will not be our last. Why? The bike ride is amazing, relaxing, stress-free, filled with wonderful views, has cool attractions (Perry Monument, a hike to the observation platform in the Natural Area, Presque Isle Lighthouse) and it is a National Recreation Trail. Further, I would suggest bringing a picnic lunch and plenty of water along since it is a loop trail and when you wish that this biking experience could continue, you will be prepared to grant your own wish by continuing on the loop for another go-round. The toughest part will be to decide the view you want when you stop for your lunch break—so many picturesque spots available to dine with a view!

Unlike our last ride here, the lake levels had increased to the point that the bike trail by the Perry Monument was flooded but it was a minor issue and gave us an opportunity to jump off our bikes and more thoughtfully explore the monument and historical placards. Thinking about our experience, I would strongly suggest a trip in the off-season. Walking along the beaches and riding on the multi-purpose trail are both experiences enhanced by smaller crowds. Nothing ruins my zen as fast as the worries associated with sharing the trail with walkers while on my bike. No worries walkers, my zen is also ruined when sharing the North Shore Riverwalk Trail with bikers when I am walking with Joseph to a football game in Pittsburgh. Yes, it does cut both ways and humans are only humans and are easily led astray. With that thought, as a biker on Presque Isle, my recommendation remains steadfast—go off-season.

Caution: Bikers and walkers please be courteous and conscious of folks when sharing multi-purpose trails so accidents can be avoided. Bikers, proceed very slowly when approaching walkers and use your bells/horns to alert walkers as you are approaching them from both the rear and head-on. Bikers, please remember walkers can be in deep conversations with their companions, talking on their cell phones, or listening to music with headphones which all result in diminished awareness of potential dangers. Walkers, don't form a blockade by spreading your group the entire width of a trail. Walkers, understand that a biker swerving off a trail to avoid a collision can result in a serious injury to the biker and please keep in mind that bikers can't stop on a dime or magically hover in place.

Opportunity: When visiting off-season, jump on the Internet and check on the opening and/or closing date for Sara's Restaurant. It is located on the right side of the road at 25 Peninsula Drive, just past the Tom Ridge

Environmental Center and before one drives onto Presque Isle. To me, it is a great burger and hotdog joint and I highly recommend a stop there when you come to visit Presque Isle. For example, in 2024 it opened at 11:00 AM on April 1st, perfect timing for off-season bike riding or beach meandering. Also, when on their site, don't forget to print off coupons—eating super food while saving money is just perfect.

I have many memories of Presque Isle going back to the early 1960s. Mom always loved the beaches there and she would take us to visit overnight with Paul driving his car. Before Interstate 79 was constructed, it really was a long haul on Pennsylvania Route 19. I have no way to confirm my memory but I think it was over four hours to go there from our house in Pittsburgh and much longer when we stopped for lunch in one of the small towns along the way. I still remember when Interstate 79 finally opened the entire way, suddenly going to Erie was a day trip. One Mother's Day (must have been in the late 1960s when I-79 was completed), Paul surprised Mom by taking her on a picnic lunch at one of the beaches on Presque Isle. Mom was just so excited and Diane, Paul's wife, made a great lunch with fried chicken, potato salad, watermelon, and cake. It was a perfect off-season visit and Mom loved it.

As mentioned at the beginning of this section, Presque Isle is all about the water. In fact, if we came on our quest after I bought my kayak, I know we would have been checking out more of the park. I love the thought of kayaking on Lake Erie within the shelter of Presque Isle Peninsula and kayaking on the interconnecting ponds that are on the peninsula itself. This possibility reminds me of my excitement when Donna and I visited Isle Royale National Park for our 39th wedding anniversary. We watched kayakers not only out on Lake Superior but on some of the ponds located on Isle Royale itself. Keeping all of this in mind, my pick for the **Best Water Park in the Pennsylvania State Park System** is **Presque Isle State Park**.

Hearing—Ring-billed gulls screaming; sight—view from tower at Tom Ridge Environmental Center, picturesque lighthouse, gleaming waters; touch—walking on the beach.

87. PRINCE GALLITZIN

This is an impressive park with 6,249 acres and the 1,635-acre Glendale Lake. Further, State Game Land 108 adjoins sections of the parkland. Glendale Lake is not just an oval or rectangle-shaped body of water but spreads out in many directions producing interesting coves and containing 26 miles of shoreline. There are amenities galore including two marinas, nine boat launching sites, boat rentals, swimming beaches/food concession, and picnic areas with four pavilions. There are 32.65 miles of hiking trails, a 2.3-mile multi-use trail open to bikers, 20 miles of mountain biking and snowmobiling trails, horseback riding trails with an adjacent off-parkland riding stable, and seven miles of cross-country skiing trails. The campground is on a peninsula and is a large operation with 391 sites, camp store, swimming beach, and boat rentals. This is another state park where I strongly advocate reviewing the corresponding Pennsylvania Recreation Guide to clearly understand all that awaits a park visitor.

In my mind's eye, I still see us arriving at the Prince Gallitzin park office on a sunshine-filled day and just saying, wow! From this location, we had a wonderful view of Glendale Lake spreading out before us and it was simply stunning. The park office and the landscaping all appeared brand new (our quest visit was in 2018) and so welcoming with the backdrop of the sparkling lake waters. A portion of the landscaping includes a Patton Paver Historic Walk which is impressive to see and learn about the pavers. Donna and I hiked the Point, Footprint, and Campground Trails.

The campground really is like a small town and must be a lively place for family camping adventures. We went on a geocache adventure with Joseph here last year during camping season and the camp store had a sandwich board sign out front beckoning hungry campers to enjoy a funnel cake. I am sure that this sweet treat along with many food items makes this store very popular with campers of all ages. On the way out, the three of us stopped at Headache Hill and climbed up some flights of stairs to the top of Headache Hill Water Tower. This is a great stop when visiting because the nice view from the top of the tower rewards your efforts to make it to the roof.

Sight—spectacular first view of Glendale Lake; smell—delicious aroma wafting out of the Crooked Run Campground camp store; touch—bending down to touch history in the form of a Patton paver.

88. PROMISED LAND

Promised Land! We were very excited to make this a hub park for five days. Why the excitement for a first time visit? Many times over the past thirty years we passed the exit sign for this park on Interstate 84 when driving to and from Acadia National Park but never found the time to take the exit. Silliness always broke out as we declared to one another that if we only knew we could drive to the "Promised Land," we would have taken a road trip there a long time ago. Each time between rolling laughter, we promised ourselves that someday our destination would be Promised Land State Park instead of Maine. Thanks to our quest, someday was now!

So with our quest winding down in August 2022 and with much anticipation, we finally allowed ourselves to follow the exit sign for Promised Land State Park. Wow, we were not disappointed and only wish we came here sooner. It consists of about 3,000 acres and is surrounded by a 12,464-acre chunk of Delaware State Forest that includes 2,845-acre Bruce Lake Natural Area. In addition, there are two lakes; namely, 173-acre Lower Lake and 422-acre Promised Land Lake. The lakes are well used with fishing permitted in both and swimming allowed in Promised Land Lake. There are two boat launch sites on Lower Lake and three boat launch sites on Promised Land Lake. Mooring sites are available in both lakes and there is a boat rental concession across from the beach on Promised Land Lake. Not only can rental boats be picked up at the concession area but also at Pickerel Point on Promised Land Lake and at Lower Lake. The main beach and refreshment stand are located in the Day Use Picnic Area with another beach located at the end of Pickerel Point. The picnic grounds feature parking, picnic tables, two pavilions, water, restrooms, sand volleyball, basketball, and the convenience of the nearby beach, refreshment stand, and boat rentals.

Other recreational opportunities include hiking, biking, orienteering, geocaching, camping, touring a museum, and attending programs for children. Promised Land is blessed with six campgrounds and a horse camping area. Beachwood Campground with 106 sites, Northwoods with 48 sites, Rhododendron with 63 sites, and Hemlock Hill Horse Camping are clustered by Lower Lake. We stayed in Beechwood Campground which is closest to the lake. Our site, #368, offered a great flat spot for our tent and was convenient to our camp host and the showerhouse/restrooms.

Lower Lake, Promised Land State Park

Deerfield Campground with 34 sites for rustic camping (flush toilets), Pickerel Point with 75 sites, and the Pines with 58 sites for rustic camping (flush toilets) are scattered around Promised Land Lake. The Pines Campground is connected to the Day Use Picnic Area by a paved trail. The Pickerel Point Campground is on a peninsula with a swimming area and boat rentals at the tip. It is close to the Masker Museum which is the largest museum in the state park system and is divided into two sections, one focusing on natural history and the other, the CCC. A bonus is that it is housed in a historical building constructed by the CCC. The Point Deerfield Campground is close by to the Promised Land Auditorium which is used for special events. This auditorium sits between the Point Deerfield Campground entrance and the Packer Museum. Programs for children include a nature arts and crafts program and a fishing program that includes loaner poles, bait, and tackle.

Promised Land uses Delaware State Forest to full advantage. About 50 miles of hiking trails meander through the park as well as adjoining state forest land. Also, recreational choices such as horseback riding, snowmobiling, cross-country skiing, and snowshoeing utilize a combination of state park and state forest lands. For example, per the DCNR, the best cross-country skiing trails and snowshoeing trails are found in Bruce Lake Natural Area (Delaware State Forest land) and Conservation Island (Promised Land State Park land). Speaking of Conservation Island, it is located in Promised Land Lake which we accessed by means of a pedestrian bridge. At the bridge, we obtained a booklet that acts as a teaching tool for children. Included within its pages, we discovered "Pocono Plateau Senses Bingo" which enables kids to play along as they tour the island. Of course, us big kids had fun playing it as well!

Over the years of our quest, we camped at other hub parks but the spokes on this hub required more driving to reach the other parks and return to our campsite. This translated into us supplementing our camp dinners with few restaurant visits before we collapsed around our campfire each evening. Also, it meant we had less time and energy to explore our hub park on foot. During our stay, we hiked around Conservation Island as well as the Lower Lake Trail and found lots of interesting rock formations that are visible signs of the glacier that once covered this land. Next time, we want to bring our kayak and spend several days just exploring with Laura and our grandkids everything this amazing park has to offer. We are looking forward to hanging out on the beach, swimming in the lake, checking out the museum, and hiking in the Bruce Lake Natural Area.

Thinking about everything that makes Promised Land so special while considering all our other park visits, it was very difficult to pick the park in this next category. However, as Donna loves telling me, "Joe, just put on your big-boy pants and go for it." I am happy to choose **Promised Land State Park** as my pick for the ***Best Overall Pennsylvania State Park***. Again, not easy since there are so many worthy selections but this park just checked off so many boxes in my mind that it makes perfect sense.

Sight—large rock formation with a huge tree tenaciously anchoring itself amongst the stone and slight crevices, puffy white clouds in a gorgeous blue sky reflected in Promised Land Lake; smell—morning bacon, pine nuts roasting in a skillet fired by our trusty Coleman stove; taste—amazing Italian dish that included the aforementioned pine nuts, sauce, cheeses, and plenty of Italian spices.

89. PROMPTON

This is the only state park that we visited that did not have a state park sign. The 290-acre Prompton Lake and dam are operated by the Army Corps of Engineers. Amenities include a boat launch, fishing, picnic tables, restrooms, picnic pavilion above the dam, disk golf, and 22.9 miles of hiking trails. We made the boat launch site our first stop. There is a kiosk there that has a large map showing Prompton State Park and its hiking trails which Donna photographed as her state park sign. We ate our picnic lunch at the pavilion and afterwards, we checked out the dam, walked along the lake shore, and explored a small inlet. The inlet was filled with water lilies in bloom, and closer to the shoreline, pickerelweed was blooming. Growing near the shore of the inlet we found cardinal flowers in bloom. Afterwards, we found two geocaches before returning to our truck.

Sight—wildflowers in bloom, no traditional park sign.

90. PROUTY PLACE

This remote five-acre park is surrounded by Susquehannock State Forest. We came down Long Toe Road which is very scenic as we drove by several beaver dams. Upon arriving in the park, we found seven spring wildflowers in bloom including trout lily and red trillium. The wildflowers were all very close to the parking area. There is a small roofed structure that contains a disabled hand-pump well. The park functions as a trailhead for trails and streams within the state forest.

Hearing—peaceful, hushed environment; sight—vast forest, wildflowers in bloom.

91. PYMATUNING

This park is all about the 17,088-acre lake that is Pymatuning Reservoir. The reservoir spans the Pennsylvania and Ohio border and is the home to Pymatuning State Park Pennsylvania and Pymatuning State Park Ohio. It is the largest lake in Pennsylvania and Pymatuning State Park with 16,892 acres is the largest state park. This is a huge recreation area and obtaining a Pennsylvania Recreation Guide for Pymatuning is a must to gain some understanding of the complexity of the lake, park, and surrounding area. For example, there are two natural areas in the park; namely, Black Jack Swamp Natural Area and Clark Island Natural Area. Amenities include marinas, launch sites, boat rentals, fishing, three public beaches, a campground beach, numerous picnic tables, 10 picnic pavilions, restrooms, three campgrounds, seven miles of hiking trails, and the famous spillway. Adjoining or nearby the park are a Pennsylvania Fish and Boat Commission Hatchery, a Pennsylvania Game Commission Wildlife Learning Center, Pennsylvania Game Commission Pymatuning Waterfowl Area, and State Game Lands 214.

Donna and I hiked a portion of the Spillway Trail, the Sugar Run Trail by the dam, and we walked around the dam area. Later, we enjoyed our time at the spillway fish and fowl feeding area. It really is a tourist attraction all by itself and we quickly learned why. We bought some loaves of bread at the spillway concession stand and just had a blast feeding the carp, ducks, and geese. Perfect stop for kids of all ages and to see the crazy antics of waterfowl walking across huge groups of carp to chase down pieces of bread brought on lots of smiles and laughter. Plus, the lore of the lake is intense and after our visit I understood why my brother and his buddies loved it as a fishing destination.

Sounds—spillway feeding frenzy; sight—ducks turning a large gathering of hungry carp into a roadway, vastness of the waters of the lake.

92. RACCOON CREEK

This park is well known for its Wildflower Reserve which has an amazing reputation. However, there are many more attractions contained within the 7,572 acres of parkland and 101-acre Raccoon Lake. Amenities include two boat launches, boat rentals, swimming beach, picnic areas, restrooms, 172-site campground, a historical site, and 44 miles of hiking trails. A 19.5-mile backpacking loop trail is a wonderful way to explore the park with two primitive campsites that each include five Adirondack shelters and five tent sites only available to backpackers. There also are 19 miles of mountain biking trails and 16 miles of horseback riding trails.

I knew about this park long before we visited during our quest. My grandparents, Frank and Mary Brzozowski, immigrants from Poland, owned farmland that was obtained by the federal government under the Emergency Conservation Work Act in the 1930s. Their property eventually became part of Raccoon Creek State Park. My dad's youngest brother, Walter Brzozowski, often told me about visits there when he was very young. My uncle said that his older brothers and his dad would bring their rifles there to target practice. He also spoke about a story my dad told him regarding the stream that flowed through the property. Dad told him that the stream pools were so cold in the summer, that they would use a pool to cool down their beverage bottles. Several years ago, I paid to have the Pennsylvania State Archives searched for information about their property but it was unsuccessful. I had hoped to take my children and grandkids there so we could walk that land together and learn more about our family history. Although I have yet to learn anything about the property, I am very proud that my grandfather came to this country in 1902, started a painting business, and succeeded to the point where my grandparents purchased their home in McKees Rocks as well as the farmland.

This park was on our minds for decades because of the 314-acre Wildflower Reserve where there are over 700 species of plants and the spring wildflowers are said to be amazing. Donna and I have no explanation why the two of us have yet to make it here during the springtime. In any event, we finally arrived at the preserve for the first time in July 2020 so our favorite spring wildflowers were long gone. That being said, we enjoyed hiking on the 4.5 miles of trails which provided many beautiful views of Raccoon Creek from the heights and at stream level. Looking at the stream, I can't help but wonder if this is the one that ran through my grandparents' land. Unfortunately, I did not find myself totally lost in the moment because of an overwhelming amount of noise pollution. Pennsylvania Route 30 runs right along the entrance of the preserve as well as a portion of the trails within. Truck traffic was very frequent and loud but that was not the only noise that shattered the tranquility of this spot. Greater Pittsburgh International Airport is not far from the park and based on the constant noise from air traffic, I would say that the park is right under the flight path of many jets taking off and landing.

Walking on the Jennings Trail in the preserve, we enjoyed finding Cy Hungerford's cabin. Cy was a very famous political cartoonist in Pittsburgh and I always enjoyed his cartoons in the *Pittsburgh Post-Gazette* until his retirement the year before Donna and I were married. Standing by the cabin, I had to laugh as another jet, at seemingly full throttle, roared overhead. I chuckled because this cabin was Cy's retreat from the city of Pittsburgh but today, he would find no refuge from modern life.

We ended our visit by checking out the lake and driving to the Frankfort Mineral Springs section of the park. There are some interesting ruins of the spa resort and we enjoyed checking out springs and letting our imaginations drift back to another time. The history of the springs as an attraction dates from the 1790s to 1912. The historical placards are very interesting as well as the wonderful Frankfort Mineral Springs booklet provided by the DCNR. A perfect walk through history before our long drive home.

Hearing—diesel and jet engines abound; sight—picturesque Raccoon Creek, fantastic rock formations, queen of the prairie in full bloom, bee balm flowering with its bright red blooms popping in the landscape; taste—enjoying Donna's wonderful picnic lunch at a picnic table by the preserve's parking area.

93. RALPH STOVER

This divided 45-acre park is on opposite sides of Tohickon Creek. However, except for very small slivers of land, the two sections are not directly across the creek from one another. Further, the High Rocks Vista section of the park is sandwiched between sections of Tohickon Valley Park which is a Bucks County park. There is parking within the park for the Island Picnic Grove; however, the parking for the High Rocks Vista section is within Tohickon Valley Park. It is somewhat complicated and I would highly recommend going to the DCNR site for this park and printing off the map prior to visiting. There are picnic tables, picnic pavilions, and vault restrooms at the picnic grove as well as access to the Means Ford Bridge which is limited to pedestrians but does span Tohickon Creek. Rock climbing on the 150-foot rock face found within the High Rocks Vista section is open to experienced rock climbers. Everyone else is required to walk behind the safety rails to protect themselves from the sheer drops that exist there.

We parked by the Means Ford Bridge and walked around the Island Picnic Grove before we used the bridge to cross the Tohickon Creek and walked steeply uphill along Stover Park Road which is bounded on both sides by private property until it reaches Tohickon Valley Park. We continued to walk along the road until we saw a sign for High Rocks Trail on the right. We jumped onto the trail and followed it through Tohickon Valley Park where it eventually crossed into the High Rocks Vista section of Ralph Stover. The views from the section of the trail that is parallel to the cliffs are spectacular. An additional feature are the turkey vultures circling overhead as they ride the thermals in the sky above the gorge. We also watched the vultures at very close range as they landed on the upper reaches of trees and resumed their flights. Donna and I were fascinated to see these beautiful birds spread their massive wings to obtain the rays of the sun. Turkey vultures are a familiar sight for us since we live in the Laurel Highlands but we never have had the opportunity to observe them at eye level and for such an extended period of time. The gorgeous views and the turkey vultures provided us a lot to talk about as we retraced our steps to our truck.

Sight—turkey vultures in action, Tohickon Creek Gorge; vistas all along the trail.

94. RAVENSBURG

This scenic little 78-acre park sits in the bottom of a beautiful gorge with Rauchtown Creek flowing through its entire length. Amenities include a campground with 21 tent sites and a shower house, fishing in Rauchtown Creek, and picnicking with tables, rustic restrooms, and two pavilions. The park boundaries are almost all surrounded by Tiadaghton State Forest which provides great hiking opportunities beyond the one mile of park trails. Two examples are the Mid State Trail and the Thousand Steps Trail. Combining the Thousand Steps Trail with a section of the Mid State Trail and the Raven Trail appears to provide a nice loop hike.

We hiked the Raven Trail that goes just about the length of the park and crosses Rauchtown Creek on footbridges. One end of the trail is anchored by the campground and the other by the Castle Rocks formation. Briefly, towards the campground, the trail is dual-designated as the Mid State Trail. The Mid State Trail cuts through the park as it goes through Tiadaghton State Forest. As we continued along the Raven Trail towards Castle Rocks we passed a small pond formed by the waters of Rauchtown Creek and a dam constructed by the CCC. It is very scenic with water tumbling over the dam, which has a step-down front, and collecting in a smaller pond before continuing unimpeded through the rest of the park. Once we reached Castle Rocks, we hiked paths through and around these beautiful rock formations which are tall, erosional spires of sandstone that loom through the tree-covered hillside like some ancient castle towers. A fantastic place to let your imagination go!

Sight—footbridges, neat little campground, trailhead of the Thousand Step Trail, Castle Rocks.

95. RAYMOND B. WINTER

This entire 695-acre park is located within Bald Eagle State Forest. Further, 39-acre Rapid Run Natural Area is within the park while the 407-

acre Halfway Run Natural Area is adjacent to the park and within Bald Eagle State Forest. Halfway Lake is only about six acres in size but a big draw with fishing and a swimming beach that includes a food concession, restrooms, changing rooms, beach volleyball, and playground. Other amenities include a 61-site campground, 6.3 miles of trails, and picnicking areas with picnic tables, two pavilions, and restrooms. The trails within the park, in conjunction with counterparts in the state forest, accommodate such recreational activities as mountain biking, horseback riding, snowmobiling, and cross-country skiing. Also, the park is a middle trailhead for the Mid State Trail which makes its way through the length of the park and is dual-designated on its park meanderings as the Bake Oven Trail and Brush Hollow Trail.

Raymond P. Winter was another one of our hub parks and we camped here for four days at Campsite #17. The campsite provided a nice flat area for our tent and sat diagonally across from the shower house/restrooms. We hiked the Lakeside Trail from just outside the campground entrance to the dam built by the CCC. It is a very picturesque cement and stone dam and the water puts on a grand show flowing over the edge into a pond area before continuing and eventually escaping into Bald Eagle State Forest. From here, we crossed over Rapid Run and continued on the Lakeside Trail to the Rapid Run Nature Trail. This trail loops through Rapid Run Natural Area which is very peaceful and is carried over Rapid Run by two foot bridges. Along the nature trail, we observed the devastation caused by a violent storm that simultaneously downed many massive trees and opened up huge holes in the tree canopy. The ground below went from dense shade to full sunshine which is changing the plant landscape. Where the Rapid Run Nature Trail connects to the Overlook Trail, we hung a left and made our way up this trail. It became very steep at times with many switchbacks before the overlook itself was reached along Sand Mountain Road. The outstanding vista here revealed how the park is buried within the densely forested Bald Eagle State Forest. Seeing this vista is a must when visiting but please remember that the overlook can be reached either by hiking or driving based on one's physical abilities and limitations.

Hearing—water pouring over the dam; sight—picture-perfect dam waterfall, massive downed trees, overlook vista; smell—coffee perking, bacon frying; taste—great camp meals.

96. REEDS GAP

This is a small, 220-acre park in the deep woods adjacent to two sections of Bald Eagle State Forest with Honey Creek running through its length. The campground here is limited to tent camping with 16 sites. The shower house serving the campground is reached by crossing Honey Creek on a footbridge, cutting through the Pavilion 2 footprint, and walking across Parking Lot B. If we pitched our tent here, my portable toilet would be a necessity for middle of the night nature calls! Other amenities include fishing on Honey Creek, picnicking with picnic tables and four picnic pavilions (three are reservable), and three miles of hiking trails. One of the park trails leads to the Reeds Gap Trail Spur of the Mid State Trail which continues through Bald Eagle State Forest. Another trail forms a loop by traversing the length of the park along Honey Creek and continuing through Bald Eagle State Forest to complete it.

After our initial exploration of the park, we ate our lunch at Pavilion 2 before going on the loop trail. We jumped on a footpath by the pavilion and followed it to a newly installed footbridge which we used to cross the creek. While standing on the footbridge we saw the remains of an old bridge in the creek. The loop trail was on the other side of the bridge and we followed it to the right. This section was very picturesque with the right side bounded by Honey Creek while the left side was heavily forested and displayed thousands of white pine seedlings growing at the feet of their parents.

Shortly, the trail led us to the ruins of a historical dam which had been used for water storage in conjunction with a water-powered sawmill in the 1800s. We continued along the trail through the state forest and eventually returned to the campground area where we crossed Honey Creek on the footbridge by Pavilion 2 to return to our truck in Parking Lot B. During our visit, we heard no traffic on New Lancaster Valley Road, which cuts through the length of the park, nor did we see other park visitors or campers at the campground. Thus, our time here was very tranquil and we both became totally enveloped by the natural surroundings. My experience at this isolated park was phenomenal and continues to strongly impact my soul. Writing these words brings with it a sense of overwhelming love for Donna as well as those vast stands of pine seedlings. Very hard to convey my feelings through words but the magic of those moments continue to reverberate within me.

Hearing—standing on the new footbridge listening to the murmur of Honey Creek, overwhelming silence in the forest; sight—thousands and thousands of white pine seedlings projecting the richness of life in this forest, dam ruins from long ago; smell—freshly cut lumber on newly constructed footpath bridge.

97. RICKETTS GLEN

This 13,193-acre park is all about the 22 waterfalls found in the 1,201-acre Glens Natural Area. This collection of waterfalls had such an amazing impact on visitors that a decision was made to make it a national park. However, WWII intervened and the idea was dropped so it opened as a state park in 1944. In 1969, the Glens area within the park became a National Natural Landmark and in 1993, it became The Glens Natural Area within Ricketts Glen State Park. State Game Lands 57 adjoins the park and State Game Lands 13 is nearby. In another interesting twist, the Pennsylvania Fish & Boat Commission controls a section of land that is on the borders of both the park and State Game Lands 57. This dry land was once underwater, consisting of Mt. Springs Lake and Ice Dam No. 1. This expanse of water was once used in the production of ice but, due to hazardous dam conditions, it all was drained many years ago.

Along with the waterfalls, the other big attraction is 245-acre Lake Jean. Amenities include fishing, two boat launches, dry mooring, boat rentals, and a swimming beach with a food concession. There is a 131-site campground divided into two areas near the lake, over 28 miles of trails, and picnicking opportunities aided by picnic tables, restrooms, and two pavilions. Along with hiking trails, there is a loop trail that can be used for horseback riding. I would suggest obtaining a Pennsylvania Recreation Guide for Ricketts Glen before attempting a waterfalls hike since it contains important information including an excellent Falls Trail System map.

The waterfalls at The Glens Natural Area have had such an impact on me that I can remember the five times Donna and I visited here. During all but our last visit, we parked at the Glens Lot Trailhead parking area which is directly off of Pennsylvania Route 118. When parking there, we always

The Glens Natural Area, Ricketts Glen State Park

walked across Route 118 to the Evergreen parking area and viewed Adams Falls before recrossing Route 118 and hiking to the other 21 waterfalls. We love this route since we visit all 22 falls and actually see Harrison Wright, Sheldon Reynolds, and Murray Reynolds twice. On our passport visit, we attempted to park at the Lake Rose Trailhead parking area but it was full so we parked at the Beach Lot #2 Trailhead parking area. The Lake Rose Trailhead is the closest parking area to the Falls Trail System so keep it in mind when planning a visit to see the waterfalls.

Viewing any waterfall on this hike is breathtaking and the overall effect of seeing each and every one of the 22 waterfalls is awe-inspiring. Each waterfall is worthy of investing as much time as necessary to fully appreciate its uniqueness. We approached each hike this way until the last one because Donna, Duane, and I arrived late on a fall day and we were concerned about the sunset and darkness that it would bring. Yes, it was an amazing experience despite our fast circuit of the route but the ability to linger produces its own special magic and was missed. In my mind, coming across each waterfall along the trail is like watching a continuous fireworks display. One fades away as you catch another along the trail and this process continues until the last one explodes in your vision. I have experienced nothing like this in all my years of hiking and I understand completely why a proposal went forward to make this a national park! Selecting the best park for each category is a tough process but not for this category. There is no doubt in my mind that **Ricketts Glen State Park** is the ***Best Pennsylvania State Park for Waterfalls***. With 22 waterfalls ranging in height from 11 feet to 94 feet, there just is nothing like it.

Caution: Please keep in mind that sections of the trail are steep and that any stone steps and stone paths that are in close proximity to a waterfall can be wet and slippery. On this trail we always wear waterproof hiking boots, carry extra water and energy snacks, and use our hiking poles for both balance and traction.

Hearing—roaring of the waterfalls; sight—the bursting, tumbling, splashing, sparkling waterfalls.

98. RIDLEY CREEK

This 2,600-acre park is only 16 miles from Philadelphia and with hiking trails, a paved multi-use trail open to bikers, numerous picnic areas, fishing along Ridley Creek (which flows through the length of the park), and a horse stable and riding trails, it provides a nice city escape. Additionally, the historically significant Colonial Pennsylvania Plantation is in one corner of the park and adjacent to the opposite end of the park is the 650-acre Tyler Arboretum. Both have fee-based admissions and provide park visitors with additional reasons to come to the park and stay for the entire day. The park office is located in the Hunting Hill Mansion that was built in 1915. The mansion was constructed around a 1789 Pennsylvania stone farmhouse and it serves as the reception center for the park.

Surrounding the mansion are formal gardens and the mansion and garden complex is offered as a wedding venue. During our visit, a bride-to-be and her family were touring the complex as a potential wedding/reception site. The guide told the family that the stable, located near the mansion, provides horse-drawn carriage rentals which sounded fantastic to us. Donna and I enjoyed going inside the mansion to obtain our passport and to check out the beautiful interior. We also enjoyed walking around the formal gardens and strolled along the Mansion Garden Trail. From this trail we moved onto the Yellow Trail and followed it to where it crossed the paved multi-use trail and used it to return to the parking lot and our truck. At this point, we removed our bikes from the bike hitch and biked the entire four-mile multi-use trail that let us experience a good portion of the park grounds which included a nice ride along Ridley Creek before we biked back to our truck.

Sight—beautiful stone mansion, bubbling fountains in the formal gardens, huge fireplace in the 1789 farmhouses, State Champion pin oak.

99. RYERSON STATION

This 1,162-acre park has many needs and has been undergoing a re-visioning process for several years. The 62-acre Ronald J. Duke Lake is no longer there because of mine subsidence damage to the dam. Further, an option to rebuild it has been abandoned because of further mine subsidence. At the same time, the North Fork of Dunkard Fork cuts the park into two sections (east and west sides) and the Iron Bridge that connected the Iron Bridge Trail on both sides of the stream is closed indefinitely because it is unsafe. As of mid-2024, the DCNR continues to work with all interested parties to determine the future direction of the park. The good news is that the park still maintains many recreational opportunities. Fishing is available in the North Fork of Dunkard Fork, a 32-site campground is available year-round, there are 13 miles of hiking trails, a swimming pool, and provisions for picnicking including picnic tables, two pavilions, and restrooms. During the winter season there are other recreational possibilities including cross-country skiing, ice skating, and sledding.

We visited the park with Sue, John, and their daughter, Katie. We hiked on Three Mitten, Polly Hollow, Deer, Iron Bridge, Box Turtle, and Lazear Trails. The trails provided us a variety of ascents and descents through varying habitats but the loss of the Iron Bridge forced us to complete two separate hikes. When we finished hiking, we all sat at a picnic table on a cold, windy, sunny March day and combined forces to produce and enjoy a wonderful picnic lunch.

Sight—stream flowing through the lakebed turned wetland; taste—European-style lunch with meats, cheeses, fruits, vegetables, and breads.

100. SALT SPRINGS

This park is operated by the Friends of Salt Springs Park in conjunction with the DCNR. The Friends own 437 acres adjoining the 405-acre state park and operate everything seamlessly to serve the community. The Fall Brook Nature Area is located in the park with Fall Brook running through a gorge and old-growth hemlock trees on both the east and west rims. The nature area, the four historical buildings of the Wheaton Farm, and the salt springs are all centerpieces of the park. Other important facets include 14.2 miles of hiking trails that meander through the park, natural area, and Friends land; a rustic campground with 16 sites located along the banks of Silver Creek; and picnicking opportunities with picnic tables, one pavilion, and restrooms in the day use area.

From our home in the Laurel Highlands, this is the most remote park we traveled to—we used our hub campsite at Promised Land State Park as our jumping off point to complete our journey to this location which is very close to the New York border. Reading about this park while preparing for our trip, Donna and I knew that our goal was to see the old-growth hemlocks, three waterfalls along Fall Brook, the salt springs, Penny Rock, the picturesque boardwalks amongst the hemlock trees on the rim, Wheaton House, the carriage barn, and the 1850s historical garden. We accomplished all of this and more while falling in love with this amazing, hidden gem. We found the salt springs, Penny Rock, boardwalks, and many of the hemlock trees, while hiking along the Hemlock Trail. We also hiked the Fall Brooks, Bunny, Cliff, and Cliff and Summit Trails before hiking through the other side of the natural area on the Gorge Trail. The natural area is gorgeous with towering, old-growth hemlocks and Fall Brook flowing through the gorge. This is one of the parks that is difficult to reach but even more difficult to leave behind. Donna and I just loved it here and know that this would be one of our go-to parks if it was near our home.

Hearing—waterfalls in the gorge; sight—huge tree trunk circumferences and heights of so many hemlock trees, Penny Rock, the three waterfalls, salt springs; touch—Penny Rock.

101. SAMUEL S. LEWIS

This 85-acre park is on Mt. Pisgah (885-foot-tall ridge) which provides a terrific view of the area including a portion of the Susquehanna River, the striking Veterans Memorial Bridge which is listed on the National Register of Historic Places, river towns, and farmlands. By the parking area there is a huge grassy field which is perfect for flying kites—no trees to snag the kites and lots of wind activity. On an earlier occasion, Donna visited the park and met a National Kite Flying Champion practicing his techniques. During our passport stamp visit, we ate lunch at the Hilltop Pavilion, enjoyed the view, and hiked all the trails. Along the trails, we checked out the Stine Arboretum containing some unique trees and the Rock Formation area which included some amazing boulders. We enjoyed taking lots of photographs of trees in the arboretum, boulders, and the vista. Before leaving, we walked over to enjoy the Susquehanna River view one more time.

Hearing—wind blowing through the trees; sight—English yew, Veterans Memorial Bridge, boulders; touch—constant winds.

102. SAND BRIDGE

This is a tiny, three-acre picnic park that is bordered on three sides by Bald Eagle State Forest. Rapid Run flows through the park and is open for fishing. A foot path connects two parking areas and it crosses Rapid Run by means of a pedestrian bridge. There is a picnic pavilion on each side of the stream and we had coffee and snacks at the one listed as Pavilion #1 on the map that is found in the Pennsylvania Recreation Guide for Ravensburg, McCalls Dam, and Sand Bridge State Parks.

Sight—rustic footbridge, woodlands; smell—coffee pouring out of our vacuum bottle.

103. SHAWNEE

We have visited this 3,985-acre park and 451-acre Shawnee Lake on many occasions since moving to the Laurel Highlands. We have found it a great spot for hiking and kayaking. The lake is open for fishing, has three boat launches, boat rentals, 183 dry boat moorings, and a swimming beach. Other amenities include 16 miles of hiking trails, nine-hole disc golf course, and picnicking with many picnic tables, five pavilions, and restrooms. The campground has 293 sites divided into several sections and Turner Camp Road, Pennsylvania Route 96, and the Pennsylvania Turnpike form somewhat of a triangle in which the campground is located. Our friends, Sue and John, tent-camped here many times when their kids were young and they always speak highly of their experiences.

Over the years, Donna and I have hiked the Lake Shore, Felton, Field, Forbes, Pigeon Hills, and Shawnee Trails and have biked the Lake Shore

Trail a few times as well. On our passport stamp visit, we circled a section of the lake by means of the Lake Shore Trail and State Park Road which enabled us to return to our truck. When visiting the park to hike, we always park in the lot by Pavilion No. 2 and twice we spotted a bald eagle after we parked. We also spotted a bald eagle when kayaking on the lake.

Shawnee Lake is great for kayaking and we always park at the Colvin boat launch area to put our kayak in the water. During a visit in September 2024, our grandson Mason fulfilled an item on his geocache wish list; namely, finding a geocache on an island. The two islands in Lake Shawnee closest to the Colvin launch site both have geocaches. Mason and I found the first one with the help of another geocacher—a 78-year-old Navy veteran who was excited to run into fellow geocachers. He used a grappling hook and rope to pull his kayak close to shore which was a super idea. We tied off on a log that was partially submerged in the lake and made it onto the island in time to help him up an embankment from his moored kayak. Mason and Laura paddled out to the second island and found the second island cache. Donna and I could not let our grandson and daughter have all the fun so we paddled out after their return to find the cache for ourselves. Oh my gosh, we faced an embankment about two feet above the waterline so while I held onto the kayak line, we simultaneously launched ourselves up and over—we tumbled into each other's arms and just sat there laughing like a couple of teenagers. Yes, as a bonus, we found the cache too!

On a historical note, General Forbes and his army camped within the footprint of the park in 1758 while building a section of the Forbes Road. It is always exciting to think about that when hiking here. If visiting this park during fruit season, I would recommend the orchards in New Paris. There is soft serve in Schellsburg which is always welcomed by kids of all ages.

Also, a great place for a lunch or dinner is Jean Bonnet Tavern which was built in 1762 and is on the National Register of Historic Places.

Sight—bald eagle soaring over Shawnee Lake, smile on Mason's face with his first island geocache; taste—burgers at Jean Bonnet.

104. SHIKELLAMY

This is a very interesting park divided into two areas by the Susquehanna River; namely, the 78-acre Shikellamy Overlook and the 54-acre Shikellamy Marina. Our first stop was at the park office located in the marina on the tip of Packers Island which is in the North Branch of the Susquehanna River. When we arrived, the park ranger had just completed his day and was walking away from the locked door of the park office. He was kind enough to reopen it so we could obtain our passport stamp. We thanked him for taking the time at the end of his day and told him how much we appreciated his effort. However, we were not totally surprised since we met many DCNR employees who were kind and generous with their time throughout our long quest.

The marina area includes picnic tables, pavilions, restrooms, swings, a 1.5-mile paved bike trail, and a butterfly garden. All the other amenities relate to the river including a marina with 73 slips, huge parking lots for trucks and boat trailers, and two boat launches. We walked around a bit and checked out the butterfly garden but did not make it to the Point Sitting Area before leaving. I would like to add two comments on the marina. Please call ahead or check the website to determine if the seasonal boat rental concessionaire is in operation because the park is seeking a new partner to run it. Second, the world's largest inflatable dam is in seasonal operation on the Susquehanna River just two miles downstream from the park. When the dam is inflated, it forms the 3,060-acre Lake Augusta.

The route to reach the Shikellamy Overlook, which sits on top of a 360-foot cliff, includes two bridges, one to cross the North Branch of the Susquehanna River and the other to cross the West Branch of the river. The views from the overlooks along the Deer Trail should not be missed since they are spectacular. The unfolding panorama on our walk included the confluence of the West and North Branches of the Susquehanna River, portions of Northumberland and Sunbury, and the Shikellamy Marina section of the park. There are picnic tables, pavilions, restrooms, and a few miles of trails at the overlook. We walked the Deer Trail loop and another loop we created by walking the Oak Ridge Trail, a portion of the Deer Trail and the Dry Hollow Trail which returned us to our truck.

Sight—the amazing overlook views along the Deer Trail.

105. SIMON B. ELLIOTT

This 318-acre park is located directly off of an exit of I-80 and surrounded by Moshannon State Forest. There are hiking trails that lead into the state forest and a parking lot is plowed during the winter months to provide parking for visitors planning on snowmobiling and/or cross-country skiing. There are picnic tables, pavilions, and restrooms available for picnickers with the park providing a beautiful setting amongst the pines and oak trees.

The park has a nice, old-fashioned atmosphere with the park office in a log cabin as well as six rustic cabins built by the CCC. The rustic campground has 25 sites (non-electric) along with restrooms but no showers. We have not camped here but I would imagine road noise from I-80 could impact the rustic campground at night. An interesting feature of the park is that it once held a tree nursery to provide seeds for reforestation in other parks and forest land. The production facilities closed in 1978 but seeds continue to go to other state tree nurseries. Before going back to our truck, we checked out the tree seed orchard, the Simon B. Elliott monument, and hiked a portion of the Old Horse Trail that entered the state forest before circling back into the state park.

Sight—very rustic buildings that transport one to another era, beautifully forested land.

106. SINNEMAHONING

This is a beautiful 1,910-acre park on a narrow swath of land in a steep mountain valley with First Fork Sinnemahoning Creek running through it and forming the 145-acre George B. Stevenson Reservoir near the end of the park. Portions of both Elk and Susquehannock State Forests border sections of the park. Picnickers can find picnic tables, pavilions, and restrooms; there is a boat launch and mooring spaces on the reservoir; the five-mile Lowlands Trail follows along the First Fork; and there is a 35-site campground with restrooms and showers. There is no swimming in the park but during the winter months there are opportunities for snowmobiling, cross-country skiing, and ice skating if the weather permits.

Our first stop was at the south entrance where we parked and checked out the reservoir. Next, we visited the park office and Wildlife Center which is a beautiful, LEED-certified building. Along with park offices it contains classrooms, exhibits, information on the Pennsylvania Wilds, and a gift shop. On the advice of a park ranger, we walked down a hill behind the building onto the Lowland Trail which is on an old railroad bed so it is flat and wide and followed it to the Wildlife Viewing Area where this section of the trail ends. Along the way we saw some wildflowers (first time we identified a cuckoo flower) and topped off this wonderful nature hike when we reached the viewing area and used our binoculars to see a bald eagle sitting in its nest. On returning to the Wildlife Center we had a picnic lunch at one of the outdoor picnic tables before leaving.

Hearing—very quiet along the Lowland Trail; sight—outstanding architecture of the Wildlife Center, exhibits, cuckoo flower, bald eagle.

107. SIZERVILLE

This 386-acre park is almost totally surrounded by Elk State Forest. The East and West Branches of Cowley Run flow through the park and provide fishing opportunities while adding to the beauty of the woodlands. Other amenities include opportunities for picnickers with picnic tables, six pavilions, and rustic restrooms; many trails including five miles of hiking trails formed into a series of six loops, a trailhead for the 33.5-mile Bucktail Path hiking trail, and winter snowmobiling and cross-country skiing trails that extend to trails within Elk State Forest; and swimming with both a swimming pool and wading pool. The campground has 28 sites with restrooms and showers.

We hiked the North Slope, Sizerville Snowmobile, and Bottomlands Trails. Along the Sizerville Snowmobile Trail we found the plaque dedicated to CCC Camp S-85 which was located here from 1933 to 1935. We were really surprised and excited to find 22 spring wildflowers during our hike even though the Pennsylvania Recreation Guide for Sizerville State Park mentioned an abundance of spring woodland flowers—seeing is believing. We ate lunch at a picnic table beside the East Branch of Cowley Run and spotted fiddleheads popping up along the bank—a beautiful photo opportunity.

Hearing—tranquil atmosphere along the Snowmobile Trail; sight—freshly minted fiddleheads in conjunction with the stream, red trillium, sharp-lobed hepatica, foamflower, ginger.

108. SUSQUEHANNA

This 20-acre park is located along the West Branch Susquehanna River in the city of Williamsport. I remember it was a bit confusing as we approached on Arch Street. The park entrance is to your right just prior to crossing the Arch Street Bridge. This riverfront park comes with a nice view of the river, restrooms, picnic tables, a pavilion, boat launch, and an in-season (May-October) chance to purchase tickets to ride on a paddle wheeler named the *Hiawatha*. The *Hiawatha* offers a regular one-hour cruise as well as many specialty cruises throughout the sailing season. We visited in September but it was during COVID so the *Hiawatha* was not sailing. Before leaving we enjoyed a picnic lunch at one of the many picnic tables.

Sight—a sunshine-filled fall day produced a sparkling river.

109. SUSQUEHANNA RIVERLANDS

This 1,044-acre park is one of the three new state parks created by former Governor Wolf and announced on September 27, 2022. We visited in early March 2023 and found a large quantity of snowdrops blooming along Codorus Creek where it flows into the Susquehanna River. We initially parked at the section of the park near the river before a local resident we met there guided us to the parking lot up the hill so we could access the Overlook Trail. The trail traveled along the edge of a farmer's field and through a wooded area before it led us to the overlook at Schull's Rock. Beautiful rock outcrops form the foundation of the overlook and the views of the Susquehanna River were wonderful. The DCNR cautioned that private residences and farm fields within the park were off-limits. The areas to avoid were well marked on our visit so we experienced no problems avoiding them.

Sight—snowdrops, views from the overlook; touch—gusting winds on the rock outcrops.

110. SUSQUEHANNOCK

This 224-acre park is divided into several segments on both sides of the Susquehanna River and features many beautiful views that can be reached by accessing the main section of the park containing the park office as well as the park sections labeled the Pinnacle Overlook and Urey Overlook. These two park sections are farther upstream from the main park and on opposite sides of the river from each other with Urey Overlook located close to Samuel S. Lewis State Park. This is a very interesting but difficult park to describe and understand. I would highly recommend obtaining the Pennsylvania Recreation Guide for Susquehannock State Park before visiting.

Donna and I were both caught off-guard and amazed when we arrived in the area. Driving to the park office we saw road signs pointing the way to many appealing outdoor areas and when we obtained our copy of the guide, it revealed tons of outdoor areas just waiting to be explored. These included two wildflower preserves; namely, Ferncliff Wildflower and Wildlife Preserve and Shenks Ferry Wildflower Preserve. Both really piqued our interest and the guide provided many more goodies including the Mason-Dixon Trail, Muddy Run Recreation Park, and the Bald Eagle Sanctuary. At this point, we both agreed that a week-long camping trip would be a great idea for a future trip.

The main park grounds include picnic tables, picnic pavilions, restrooms, trails, overlooks, and a historical house. Once we obtained our passport stamp, we followed the Overlook Trail to Hawk Point Overlook and Wisslers Run Overlook. Hawk Point and Wisslers Run are great spots for views from the 380-foot plateau that the park sits on. Along with the views, informational placards provided us with invaluable information. From our vantage point at Hawk Point, we used our binoculars to observe Mt. Johnson Island which is the world's first bald eagle sanctuary. Between the two overlooks, Hawk Point was our favorite because the views were less altered by industry. But Wisslers Run provided great views of the Conowingo Islands with rock formations that gave off a national park vibe.

From Wisslers Run, we followed the Overlook Trail back towards Hawk Point and went on the Nature Trail to Park Road where we walked to the James B. Long House, built in 1850. There is very interesting history associated with the house but it is closed to the public because the interior is not safe. Hopefully, funding will be found in the future so visitors can explore the interior as well as walk around the exterior which is picturesque in itself. Before we left, we sat at a picnic table, sipped our coffee, and reflected on the wonderful views and the spring wildflowers that we came across on the trails.

Sound—hushed atmosphere at the overlooks; sight—rock formations in the river, amazing vistas, large groups of false Solomon's seal in full bloom.

111. SWATARA

This 3,520-acre park sits in Swatara Valley which is between Blue Mountain and Second Mountain, and State Game Lands 80 and State Game Lands 211 are in the mountainous terrain on both sides of the valley. At the same time, there is no park office, no picnic areas, no trash receptacles, no campground, and only rustic restrooms. At first, with all of this taken together, Swatara State Park exudes isolation but the spell is quickly broken because Interstate 81 runs along the length of one side of the park and Pennsylvania Route 443 runs along the opposite side.

That being said, the park shines for many other reasons. Swatara Creek flows through the entire length of the park providing fishing opportunities and a wonderful water trail with three boat launches for non-powered watercraft. There are 18.2 miles of hiking and biking trails, a 27.2-mile mountain biking trail system, 12.8 miles of trails open to horseback riding, and two miles of the Appalachian Trail go through the southern section of the park. A portion of the bike trails is the Swatara Rail Trail which is 10 miles point-to-point, extending from the Lickdale Trailhead by Exit 90 of I-81 to a location near Exit 100 of I-81. To see much more of the

Sand Siding Trail, Swatara State Park

park, an 11-mile loop is suggested by the DCNR as follows, "using the Swatara Rail Trail and Bear Hole Trail and crossing the creek at the Waterville Bridge and the Swopes Valley Road."

Based on my research, I knew Swatara would be one of our biking parks and that we would utilize the 11-mile loop outlined in the Pennsylvania Recreation Guide for Swatara State Park. Wow and wow and wow, again! The loop was beyond amazing and provided us with an entertaining variety of biking experiences. Biking from the parking area of the Swopes Valley Trailhead, we made a left onto Swopes Valley Road, crossed over Swatara Creek, and continued on Swopes Valley Road until we made a left onto the Swatara Rail Trail (a right on the Rail Trail would lead us to a dead end near Exit 100 of I-81). The Rail Trail, for the most part, followed along Swatara Creek. Mostly flat, this section had both dirt and gravel surfaces and lots of beautiful scenery. We briefly took a left onto Sand Siding Trail so we could bike across a wonderful, two-span, rail-to-trail bridge that just screamed out to be checked out and photographed. We recrossed the bridge, made a left, and resumed our ride on the Rail Trail.

Donna and I have biked on paved bike trails before and love those opportunities; however, we were in for a surprise because the typical paved bike trail was not the experience we encountered next. We rolled right onto an old paved road that now serves as part of the Rail Trail. It really was fun and amazing to bike along a roadway with no worries about vehicles! The Rail Trail goes past the Waterville Bridge but we turned left to cross the bridge to continue on our loop. By biking across Swatara Creek on the Waterville Bridge, we were ever so briefly biking on the famous Appalachian Trail which was really a cool experience. It was over in a few heartbeats and off we went, turning left onto the Bear Hole Trail where we saw the ruins of locks from the Branch Canal, which was destroyed by a huge flood in June 1862. Biking up a steep grade on the Bear Hole Trail reminded us of the hills we biked on the carriage trails at Acadia National Park—strenuous but doable. The great thing about a hill is all the fun zipping down from the top and the Bear Hole Trail did not disappoint. The noise from I-81 was very noticeable when we were biking a big chunk of the Bear Hole Trail since most of it runs close to the highway. However, it was only a minor distraction since the ride was exhilarating and filled with an abundance of beauty.

There was one more fun activity just before we found ourselves back at the Swopes Valley Trailhead. There is a fossil site along the trail and visitors are encouraged to look for them. Donna and I had lots of fun scrambling up the fossil hill and looking for fossils and talking about how much fun it would be to bring our grandkids here. No, we found nothing, but still enjoyed the hunt. The loop came to an end too soon but gave us much to discuss in the truck as we drove away.

Now it is time to recognize **Swatara State Park** as my choice for the ***Best Pennsylvania State Park for Biking***. The loop is like nothing I have experienced in a short, 11-mile trail. Donna and I absolutely loved it. Add to this amazing experience for bikers, there is a section of the park devoted to a six-segment trail for mountain bikers. Combining all the available biking experiences together, makes this park a biker's nirvana.

Sound—patches of peace and quiet along the biking loop; sight—picturesque rail-to-trail bridge, Appalachian Trail sign, famous Waterville Bridge, lock ruins.

112. TOBYHANNA

This is a 5,440-acre park with the 170-acre Tobyhanna Lake within its boundaries. It is connected to Gouldsboro State Park by the 3.2-mile Frank Gantz Trail and a section of the park borders the Tobyhanna Army Depot. Amenities include fishing, swimming beach, boat launch, boat rentals, four picnic areas, a picnic pavilion, restrooms, and campground with 135 sites. There are 10 miles of hiking trails and the 5.1-mile Lakeside Trail can also be used by bikers and snowmobilers when there is enough snow.

On arrival, we stopped at the park office, collected three passport stamps, and enjoyed a conversation with the ranger about our quest and our progress. She was very happy for us and suggested we walk along the Lakeside Trail to the dam. We enjoyed the walk, scenery, and the wonderful berries that we found along the way. There were large, long concrete slabs that we used to cross the stream just below the dam as we made our way on the loop before retracing our steps to where we parked the truck.

Caution: Part of the park borders the Tobyhanna Army Depot and the DCNR warns that visitors to remote/undeveloped sections of the park may find unexploded ordnance (UXO). Please remain alert and don't touch anything that appears to pose a UXO threat. Also, take note of the location and report your information to the park office. There are more details on the Tobyhanna State Park website regarding this subject.

Caution: Tobyhanna Lake will begin to be drawn down in the spring of 2025 for the construction of a new dam. The project is projected to be completed in September 2026 but please check the Tobyhanna State Park website for updates. During this project the lakebed and dry creek beds will be off limits because there could be UXO in these areas.

Sight—sparkling lake; taste—delicious berries.

113. TROUGH CREEK

This 541-acre park is in a gorge with Great Trough Creek flowing through it and into Raystown Lake. Raystown Lake is a 8,300-acre reservoir created by the U.S. Army Corp of Engineers and is a huge tourist attraction. U.S. Army Corp of Engineers land and Rothrock State Forest borders the park. There is a lot packed into these forested acres with adjacent forest and Army Corps land adding to the recreational possibilities. Fishing is available along Great Trough Creek and in Raystown Lake which can be reached by using the Terrace Mountain Trail (27-mile point-to-point trail that traverses Trough Creek State Park). There is a canoe/kayak launch that enables paddlers to proceed along Great Trough Creek to Raystown Lake. Picnickers have many choices with five picnic areas, three pavilions, and restrooms. There is a 29-site campground with rustic restrooms but no showers.

Attractions include the historical Paradise Furnace ruins, iron master's home (now park rental), dam ruins, Copperas Rocks, Rainbow Falls, Balanced Rock, and an ice mine.

On our quest visit we parked at the Copperas Rock parking area to check out the Rocks and access Copperas Rock Trail. We hiked that trail to the Ledges Trail. This trail has great overlooks and is worth the effort. The Ledges Trail leads to Abbot Run Trail and Raven Rock Trail. We followed Raven Rock Trail to Balanced Rock. Balanced Rock is great to see from this viewpoint as well as way down below where the view provides a perspective that makes the rock seem like it is in a very precarious position. We continued along Raven Rock Trail and eventually returned to Balanced Rock. We hiked the Balanced Rock Trail down (some cool CCC-created stone steps along the way) to see Rainbow Falls which was flowing very well in March 2019. From there we continued down across footbridges and hit some water along the trail which is parallel to Great Trough Creek. We passed over the creek on a fun, picturesque, suspension bridge that has some bounce to it.

After crossing the bridge, we walked across Trough Creek Drive and started the Boulder Trail. This was a bit of a challenge but all the boulders and other rock formations were so interesting and magical that I found my imagination going wild—one looked like a pirate ship. Donna and I were discussing the trail as we went along and how much fun it would be for kids to explore. The trail went sharply down to Great Trough Creek where we checked out the ice mine and dam ruins. We had our lunch at a picnic table that provided a great view of this spot along the creek. The only problem was the steep climb back up while retracing our steps on the Boulder Trail but going through all the boulders and other rock formations provided as much fun as earlier. At the bottom, we walked along Trough Creek Drive to return to our truck.

Hearing—flow of water providing comforting background on much of our meandering; sight—Balanced Rock, Rainbow Falls, rustic trail bridges, amazing rock formations.

114. TUSCARORA

This 1,618-acre park includes 96-acre Tuscarora Lake and is adjacent to a portion of State Game Lands 227. Locust Creek flows through the park and continues into State Game Lands 227 after passing through a dam. The lake includes a boat launch, boat rentals, fishing, and a swimming beach. There is no campground but there are numerous picnic tables, two pavilions, and restrooms. We sat at a picnic table and enjoyed lunch with a lake view. Afterwards, we hiked a small loop formed by the Old Log, Forest Edge, and Laurel Trails. We found a geocache along the Old Log Trail which was nice since Tuscarora was the 100th park on our quest.

Sight—sparkling lake waters, geocache.

115. TYLER

This 1,711-acre park is about a 40-minute drive from Philadelphia which must make it very appealing to a huge number of day visitors. Neshaminy Creek flows through the length of the park and includes fishing, boating, and boat rental opportunities. Other amenities include picnic tables as well as restrooms and a pavilion, horseback riding trails, many miles of paved and unpaved multi-use trails, Langhorne Players Theater (old mill converted for use by community theater group), the Tyler Park Center for the Performing Arts (old barn converted to artists dwellings, workshops, studios), and the Schofield Ford Covered Bridge.

 Our visit started with a bang. We just exited our truck to take our lunch to a picnic table located by Neshaminy Creek and the pedestrian causeway, when thunder and lightning started followed by a downpour. We ate our lunch in our truck while it poured for about 15 minutes. Afterwards, the sky cleared and we walked across the causeway and hiked towards Schofield Ford Covered Bridge. We reached the bridge by hiking on the Mill Dairy Trail and the Covered Bridge Trail—some nice views along the way and the bridge is a beauty both outside and inside. The weather became unsettled again by the time we reached the bridge and we sheltered inside until this second storm passed. Much to our surprise, when returning to the causeway, we found it flooded out by the heavy rains which caused the stream to rise substantially. Our estimate was that the water rose by over two feet since we first crossed. There were telephone pole-sized guardrails on both sides of the causeway decking, so we took our boots off and gingerly walked across it in several inches of water as thunder booms were again heard in the distance. We would have never attempted the crossing if the water had reached the level of the guardrails because the speed of the current, coupled with the increased length of the crossing, would have substantially increased the potential for disaster.

Sound—thunder booming; sight—lightning zigzagging in the sky, gorgeous covered bridge, Neshaminy Creek overwhelming the pedestrian causeway.

116. UPPER PINE BOTTOM

This five-acre park is located on Pennsylvania Route 44 and is surrounded by Tiadaghton State Forest. Although small in size, it acts as a trailhead for trails within Tiadaghton State Forest and Upper Pine Bottom flows through the park so fishing is a possibility as well. We used this tiny park as a snack stop along our drive and enjoyed a cup of hot coffee and some fruit before continuing on.

Sound—tranquil spot with little traffic; sight—forest and stream view.

117. VARDEN CONSERVATION AREA

This is a 444-acre park with a very interesting history. The DCNR published a brochure entitled, "The History of the Varden Conservation Area" which provides great information on the use of the land before it became a conservation area. The park is divided into two tracts by Pennsylvania Route 296 and private land. The two areas are named the Tannery and Mid Valley Tracts and based on our research, we focused our efforts on the Tannery Tract. Amenities include hiking trails, restrooms, and the pond located within the Tannery Tract is open for fishing.

We viewed the pond from the Pond Trail and it was like a mirror reflecting the puffy white clouds as well as the deciduous trees growing by the trail. We followed this trail to the footbridge where we picked up the Tannery Trail which brought us to the Varden Chimney built in 1790. We also visited the old cemetery which is just across a dirt road from the chimney. From the cemetery, we retraced our steps to the point where the Tannery Trail branches to the left and checked out the Brooks Dairy Barn which needs some structural intervention. We grabbed some photographs of old farm implements before again retracing our steps to the split and making our way back to our truck.

Sight—historical chimney and cemetery.

118. VOSBURG NECK STATE PARK

This is one of the three new state parks created by former Governor Wolf and announced on September 27, 2022. It is located on Vosburg Neck which is an oxbow on the North Branch of the Susquehanna River. It shares Vosburg neck with Camp Lackawanna which is owned by the Presbytery of Lackawanna, PC (USA), and a small segment of private land within the park per the Howland Preserve Trail Map. More information on Camp Lackawanna can be found on their website. This 669-acre park is filled with history including buildings, canal bed, rail bed, and cemetery.

When we visited the park, a temporary banner was used as the state park sign. The trail maps located at the barn were labeled the Howland Preserve and no DCNR map was available. We crossed Vosburg Neck Road from the parking lot and followed the Vista Trail up to an overlook that provided a narrow view of the river and some farmland beyond. There were some picturesque old stone walls as we hiked back down on the Howlin Down Trail. Crossing the road again, we made our way to the river and checked out the very visible canal bed. We were happy to return to the truck and enjoy our thermos of hot coffee since we ran into some snow while hiking the upper sections of the Vista and Howlin Down Trails and the bleak, windy day made the coffee that much more enjoyable.

Sound—very quiet and peaceful location; sight—historical buildings, stone walls, canal bed, snow; smell—coffee; touch—cold winds blowing.

119. WARRIORS PATH

This 349-acre park is bounded on three sides by the Raystown Branch of the Juniata River which flows into Raystown Lake. The land that the park sits on is a result of river meandering—the river curves back and forth forming a series of chunks of land bounded by the river on three sides. DCNR recognizes the river meandering in this area as one of the best examples in Pennsylvania. Amenities include three miles of hiking trails, picnic tables, a pavilion, restrooms, boat launch site, and fishing.

There is a series of loop trails through the park. We hiked portions of the Broad Top, Warriors, River Trail, and Deer Trail Loops. Rock cliffs across the river formed a beautiful backdrop on a portion of the River Trail Loop. We returned to the start of this little hike by again utilizing portions of the various loop trails.

Sound—zen-like atmosphere throughout this little park; sight—rock cliffs plunging into the river.

120. WASHINGTON CROSSING

This park has much to recommend it for recreation purposes including biking on the Delaware Canal Towpath, picnicking, boating on the river and canal, and fishing in the river. However, to me it is all about the history as it was established for the preservation of the history at this site in 1917 and named a National Historic Landmark in 1961. This park is part of the trifecta of parks in Pennsylvania regarding General George Washington and the Continental Army. The other two parks are Fort Washington State Park and Valley Forge National Historical Park (established as the first

Pennsylvania state park in 1893 and gifted to the United States in 1976). Both the DCNR and Friends of Washington Crossing Park jointly are in charge. Some fees may be encountered depending on what is accessed when visiting. Also, the Bowman's Hill Wildflower Preserve found within the park is operated by a non-profit and there is an admission to enter the preserve which is enclosed by a fence.

The park is divided into two sections by private property, one is the upper section which includes graves of colonial soldiers, Thompson Neely Farmstead and Grist Mill, Bowman's Hill Wildflower Preserve, and Bowman's Hill Tower. The lower section includes the visitor center, monument, McConkey's Ferry Inn, Durham Boat Barn, and many other historical buildings. The Delaware Canal and Towpath passes through both sections of the park which provides the opportunity to bike between the two.

Understanding the historic events that occurred here begins with the park office and visitor center. We enjoyed the museum-quality displays and movie very much. After viewing the film, we were able to obtain a tour of the historical park grounds conducted by a ranger for a modest fee. This small investment was well worth the cost based on the historical information provided. The tour included an amazing look at the Durham Boat Barn which houses replicas of the Durham boats that were used by General Washington to transport his troops across the Delaware. As relayed by our guide, the historical facts of this crossing pertaining to the difficulty and physical demands on both soldier-passengers and boatmen greatly impacted me that day and still does.

After the tour, we walked along the Delaware Canal Towpath before retracing our steps and driving to the upper section of the park. We briefly walked around the Thompson-Neely Farmstead before taking the trail that

Continental Army Graves, Upper Section Washington Crossing State Park

led us to the colonial soldiers' graves. Along the path to the graves we encountered a wide stream that was impossible to cross without either removing our boots or taking the option of submerging our boots. It was in April with the waters very cold and running high so even though our choice was obvious, it was chilling!

There were some very emotional moments when viewing the graves and thinking about all the suffering these soldiers went through coupled with the fact that they did not survive to make the Delaware River crossing. We retraced our steps (once again removing our boots and socks) to the parking lot and drove up to Bowman's Hill Tower. It was a strenuous climb up the many stairs but the views were well worth the effort. Since we were going to reroute our drive to avoid going across the narrow bridge again, we decided to skip the wildflower preserve to give ourselves more time to drive to our accommodations. We knew we would be hitting Philadelphia during rush hour and that major traffic jams were on the horizon.

Wow! We in Pennsylvania are so blessed with all the history found in our state parks. I must say that due to the history that occurred here, along with my personal belief that the United States would not exist without the successful crossing, I have no doubts in naming **Washington Crossing State Park** as my choice for the ***Best Pennsylvania State Park for History.***

Caution: Please be cautious driving to the park. Donna and I were diverted by flooding off of Pennsylvania Route 32 and the detour took us across the Delaware River into New Jersey. Coming across the bridge, we made a right onto New Jersey Route 20 which led us to the point where it was necessary to cross Washington Crossing Bridge into Pennsylvania and the lower section of the park. This bridge is very, very narrow (7.5 feet for each of the two lanes) and was difficult to cross with traffic flowing in both directions. It really caused us lots of anxiety because Donna was driving her new car. When we spoke with two rangers at the park office and visitor center, they told us horror stories of numerous accidents on the famous bridge as well as long back-ups when drivers of vehicles going in each direction on the bridge found it impossible to safely pass each other.

Sound—the quiet solitude Donna and I experienced by the colonial soldiers' graves, the park ranger retelling the experiences of soldiers and sailors crossing the river; sight— Durham Boat Barn, views from Bowman's Hill Tower; touch— running my hand over a section of the stonework wall of McConkey's Ferry Inn which likely was erected only 14 years or so after the famous crossing.

121. WHIPPLE DAM

This 256-acre park with 22-acre Whipple Lake is almost entirely within Rothrock State Forest. Visitors looking to picnic will find three large pavilions, many picnic tables, and restrooms all within a very woodsy, cozy environment. The lake has a swimming beach with a snack bar and changing area as well as boat rentals and fishing. Fishing is also available along Laurel Run which runs the entire length of the park while entering and exiting Whipple Lake. The imprint of the CCC is heavy in this state park just like in so many others; however, in 1987, the 32-acre "day use section" was placed on the National Register of Historic Places as the Whipple Dam National Historic District. Walking around this area is like stepping back in time to the days when both national parks and the state parks were touched by the Herculean efforts of the CCC.

On our visit, we walked around the beautiful and picturesque historic district and Donna took numerous photographs of the amazing CCC sites. Our favorite was the ranger office which is a really special, log cabin-style building. To finish our visit, we hiked the Whipple Lake Trail which is a loop. The trail provides some great views of the lake and the day use area. And as the trail leaves the lake behind, it parallels Laurel Run on and off before crossing the stream and looping back towards the lake. The scenery, both natural and manmade, along this trail made for a whimsical hike. One CCC creation really sticks in my mind. Just picture two beautiful pillars created by stone masons and supporting a small roof that provides shelter to a picnic table that is built inside of and around the pillars. It is really cool and well worth a look to admire and photograph.

Sound—a hush in the air produces a timeless, zen-like atmosphere; sight—CCC structures exuding old-time charm.

122. WHITE CLAY CREEK PRESERVE

This 3,050-acre park consists of three segments with White Clay Creek flowing through the entire length of the largest segment. It is a very complicated park to visit with three non-contiguous segments, three state borders (Pennsylvania, Delaware, Maryland), and Delaware White Clay Creek State Park bordering two segments. Based on these factors, it is important to obtain the Pennsylvania Recreation Guide for White Clay Creek Preserve and download any available trail maps prior to visiting. Points of interest in the park include London Tract Meeting House and adjacent historical cemetery, Tri-State Marker (Maryland, Pennsylvania,

Delaware), Arc Corner Monument, and fishing opportunities along White Clay Creek which is a National Wild and Scenic River.

On arrival, Donna and I explored the cemetery at the London Tract Meeting House (built in 1729) which includes burials from before the Revolutionary War as well as burials of Revolutionary War veterans. Next, we drove to a parking area at the end of Arc Corner Road where there is a trailhead for the Arc Corner Connector Trail. We took this trail to the Tri-State Marker Trail which is somewhat of a loop trail (using a small segment of the connector trail) that took us to both the Tri-State Marker and the Arc Corner Monument. The trail was well-blazed and fun to use as state welcoming signs always greeted us as we seamlessly crossed state borders. The forest was dense with some wonderful spring wildflowers including the showy orchis which was the first time we saw this beautiful little orchid in Pennsylvania. We enjoyed taking selfies as well as pictures of each other with our boots and arms in two states as well as with the Tri-State Marker where we stood on the corner of three states.

Sound—wonderful silence interspersed with the reverberations of the melody produced by the flowing waters in the creek; sight—White Clay Creek, Tri-State Marker, Revolutionary soldiers' markers, showy orchis in bloom.

123. WORLDS END

This 780-acre park is a super park for family vacations. It is surrounded by Loyalsock State Forest so plenty of room to roam on hiking trails that venture from the park into the surrounding forest. At the same time, there are opportunities for snowmobiling and cross-country skiing within the park in the winter and nearby trailheads provide further opportunities to pursue these sports in the state forest. Loyalsock Creek flows through the park providing fishing and boating opportunities. Also, there is a dam along the creek near the park office which provides a swimming area. The office has some really great taxidermy displays that will entertain visitors of all ages. We really enjoyed the black bear since we never saw one in the wild that has cinnamon-colored fur which is very striking. The park has an unusually large cabin-colony thanks to the efforts of the CCC with 19 rustic cabins as well as a separate 70-site campground further along Pennsylvania Route 154.

We have visited this beautiful park twice. The first visit we hiked the Worlds End Trail to the Worlds End Vista which provided a great view and is flagged in the DCNR Recreation Guide for the park. We retraced our steps and drove to the campground where we accessed the Canyon Vista Trail which is a four-mile loop. Great hike with some challenging steep sections that leads to the Loyalsock Canyon Vista which is another photo opportunity flagged by the DCNR, and it did not disappoint with super views of the Loyalsock Creek Gorge. Directly across Cold Run Road from the vista sits the Rock Garden. We had a blast acting like kids and scrambling amongst the boulders/rock formations. Both the Loyalsock Canyon Vista and Rock Garden are very well loved because folks can drive to this location from down below and tons of people roam the area. The good news for us on this first visit was it was in the spring so we found numerous wildflowers on our hike but very few people.

We visited in mid-July to obtain our passport stamp. The swimming area was very busy with visitors enjoying the cool, refreshing water. Duane was with us on his motorcycle so we obtained driving directions from a ranger and drove to the Canyon Vista/Rock Garden parking area. Wow!

Big change from our spring visit with large crowds at both attractions. Just like all tourist spots, the best time to visit is off-season.

During our first visit, we missed out on Big Mike's Steaks & Hoagies at the Historic Forksville General Store. Big Mike's is seasonal so check out their information online because Big Mike and his delicious food should not be missed. It is located right by the Historic Forksville Covered Bridge (we found a geocache there) and very near Worlds End State Park. The food is fantastic, there is a walk-up window for ordering and pick-up, and a wonderful grouping of picnic tables sit right along Loyalsock Creek. By the way, don't pass up Big Mike's because of poor weather since there is seating in the general store as well.

Sound—lots of brave souls carrying-on as they jump into the cold water of Loyalsock Creek during a hot summer day; sight—Worlds End and Canyon Vistas, Rock Garden; taste—hoagie from Big Mike's.

124. YELLOW CREEK

This 2,981-acre park and 720-acre Yellow Creek Lake is a big complex and includes a large Boy Scout camp. The lake almost stretches the entire length of the park with Yellow Creek flowing in one end of the lake and out the other. The lake provides fishing opportunities as well as boat rentals, four boat launches, and a swimming beach with snack bar. Other amenities include five miles of hiking trails, 18 miles of mountain biking trails, and picnicking spaces that include picnic tables, restrooms, and three pavilions. There is no campground but a private campground is nearby.

We hiked or kayaked at this park on numerous occasions because it is only 40 minutes from our home. We usually start our adventures by going to the parking area at Grandpaps Cove. No matter the season, this location is always peaceful and we find it a great place to launch our kayak and to gain access to hiking trails. The kayaking is enjoyable and gives us plenty of opportunities to see wildflowers in bloom on the water, near the shoreline, and on the shoreline itself. We usually hike the Simpson Trail to the Damsite Trail and back. However, there are loops in the trails and so many unofficial trails (created by mountain bikers going their own ways) that we still find following the main trail to be confusing at times. I have no problem with mountain bikers and hikers sharing multi-use trails but sometimes enthusiasm leads bikers to strike off through the woods instead of designated trails which causes confusion for hikers attempting to navigate from point A to point B on designated trails. At the same time, whether it is hikers or bikers going off the trail system, the results are the same; namely, erosion, destruction of plants, and all-around degradation of the environment. All of us need to appreciate the wonderful gift that our parks represent and always do our best to respect the environment so everyone now and in the future can enjoy nature at its very best.

Enough said on that subject and now to our passport stamp visit. It was in July and we hiked the Ridgetop Trail, feasting on blackberries. Afterwards, on the way to the park office, we pulled into the parking lot for the Environmental Learning Classroom. It was not open but we checked out Dragon Pond. We went on a little stroll around the pond which is designed to provide fishing opportunities for visitors with disabilities as well as for children that are 12-years-old or younger. When we were there, young families were relaxing and enjoying this wonderful fishing opportunity with their youngsters.

Sound—Boy Scouts at their shooting range; sight—water lilies in full bloom.

To end this section, here is the list of my favorite park and my runner-up in each category:

Biking Parks
Swatara

Lehigh Gorge

Camping and B & B Parks
Bald Eagle—Nature Inn

Hickory Run

Family Vacation Parks
Little Buffalo

Worlds End

Hiking Parks
Laurel Ridge

Cooks Forest

History Parks
Washington Crossing Historic Park

Caledonia

Overall Parks
Promised Land

Ohiopyle

View Parks
Hyner View

Cherry Springs

Water Parks
Presque Isle

Pymatuming

Waterfall Parks
Ricketts Glen

Lehigh Gorge

Wildflower Parks
Ohiopyle

Raccoon Creek

Pennsylvania's 20 Mighty State Forests

OUR APPROACH TO THE STATE FORESTS WAS TO KEEP THINGS SIMPLE WITH THE UNDERSTANDING THAT AN IN-DEPTH APPROACH WAS IMPOSSIBLE BASED ON THE OVERWHELMING SIZE AND DIVERSITY OF THESE LANDS.

While we were planning our overall approach to our park and forest visits, we decided to keep things very simple with regard to our state forest visits. It was an easy decision based on the overwhelming size and diversity of these lands and our previous experiences with Forbes State Forest which we consider our "home" forest. Prior to beginning our quest, we had explored these woods for over 30 years but we just scratched the surface of the treasures held within its vast acres.

We planned to visit each of the Forest District Headquarters, obtain our passport stamp, corresponding map and Recreation Guide, speak to a ranger or other staff if possible (COVID), and obtain trail maps and handouts that appeal to us for future visits. We had no expectations of any forest visits during our quest and would rely on fate—chance encounters while driving to state parks and Forest District Headquarters such as responding to roadside forest signs proclaiming vista views or hiking on state park trails that just happen to lead into state forests.

Now, onward to the state forests . . .

1. BALD EAGLE

193,424 acres in Centre, Clinton, Lycoming, Mifflin, Snyder, and Union counties

Our harrowing trip through Bald Eagle State Forest on a drivable trail was exactly that and led to the loss of Duane's motorcycle. However, I do remember the beauty that surrounded us as we halted to have our lunch and regain both our wits and strength before resuming our travails on the drivable trail. I just wish the circumstances that found us in the heart of this amazing forest would have been different so we were in a zen-like state instead of a state of panic! I know driving through the woods on a better road would have weaved together magic moments where our senses soaked up the "wildness" of the landscape, enabling us to relish and savor it all.

The good news is that great experiences in Bald Eagle State Forest were ahead of us later in the week. We drove on McCalls Dam Road, for the most part, an "improved dirt road" traveling between a great restaurant just off of an exit on Interstate 80 and our campsite at Raymond B. Winter State Park; at the same time, we used this road to travel from our campsite to McCalls Dam State Park for our quest visit. Despite our initial fears, we found McCalls Dam Road to have a solid, gravel surface (some of it was paved) and everything we initially hoped for in planning this drive into the woods came to fruition. For example, the three-mile drive between our campsite and McCalls Dam was awe-inspiring with the beauty and serenity of the forest being all-consuming. To add to the experience, we did not encounter another vehicle during our round trip—just us and nature.

Coming back to our campsite at Raymond B. Winter from Shikellamy State Park on Interstate 80, the three of us realized we were very hungry. While I drove, Donna checked out potential restaurants on her phone and found Kavkaz on 3379 E. Valley Road just off Exit 192. Oh my gosh! If I had suddenly stumbled upon some of my dad's long lost relatives from Poland, I could not have been treated better and that is exactly how I remember the kindest and most welcoming restaurant owner I have ever met. What a true gem of a human being!! His restaurant provided fantastic food that was a mix of Middle Eastern and Eastern European offerings.

The interior of the restaurant was closed because of COVID but there were picnic tables for outside dining in good weather. Duane took a stroll and found the owner sitting at a picnic table on the other side of the restaurant building from our location. He came back to us and I returned with him to meet the owner while Donna was gracious enough to wait for our food. The long and short of it was that Duane and I had a blast accepting the amazing hospitality of the owner—just the most caring, joyful person we could hope to run into during COVID or at any other time. I truly felt like he was indeed a cousin that I had never met before and it was a quick bonding experience of long lost relatives finally meeting during a time of adversity. We were with the owner so long that the food came before we returned and Donna asked them to pack it to go instead of using a picnic table. She finally came and got us and drove us back to our campsite via McCalls Dam Road. It was a beautiful ride in the fading light and we were able to experience Bald Eagle State Forest in the dark which made for an otherworldly experience as the headlight beams were continuously swallowed by complete darkness. Donna did a terrific job of keeping the car on McCall Dam Road during our seven-mile trek from Eastville to our campsite where we enjoyed our amazing meal.

Two places on my list for a future visit to Bald Eagle State Forest are Halfway Run Natural Area and Rosecrans Bog Natural Area. We can camp at Raymond B. Winter State Park and visit both. Halfway Run is on the doorstep of the state park and Rosecrans is just north of Kavkaz restaurant!

2. BUCHANAN

71,638 acres in Bedford, Franklin, and Bedford counties

Driving from Buchanan's Birthplace State Park to Cowans Gap State Park, we took Tower Road (gravel surface) into Buchanan State Forest to reach Big Mountain Overlook/Tower Road Vista. Tower Road comes to a dead-end where there is parking and a short trail out to a rock outcrop and an amazing view. We drove back and took Aughwick Road (paved) through the State Forest to reach Cowans Gap State Park. It was a very scenic drive and upon leaving the park, Aughwick Road continues through another section of the state forest.

A historical site within the forest is on my list to explore in the future. It is the Sideling Hill POW Camp where German POWs were held during WWII. The prospect of reaching this site is really exciting for me because there were many books on WWII in my dad's office library and as a kid and later a teenager, I decided reading as many of his books as possible might help me understand the dad I lost as a child. My love for reading and collecting books began in his office as I methodically attacked the library shelves. Along the way, I became a WWII buff and over the years have collected many autographed books on this subject. Now as I age, I have been donating many to a veterans' organization through a fellow North Catholic High School alumnus who is a retired Navy pilot.

3. CLEAR CREEK

14,431 acres in Forest, Jefferson, and Venango counties

On our way to visit the Clear Creek Forest District Headquarters we saw a sign for Bear Town Rocks. Upon arrival, we inquired about it and we were provided a DCNR brochure entitled, "Clear Creek & Callen Run Tracts" which contains a trail map and information on Bear Town Rocks. Bear Town Rocks appeared to be perfect with huge sandstone boulders from about 320 million years ago and a beautiful overlook perched on the top of the tallest one and all waiting at the end of the trail. The trailhead is located at Shelter No. 5 in Clear Creek State Park or it can be accessed from a parking lot near this shelter just off of Pennsylvania Route 949. Either way, the trail crosses Route 949, entering Clear Creek State Forest and begins climbing upwards to Bear Town Rocks. It is a very scenic trail and the rocks are magical. We enjoyed wandering around the boulders and did some geocaching which was a bonus. It was fun reaching the overlook on top of a huge boulder and the view was outstanding. On the way back down to our truck, we increased the length of our hike by taking the Trap Run Trail which eventually loops back to the Bear Town Rocks Trail. We find it rewarding when we can do loop trails or add a loop trail so there are different experiences coming and going on a potential point-to-point trail.

We would love to go back with our grandkids to see Bear Town Rocks and add a few more trails in the state forest during our visit. Camping at Clear Creek State Park for a few days would enable us to do just that. The same DCNR brochure we used to hike the Bear Town Trail shows some other loops to check out. A description of the Pine Loop Trail sounds like a real winner as follows, "It winds through unique rock formations and along a cascading stream."

4. CORNPLANTER

1,585 acres in Crawford, Forest, and Warren counties

We visited the Cornplanter District Office in North Warren during COVID. The office was closed to the public but a ranger spent some time talking to us in the parking lot. We obtained a map and Recreation Guide, a Hunter Run Trail System leaflet, an Anders Run Natural Area Trail System leaflet, and an amazing Cornplanter State Forest Plants & Wildlife Guide. This DCNR guide unfolds into six sections so it is very compactible. Also, it is coated in a plastic-like substance which makes it very durable. The guide is labeled as "a Bio Diversity Snapshot" and provides quality reproductions of examples of flora and fauna found in the Cornplanter State Forest. They are broken out into the following categories: trees and shrubs (22 examples), wildflowers (16), ferns and fern allies (8), fishes (10), freshwater mussels (10), insects (9), reptiles and amphibians (12), birds (20), and mammals (20). It is an amazing mini-field guide and is perfect to teach children as well as a neat little ID tool for adults. Bravo to the DCNR for making it available to visitors.

On our next trip to visit the Allegheny National Forest we plan to explore the 96 acres of the Anders Run Natural Area. The Anders Run Trail consists of smaller and larger loops that go through this old-growth area. The DCNR leaflet includes the following: "Dominant, old-growth hemlock and white pine forest is estimated to be over 200 years old and also includes oak, maple, birch, and beech."

5. DELAWARE

82,214 acres in Monroe and Pike counties

We drove through a chunk of the forest going from Interstate 84 to Promised Land State Park on Pennsylvania Route 390 which provided a scenic beginning to our time spent camping at the park.

An area on my list for a future visit to this forest is Bruce Lake Natural Area. Donna and I would hike Promised Land's Rock Oak Ridge Trail into the Bruce Lake Natural Area and follow the Bruce Lake Trail to Bruce Lake and beyond to Egypt Meadow Lake. Donna and I really want to explore Bruce Lake since it is a natural glacial lake.

6. ELK

Over 217,000 acres in Cameron and Elk counties

We stopped at the Elk County Visitor Center which is near Benezette and found it to be an amazing place. It is a beautiful facility with displays and learning opportunities about Elk that are first class. The center is located within Elk State Forest. A bonus is that there are many hiking opportunities within the forest very close to the center which makes for a great family or adult-only outing. Visiting Sizerville State Park via Pennsylvania Route 155 provided us with great views of the forest as well as driving on Pennsylvania Route 872 when we were on our way to Sinnemahoning State Park's park office and wildlife center.

A return to Sizerville State Park to check out spring wildflowers is in our future and would give us a chance to hike two trails in Elk State Forest.

The Sizerville Nature Trail is across the street from the park's campground. It is a three-mile loop that is entirely in the state forest and has many educational stopping points and a scenic vista. I would also like to check out Johnson Run Natural area which is a 216-acre tract containing old-growth hemlock. The trailhead for Bucktail Path, which provides a means to visit Johnson Run, is just off of Pennsylvania Route 120 in Sinnemahoning.

7. FORBES

Approximately 59,000 acres in Fayette, Somerset, and Westmoreland counties

As mentioned in the introduction to this section, Forbes State Forest is our "home" forest so lots to discuss. For example, several miles of the Laurel Highlands Hiking Trail are within Forbes State Forest. One section, miles 39 through 43, passes through a scenic area that includes Beam Rocks. The other section is mile 36 to 37 which includes crossing over the Pennsylvania Turnpike on a newer pedestrian bridge which is fun to do. Kids love waving to the folks on the turnpike and getting the truckers to activate their air horns.

As mentioned in the Linn Run State Park section, Donna and I absolutely love Grove Run Trail. This loop trail begins and ends in Linn Run State Park but for the most part, it is in Forbes State Forest. There are several great trails that we can access from Grove Run and sometimes we shorten the hikes on these trails by using other trailhead parking areas. A really scenic hike we enjoy begins by hiking Grove Run Trail to Fish Run Trail to Laurel Summit State Park's parking area where restrooms and picnic tables are located. From that point, we hike along Wolf Rocks Trail to Hobblebush Trail which descends along a beautiful little stream to Fish Run Trail which returns us to Grove Run Trail and finally back to the Grove Run Trailhead. Just prior to reaching Laurel Summit State Park, Fish Run Trail briefly crosses into Laurel Ridge State Park before returning to Forbes State Forest. This hike can be expanded by having a picnic lunch in Laurel Summit State Park's picnic grove and checking out both Spruce Flats Bog & Wildlife Area as well as the Wolf Rocks Vista before resuming the original hike by descending Hobblebush Trail.

Spruce Flats Bog is an amazing 28 acres that is not directly accessed but viewed by means of a raised walkway and observation deck. Donna and I have a wonderful time getting down on our hands and knees on the walkway deck to find small cranberry and tiny sundew plants as well as purple pitcher plants and cotton grass all growing in the bog. Also, we always take time to enjoy the overall view of the bog from the observation deck and read the interesting facets of the bog on the educational posters. The tree line is a thing of beauty and how it is formed and the type of trees growing there is a fascinating story.

The hike to Wolf Rocks is really fun and not too tiring for young kids or older adults. Wolf Rocks Trail, just past where Hobblebush Trail joins it, turns into a loop which is nice since terrain and scenery will vary going to and returning from the vista. We have hiked this trail in all seasons and once, there was sufficient snowpack for us to go cross-country skiing along the trail. The Wolfs Rock Vista is gorgeous and the rocks provide a nice place for a snack before turning back. Please be cautious during snake season because occasionally we have spotted rattlesnakes sunning on the rocks at the vista. Please let the snakes enjoy the sunshine—plenty of rocks for people to enjoy without bothering these beautiful creatures.

I want to make a note here about Hobblebush Trail which can be an elusive turn-off from the Wolf Rocks Trail. Just remember when hiking from the Laurel Summit State Park's parking lot along Wolf Rocks Trail, the Hobblebush sign and the trail will be on the left. If the loop portion of the Wolf Rocks trail is reached without spotting the sign, turn around and start retracing your steps for a very brief time and the sign and trail will be on your right. Also, the outline of the Hobblebush Trail is displayed on the trail map found in DCNR's Pennsylvania Recreation Guide for Linn Run State Park but it is not labeled—just left blank. It is easy to recognize on the map because it is properly shown as branching off from Fish Run Trail and connecting to Wolf Rocks Trail. The Hobblebush Trail is labeled in another trail map the DCNR provides which is titled, "Pennsylvania Bureau of Forestry Laurel Highlands Trail System."

There are many ski touring trails within Forbes State Forest as well. The only trails that Donna and I use for skiing are the Laurel Mountain Cross-Country Ski System trails. There is a warming hut and the Pennsylvania Cross Country Skiers Association (PACCSA) maintains an outstanding presence. The PACCSA does so much for cross-country/Nordic skiers including trail maintenance, grooming, maintaining a webcam to show snow conditions (see paccsa.org), maintaining a ski patrol, keeping the warming hut warm and having some food available at very reasonable prices, providing ski lessons, and so much more. If you love cross-country/Nordic skiing please support the PACCSA with a membership and/or donation because they are a super volunteer-based organization that brings lots of joy to the mountains. The DCNR produces a great map for this ski trail system entitled, "Pennsylvania Bureau of Forestry Laurel Highlands Trail System."

I can go on and on about this trail system but I will share just a few highlights. I love jumping on Summit Trail just behind the warming hut and skiing down to Spruce Run Trail and skiing along that trail. Starting out on Summit, the upper section is lined with mountain laurel and rhododendron covered in snow and forming a magical landscape going down a gentle decline before hitting a nice little hill which is fun skiing down. At the bottom, there are some cool wooden bridges to ski across and the hemlocks are gorgeous, weighed down with snow, and forming a scenic parade to Spruce Run Trail. Skiing along Spruce Run Trail with Spruce Run flowing parallel to the trail along a slightly downhill section is my very favorite segment of all the skiing trails here. My zen moments include an iced-over Spruce Run, hemlocks towering over the trail dressed in white, and at a much lower level, beautiful rocks, mountain laurel and rhododendron all flocked in more of the white stuff. Another great segment is Silvermine Trail with huge hemlocks, groomed trails, and the solitude of just Donna and I skiing side by side. Last but not least on my trail highlights is Black Bear Trail which in combination with Silvermine, forms a great loop trail. What is absolutely amazing are the rock formations as you ski Black Bear near where it meets Silvermine.

The following are other areas within Forbes State Forest where we have hiked: Blue Hole, Lick Hollow Area/Pine Knob Overlook, Mt. Davis, North Woods Trail System, Roaring Run Natural Area, and Quebec Run Wild Area. Over the years we have visited these areas many times with John and Sue and their family as well as on our own and with our family. The DCNR, as always, can be counted on to provide great pamphlet guides covering these areas. Here is the corresponding list of titles: "Forbes State Forest Pennsylvania Bureau of Forestry Blue Hole Division/Barron Tract," "Pennsylvania Bureau of Forestry Lick Hollow Area & Whitetail Trail,"

"Forbes State Forest Pennsylvania Bureau of Forestry Mt. Davis Area," "Forbes State Forest Pennsylvania Bureau of Forestry North Woods Trail System," "Forbes State Forest Pennsylvania Bureau of Forestry Roaring Run Natural Area," and "Pennsylvania Bureau of Forestry Forbes State Forest Quebec Run Wild Area." Each one of these areas is well worth a visit if you can easily take day trips to this wonderful state forest or visit several during a camping trip. I am sure that each person who visits the state forest in their area can generate a similar list which hammers home to me the vastness of our state forests and how impossible it is for me to do justice to each of the other state forests that Donna and I briefly visited on our quest.

Here are a few notes on the locations just mentioned:

Blue Hole is a deep pool of water on Gary's Run and it takes some effort to reach it—first driving on a gravel forest road and afterwards crossing Gary's Run a few times along the hike (try to go during a dry period). Blue Hole is worth the effort since the hike and observing the deep pool of water provide some beautifully rewarding moments.

Lick Hollow Picnic Area is great for family picnics and the Pine Knob Trail is a great hike up to the Pine Knob Overlook which does not disappoint by providing fantastic views. From the overlook, we usually jump on the Whitetail Trail which follows Pine Knob Road, an improved gravel road, for a length of time before going back into the woods. We usually hike this trail for several miles before retracing our steps back to the picnic grounds. Another nice hike is created by parking one vehicle at Lick Hollow and another at Quebec Road and hiking from one vehicle to the other while enjoying a backpack lunch along the way.

Mt. Davis has provided us with many rewarding repeat visits with all the seasons delivering great outdoor moments. If you are physically able, hiking up to the fire tower at the summit is fantastic, if not, it can be reached by driving. It is really fantastic to hike through the Mt. Davis Natural Area which provides the wonderful experience of walking amongst the stunted canopy at the top of the mountain which is the tallest point in Pennsylvania at 3,213 feet. The fire tower views are outstanding and well worth taking the time to walk up the many, many steps.

The North Woods Trail System deserves a whole day visit. It is set up as a cross-country ski area with a warming hut but is great anytime of the year. The Laurel Highlands Hiking Trail (LHHT) weaves through the ski trails and the many ski loops in combination with the LHHT provide numerous hiking combinations.

Roaring Run is a great place to hike but best during drier periods because of many stream crossings. We start off at the parking lot just off of Pennsylvania Route 31 which means we always hike the McKenna Trail at least one way as well as Painter Rock Trail; however, our hikes through the natural area vary after that because of many loop trails in conjunction with the LHHT which traverses the area. There is so much beautiful scenery including many streams and great views from rock formations along Painter Rock Trail.

Quebec Run Wild Area provides many trails and depending on how we are feeling, we hook them together for larger or smaller loops that bring us back to the parking area where the Whitetail Trail comes in. Scenery is varied and beautiful (hills, streams, rocks, hardwoods, softwoods, mountain laurel, rhododendron) which makes us keep coming back for more.

Looking back at all the time we have spent hiking in Forbes makes me appreciate the treasures found in our state forests even more. At the same time, I know there is so much more to see in our "home" forest and look forward to more repeat hikes as well as new explorations. One goal that comes to mind immediately is visiting Wharton Iron Furnace. The many relics from the early days of iron production always intrigue me.

8. GALLITZIN

24,283 acres in Bedford, Cambria, Indiana, and Somerset counties

This is another state forest that is close to home. We have hiked the Charles F. Lewis Natural Area within the Rager Mountain Division of Gallitzin on numerous occasions. I just love the hike up through a beautiful hollow with a rapidly flowing stream, sweet little waterfalls, and rock formations to our left as we climb the trail from the parking lot. This natural area has gorgeous scenery and is a wonderful place for spring wildflowers. There are two loop trails that when combined provide wonderful views including an outcrop where a perfect view of the Conemaugh Gap can be experienced. We tend to hike in early spring and late fall but my favorite hike was with Donna and Laura on a New Year's Day hike with temperatures hovering in the 50s. There are some beautiful sandstone outcroppings that will be reached no matter if one selects the short loop or the long loop. To me, meandering through the rock formations is always a wonderful highlight. Those outcrops are known for rattlesnakes so in snake season, be careful, observe, and do no harm on your hike through the rocks.

We also visit the Babcock Division occasionally. We have hiked portions of the 26-mile Lost Turkey Trail that has its southern terminus by the Babcock Picnic Area and its northern terminus in a parking lot near the Blue Knob State Park ski area. We also have hiked the double-looped John P. Saylor Trail starting and ending at the Babcock Picnic Area. This is a great hike and while a portion of the larger loop goes through the Clear

Shade Wild Area, the entire smaller loop is within the wild area. This is always a peaceful and very scenic hike and well worth the effort to hike the entire 18 miles. A fun highlight is crossing Clear Shade Creek on a picturesque suspension bridge. Please be prepared for lots of wet trail conditions in the spring.

Each time we hike in the Babcock Division I think of my childhood home that was on Babcock Boulevard in Ross Township just outside the Pittsburgh city limits. This division of the forest was named after the E.V. Babcock Lumber Company of Pittsburgh that sold the land to the Commonwealth of Pennsylvania. Further, the road where our house and warehouse faced was named after the owner of Babcock Lumber; namely, Edward Vose Babcock who served as mayor of Pittsburgh from 1918 to 1922.

Thinking of Babcock Boulevard while hiking on the Saylor Trail stirred up a childhood memory of my pet duck, Lucky. In my mind, it is a spring morning in 1958 and I see myself sitting on the foot bridge in front of our house/office/warehouse complex, watching minnows swim in the creek while waiting for Mr. English to arrive. He brings us milk, fruits and vegetables, and this morning, a duck! Not just any duck but my very own pet duck. Lucky the Duck arrives in Mr. English's milk truck. He is a pure white chick and moves right into our house where he lives in a big cardboard box that once held Radiant Industrial Flood Lights stocked in the warehouse for my dad's steel mill customers. Time goes by and Lucky moves into a cage next to my brother's rabbits. Paul is in the business of raising rabbits and folks are always coming by with their children to buy a rabbit or two. One rabbit, we call him Patches, never was picked because one ear flopped over. It was not good for Paul's business, but to have both Patches and Lucky as pets was wonderful.

Back in the land of my memories, I see Lucky is a great buddy. I let him out of the cage when I'm playing in the yard and that wonderful duck follows me everywhere. Also, Lucky performs as a "watch dog" or in this case, a "watch duck." My duck quacks up a storm whenever someone drives down our gravel road—it does not matter if it is a car or a huge commercial truck. What really makes Lucky a very special duck is that my pet hates water. Can you imagine a duck that hates to get wet? Girtys Run, the creek that flows in front of our property, is where we try to give Lucky baths. The bathing process begins with my sister, Sandy, holding Lucky as we go down the steep hill to the bank of the stream where Sandy throws Lucky into the water. It seems that the results are the same each time with Lucky quacking wildly, swimming over to the bank, avoiding our outstretched hands, racing up the hill at a fast waddle and looking down at us as we struggle back up the hill. What a duck!

We have hiked many trails in this state forest but there is one that I think Donna and I would enjoy hiking for the first time and that is the 10-mile-long County Line Trail. A portion of the trail crosses the Allegheny Front and there is an observation deck on the trail that is said to provide a great view of Bedford County.

9. LOYALSOCK

114,494 acres in Bradford, Lycoming, and Sullivan counties

A small portion of the Canyon Vista Trail which we hiked at Worlds End State Park goes through this state forest. Also, we drove on Pennsylvania Route 154 coming and going to Worlds End and some of the woodlands of Loyalsock are visible from the highway. We could not resist driving on

High Knob Road as well and stopping at High Knob Overlook which provided us with a beautiful vista to enjoy. Along our travels in the area, we hiked a small portion of the 59-mile Loyalsock Trail—out and back and we were not disappointed. This is a perfect trail to backpack to enjoy its entire length. My hope is to someday return to the area and visit Haystack Rapids, Jacob Falls, Kettle Creek Gorge Natural Area, and Rock Run Valley. In short, the Loyalsock State Forest has many treasures that I yearn to explore.

Opportunity: Please take note that we found a DCNR "Biodiversity Snapshot" guide at Loyalsock Forest District Headquarters. It is just like the one we described in the Cornplanter State Forest section so please don't miss picking one up.

---

10. MICHAUX

Over 85,000 acres in Adams, Cumberland, and Franklin counties

During our explorations in the area, we drove Pennsylvania Route 233 from Mont Alto all the way to the Huntsdale area where we made our way to Kings Gap Environmental Education Center. This route took us through the heart of Michaux State Forest. We also briefly entered into the forest on a section of the Appalachian Trail when we visited Caledonia State Park. A return trip would be centered on hiking trails within the Meeting of the Pines Natural Area which is next door to Mont Alto State Park. This natural area obtained its name because the following species of native pines grow here: pitch pine, shortleaf pine, Table Mountain pine, Virginia pine, and white pine. I have always loved hiking through pine trees and this experience sounds like a wonderful opportunity to do just that while identifying all five species.

11. MOSHANNON

190,031 acres in Cameron, Centre, Clearfield, Clinton, and Elk counties

When visiting Black Moshannon, Parker Dam, and Simon B. Elliot State Parks as well as the Moshannon State Forest District Office, we drove through this forest since it surrounds each of these locations. While at Parker Dam State Park we hiked a portion of the Quehanna Trail within the forest; likewise, at Simon B. Elliott State Park, we hiked a portion of the Old Horse Trail within the forest.

My target for a return to the forest is the Marion E. Brooks Natural Area because I want to hike amongst a large stand of white birch that exists there. As a kid, I remember learning that our family name, Brzozowski, means land of the birch. With this information firmly stuck in my cranium, I always enjoy having a birch tree growing on our property and love finding birch trees when out hiking. While writing these sentences, I decided it is important to determine the facts and place at risk the foundation for my love of birch trees. Truth be told, no matter what I find out, I will always love my birch trees not only for what I believe is a family connection but because I enjoy snapping a small twig of a birch and tasting and smelling the wintergreen-like essence. Yes, through the magic of the Internet I determined that "birch" in Polish is "brzozowy" and "ski" means "pertaining to" so my fragment of memory is confirmed.

12. PINCHOT

Approximately 54,000 acres in Lackawanna, Lucerne, Susquehanna, Wayne, and Wyoming counties

We only had one encounter with this state forest and that was driving on Pennsylvania Route 502 going through the Montage section of the forest traveling towards Scranton and close to the Montage Ski Resort. I would like to return to this area and visit the Thornhurst section of the forest where there is an observation deck on Pine Hill and nearby there is a trailhead for the Pinchot Trail that meanders through the Spruce Swamp Natural Area.

13. ROTHROCK STATE FOREST

92,250 acres in Centre, Huntingdon, and Mifflin counties

We passed through portions of this state forest while driving to Greenwood Furnace, Penn Roosevelt, Trough Creek, and Whipple Dam State Parks. Our longest drive through Rothrock was when we drove from Greenwood Furnace State Park to Penn Roosevelt State Park. The entire 12 miles was right through the forest on gravel roads—the scenery was stunning and included driving through Alan Seeger Natural Area. The experience was like going back in time because we passed a large group of Amish as we drove through the natural area and they were the only people we encountered both during our drive and the time we spent at Penn Roosevelt State Park which seemed very isolated within Rothrock State Forest. On a return trip to this state forest, my number one goal would be to check out Bear Meadows Natural Area (located between Boalsburg and Penn Roosevelt State Park) since it is a National Natural Landmark.

14. SPROUL

305,450 acres in Centre and Clinton counties

This is the largest state forest in Pennsylvania. We drove through portions of the state forest when visiting Hyner Run, Hyner View, and Kettle Creek State Parks. We accessed the Long Fork Loop Trail of the Donut Hole Trail System while visiting Hyner Run State Park and hiked for an hour which led us into Sproul for a short period of time. On a return trip to this forest, more hiking on the Donut Hole Trail System would be the goal since views from the trail overlooking the Susquehanna River Valley should be spectacular.

15. SUSQUEHANNOCK

265,000 acres in Potter County

We drove through this state forest constantly as we visited Cherry Springs, Denton Hill, Lyman Run, Ole Bull, Patterson, and Prouty Place State Parks. On the way to Prouty Place, we stopped off at Longtoe Vista which provides a beautiful view and is one of the six vistas in this state forest. As mentioned in the parks section, we completed short hikes into the state forest at Cherry Springs State Park on the Working Forest Interpretive Trail and at Ole Bull State Park on the Beaver Haven Nature Trail. The focus of a return trip to this forest would be to go to the Forrest H. Dutlinger Natural Area to check out the old-growth timber covering 158 acres of the 1,521-acre natural area. This natural area is within the Hammersley Wild Area so a hike here should provide a remote and tranquil experience.

16. TIADAGHTON

146,926 acres in Clinton, Lycoming, Potter, Tioga, and Union counties

We drove through this state forest to reach Little Pine, Ravensburg, and Upper Pine Bottom State Parks. We also biked the 62-mile-long Pine Creek Rail Trail that was developed by the Bureau of Forestry and is a showcase within this state forest as well as Tioga State Forest. We did this over a weekend with Sue and John. Lots of fun and beautiful scenery along the entire route as well feeling a sense of being deep within the forest where civilization is not a factor. On this bike outing, we pedaled by a timber rattlesnake in its black phase sunning itself on the side of the trail. The other phase is known as the yellow phase. These color patterns are not based on seasons of the year but the coloring is permanent—some of these snakes are always in the black phase while others are always in the yellow phase. This is a great ride any time of the year and all four of us highly recommend it.

Caution: If attempting this bike ride, be prepared since help is not readily available on the entire 62-mile-long trail. This means any bike problems are squarely in the rider's purview so bring spare tubes and/or a repair kit as well as bike tools and an air pump.

Another trip into this state forest would involve hiking at least a portion of the 42-mile long Black Forest State Forest Hiking Trail. The DCNR says it all: "It utilizes old railroad grades, logging trails and foot trails to traverse some of the most spectacular terrain in Pennsylvania."

17. TIOGA

161,890 acres in Bradford, Lycoming, and Tioga counties

We drove through portions of this state forest traveling to Colton Point and Hills Creek State Parks. Also, as mentioned in the Tiadaghton State Forest section, we biked the entire 62-mile-long Pine Creek Rail Trail that was developed by the Bureau of Forestry and is showcased within this state forest as well as Tiadaghton State Forest. On a return visit, I would like to hike the 30-mile West Rim Trail with Donna, Sue and John. There are many vistas on this trail and the views should be fantastic during any season of the year.

18. TUSCARORA

95,680 acres in Cumberland, Franklin, Huntington, Juniata, Mifflin, and Perry counties

On our drives to visit Big Springs and Colonel Denning State Parks, we drove through this state forest. Also, driving to Fowlers Hollow State Park, we drove along the edge of the state forest. As mentioned in the Fowlers Hollow section, we hiked a portion of the Beaston Trail into the Tuscarora State Forest before retracing our steps. Also, in the Colonel Denning State

Park section, I mentioned we hiked the Flat Rock Trail. This is a really strenuous, 2.5-mile hike that quickly leaves the state park and for the remainder of the climb it is within the forest. The view from Flat Rock of the Cumberland Valley is just stupendous and was a wonderful experience on our 42nd wedding anniversary.

There was no doubt where Donna and I would go when we returned to this state forest; namely, Hoverter and Sholl Box Huckleberry Natural Area. Per the DCNR, "this isolated 10-acre tract contains a rare colony of box huckleberry estimated to be 1,300 years old." I am happy to relate that we made a return to this forest in 2024 and spent time at this 10-acre tract. It was an awe-inspiring experience.

Caution: Be aware that there is no parking area by the Box Huckleberry Natural Area and one must pull off on the shoulder of the road. It was a very tight space between the embankment and where my driver-side vehicle wheels cleared the road pavement—my truck was at a slant since I was on a portion of the embankment itself. We had my truck and were hauling our 14.5-foot kayak so it was somewhat a comical sight as we squeezed into the space.

---

19. WEISER

30,000 acres in 16 tracts scattered through Carbon, Columbia, Dauphin, Lebanon, Montour, Northumberland, and Schuylkill counties

To reach the Forest District Headquarters from Interstate 80, we drove on Pennsylvania Route 42 through a portion of the Roaring Creek tract of the state forest. My pick to visit on a return to this state forest is really a no-brainer; namely, Sheets Island Archipelago Natural Area. This consists of a group of islands on the Susquehanna River that is a home for songbirds, waterfowl, turtles, snakes and frogs. We can launch our kayak from the Pennsylvania Fish and Boat Commission's Fort Hunter Boat Launch. I think it would be fun, relaxing, and informative to paddle around the islands and make observations with our binoculars as well as taking some great photos.

20. WILLIAM PENN

1,683 acres in 10 tracts in Berks, Bucks, Chester, and Delaware counties

A little sliver of state forest land surrounded by French Creek State Park and containing the district forest office, Hopewell Fire Tower, and picnic grounds with a cabin built by the CCC, constitutes the Hopewell Tract of this state forest. Visiting the district office during our tent-camping stay at French Creek State Park was the only time we were within the forest. A return to state forest land would focus on the Goat Hill Wild Plant Sanctuary—the Rose Trail awaits along with the serpentine barrens which it traverses.

State Forest Exploration Targets

This summarizes the places within the twenty state forests that I would like to explore with Donna in the future:

1) Bald Eagle— Halfway Run Natural Area and Rosecrans Bog Natural Area
2) Buchanan—Sideling Hill POW Camp
3) Clear Creek—Bear Town Rocks and the Pine Loop Trail
4) Cornplanter—Anders Run Natural Area
5) Delaware—Bruce Lake Natural Area
6) Elk—Sizerville Nature Trail and Johnson Run Natural Area
7) Forbes—Wharton Iron Furnace
8) Gallitzin—County Line Trail
9) Loyalsock—Haystack Rapids, Jacob Falls, Kettle Creek Gorge Natural Area, and Rock Run Valley
10) Michaux— Meeting of the Pines Natural Area
11) Moshannon—Marion E. Brooks Natural Area
12) Pinchot—Observation Deck on Pine Hill and the Spruce Swamp Natural Area
13) Rothrock—Bear Meadows Natural Area
14) Sproul—Section of the Donut Hole Trail System
15) Susquehannock—Forrest H. Dutlinger Natural Area
16) Tiadaghton—Black Forest State Forest Hiking Trail
17) Tioga—West Rim Trail
18) Tuscarora—Hoverter and Sholl Box Huckleberry Natural Area
19) Weiser—Sheets Island Archipelago Natural Area
20) William Penn—Goat Hill Wild Plant Sanctuary

Emptying My Shirt Pocket Notes and Final Thoughts on Achieving Our Quest

While working on achieving our quest and writing this book, I have been mulling over many things and now it is time to share.

While working on achieving our quest and writing this book, I have been mulling over many things and now it is time to share. As mentioned in the beginning of this book, Donna and I enjoy spending time together in the outdoors and our decision to start our quest was a natural next step after retirement. I think we both intuitively knew this quest would be perfect for us as an older couple who finally left our jobs behind and were contemplating the "What Next" question. With our love for the outdoors, the "What Next" question was easily answered with our decision to launch our quest to visit all these wonderful parks and forests.

Why do I enjoy my time in the outdoors so much? I have seven answers to this question that boil down to the following keywords: awe, child-like, closeness, healing, health, relaxation, and spirit. I find that my chances of experiencing an "awe" moment increase substantially when I am outdoors. A few examples include: looking overhead and seeing two bald eagles battling for territory, watching family members biking towards me with a bald eagle swooping down and taking point, watching a huge turtle slide into the Allegheny River from an island beach, gliding along a ski trail side by side with Donna as the trail leads under huge, snow-laden hemlocks, and watching mist and fog suddenly lift revealing a rapidly flowing river at the bottom of a canyon. These pinch myself, "I can't believe

I am here" moments, produce in me a sense of wonder, gratefulness, and appreciation for life.

Physically being outdoors and expending vast amounts of energy while performing a fun recreational activity unleashes my inner child. I become a kid again and just enjoy doing, playing, laughing, and loving the people I am with in what amounts to a gorgeous, outdoor playpen. For example, we are in Yellowstone in July, hiking up a mountain, hit the snow line, and I instigate a snowball battle with my grandkids. We are in Acadia and I let my grandkids drag me off Sand Beach and into the very cold ocean where we splash each other, yell, and have a blast. Donna and I are cross-country skiing in Forbes State Forest and coming back from a long ski, I race her to the truck—losing spectacularly and laughing the whole way.

Feelings of closeness that shatter bad moods or reinforce good moods as Donna and I hike, bike, kayak, ski, look for wildflowers, camp, sit at a campfire, etc. Maybe it is a mindset of us against whatever the environment can potentially throw at us that has us dropping our guards, letting our vulnerabilities show, and embracing our intimacy. In the silence and solitude of the woods, holding hands communicates strength, wellbeing, and emotional synchronicity. I have noticed that there is something about being outdoors that naturally breaks down barriers between people and brings them together. I see this so many times when hiking groups meet for the first time and social awkwardness prevails until the hiking begins and amazingly fast bonding occurs. I also notice that the worse the weather conditions or trail conditions become, the faster everyone comes together!

Everyone seems to be discussing the healing power of nature, the healing power of the outdoors, forest bathing, and forest therapy. Scientific studies have been conducted on this subject and show all sorts of positive results. I first experienced this when my dad passed and I was drawn to the outdoors. We lived by woodlands and streams and I just felt so much better spending time outdoors. I also became drawn to green plants and gardening. In times of stress at school or at work or faced with the death of loved ones, I always find solace in nature.

I have shared many of my memory bubbles that popped during our park quest. These memories were filled with love, laughter and so much more that added to the enjoyment of many park visits. There have been others based on painful memories such as the death of my dad as well as events not mentioned in this book. I found these memories easier to process while being in an environment filled with the wonders of nature and the shared joy of the outdoors and for this I am very grateful.

I know that physical activity of all kinds has a positive impact on health. At the same time, experiencing physical activities outdoors makes me believe I have found the fountain of youth. When hiking, biking, kayaking, or Nordic skiing, I feel physical strength returning at levels that are never reached when I am doing exercises indoors. Nothing makes me feel more alive than coming home from several hours of skiing on our mountain and struggling to peel off my inner layer which is sticking to my back because of all the sweat.

My ability to relax increases immensely when I am outdoors. Immersing myself in the natural world soothes all of my senses and brings about a zen-like state at times that I experience in no other environment. Seeking wildflowers is the ultimate relaxing activity for me. Meandering around the woodlands and fields looking for both old and new wildflowers is just mesmerizing. Finding a new wildflower floods me with joy. Sitting around a campfire or laying in my sleeping bag in our tent listening to the sounds of nature are both very, very soothing activities. One of my favorite memories is from the Smoky Mountains where Donna and I sat on rocks by a stream reading our books. My goodness, the flow of the water, the gorgeous surroundings, my wonderful book, and the silent companionship of Donna produced total relaxation.

There is a spiritual aspect to my outdoor time as well. Seeing all the natural beauty that the parks and forests have to offer, makes me believe that God does exist and God shows his love for us through nature. I cannot visit our state parks and forests without thinking about God's amazing creativity, artistic bent, and how all these lands act as a love letter from our Creator. Also, I have such a sense of gratitude for all the folks who helped preserve these lands in the past and continue to work to preserve and enhance this vast natural canvas that God created. Hiking to a wonderfully obscure vista and sitting down and soaking it all in is a very spiritual experience for me.

All of these reasons for being outdoors dovetailed nicely with our quest. What blows my mind is all the amazing things I did not anticipate as we began our quest. I had no thoughts of writing a book, or meeting so many dedicated DCNR personnel, or meeting so many people who share my enthusiasm for the outdoors, or buying a kayak, or finding wonderful new wildflowering places, or upgrading our tent, or finding new places to visit in our vast state forests, or seeing so much of Pennsylvania, or learning about Pennsylvania history, or discovering places that we want to share with our grandchildren, or learning about great organizations that are dedicated to our state parks and forests. Experiencing the joys we anticipated along with all the wonderful unanticipated joys, I can say without a doubt that completing this five-year quest has changed my life forever. I will always be grateful that Donna and I took the leap with our "Pennsylvania State Parks and State Forests Passport" on June 1, 2018.

About the Author

I was born in Pittsburgh and spent my first 36 years there. My mom was from the West End and my dad from McKees Rocks. I have lived in the Laurel Highlands since 1988. My leisure activities include biking, cross-country skiing, kayaking, geocaching, hiking, reading, tent-camping, travel, TRX training, weightlifting, wildflower identification/photography, and writing. My favorite leisure time is time spent with family. For several years now, I have hosted my Cupa Joe class on the Virtual Senior Academy which is part of the AgeWell programming of the JCC. It is an hour-long gathering during which I usually take Zoom participants on a virtual hike. My goal with this program is to spread the message that no matter what physical limitations one is facing in their sixties and beyond, there are ways that the treasures found in the outdoors can be experienced—through physical adaptations or the use of Zoom and similar technologies.